More praise for
No Bended Knee

"Guadalcanal is not the name of an island. It is the name of the graveyard of the Japanese army."
—MAJ. GEN. KIYOTAKE KAWAGUCHI
Commander, 35th Infantry Brigade
at Guadalcanal

"The author enlightens his readers with the tactical and strategic essentials of the campaign, but he does it using the most human terms, incidents, and descriptions."
—*Marine Corps Gazette*

Edited by Neil G. Carey:

FIGHTING THE BOLSHEVIKS: *The Russian War Memoir of Private First Class Donald E. Carey, U.S. Army, 1918–1919*

NO BENDED KNEE
The Battle for Guadalcanal

The Memoir of
Gen. Merrill B. Twining, USMC (Ret.)

Edited by Neil G. Carey

PRESIDIO
PRESS

BALLANTINE BOOKS • NEW YORK

The thoughts and opinions expressed herein are solely those of the author and do not in any way reflect the official position of the United States Departments of Defense and Navy or any other government agency.

A Presidio Press Book
Published by The Random House Publishing Group
Copyright © 1996 by Merrill B. Twining

Presidio Press and colophon are trademarks of Random House, Inc.

www.presidiopress.com

ISBN 0-89141-826-1

All photos courtesy of U.S. Marine Corps except where noted. Topography by ProImage

Manufactured in the United States of America

First Edition: January 1996
First Mass Market Edition: April 2004

OPM   10   9   8   7   6   5   4   3   2   1

To Betty Carey, whose encouragement, unflagging interest, and continued enthusiasm made completion of this book a reality.

M. B. T.

". . . the bended knee is not a tradition of our Corps. If the Marine as a fighting man has not made a case for himself after 170 years of service, he must go. But I think that you will agree with me that he has earned the right to depart with dignity and honor, not by subjugation to the status of uselessness and servility planned for him by the War Department."

—GEN. A. A. VANDEGRIFT,
  Commandant of the Marine Corps,
  testifying before the Senate Naval Affairs Committee,
  6 May 1946.

Contents

Commanders should be counseled chiefly by persons of known talent, by those who have made the art of war their particular study, and whose knowledge is derived from experience, by those who are present at the scene of action, who see the enemy, who see the advantages that occasions offer, and who, like people embarked in the same ship, are sharers of the danger.

If, therefore, anyone thinks himself qualified to give advice respecting the war which I am to conduct—let him not refuse the assistance to the State, but let him come with me into Macedonia.

He shall be furnished with a ship, a tent, even his traveling charges will be defrayed, but if he thinks this is too much trouble, and prefers the repose of a city life to the toils of war, let him not on land assume the office of a pilot. The city in itself furnishes abundance of topics for conversation. Let it confine its passion for talking to its own precincts and rest assured that we shall pay no attention to any councils but such as shall be framed within our camp.

—GEN. LUCIUS A. PAULUS (229?–160 B.C.) Rome

Foreword

Guadalcanal was an immense battle—at sea, in the air, and most certainly on land. It was at this improbable place, an island in the southern Solomons chain, that the Americans and Japanese first slugged it out toe to toe in all three elements. The bitter struggle resulted in the loss of 1,200 aircraft, 49 ships, and as many as 35,000 American and Japanese lives. Although the issue was often in doubt, the Americans finally won. Major Gen. Kiyotake Kawaguchi, commander of the Japanese forces charged with destroying the U.S. Marine invaders, described his defeat for posterity in these words: "Guadalcanal is not the name of an island. It is the name of the graveyard of the Japanese army."

Kawaguchi was correct. All of Japan's victories occurred during the war's first year. After their defeat at Guadalcanal the Japanese never enjoyed another successful offensive. The gateway to Tokyo had been opened by the gallant men—land, sea, and air—who fought on a shoestring and triumphed in that horrific campaign.

While much has been written about the actions on and around Guadalcanal, Marine Corps operations there have not, until now, received the detailed evaluative treatment they deserve. The principal written record from which historians usually take departure is the 1st Marine Division's after-action report. Its sources were meager, many having been destroyed at the direction of Maj. Gen. Alexander A. Vandegrift at the low point of the battle when he believed it was likely his division would have to withdraw to the center of the island for a last-ditch fight. General Bill Twining wrote that report while

recovering from malaria in Australia—far from many of the
subordinate units whose contribution to the record would
have been invaluable.

General Twining sets the historical record straight in this
magnificent book by telling the Marines' Guadalcanal story
in all its painful reality. What he has written, without adjecti-
val embellishment, is true military history—war with the
bark on it. It is a story told in elegant detail, resounding with
the ring of truth.

Bill Twining is the ideal man to tell this story. He was in the
middle of it from the very beginning. He was a central personality in training the 1st Marine Division, the only U.S. ground
force deemed professionally capable of carrying out Admiral
Ernest J. King's brave plan to stop the southward Japanese
thrust toward New Guinea. When his superiors saw a need for
an advance echelon to deal with the New Zealanders, Twining
was selected to head it. When they wanted an aerial reconnaissance of the Guadalcanal objective area, Twining was chosen
for the hazardous job. As first the assistant operations officer
and later as the operations officer of the division, Twining was
at the heart of its operational planning and an eyewitness to the
most sensitive—and often traumatic—experiences of the end-
of-the-line unit. He watched with revulsion the timidity of the
overall tactical commander, VAdm. Frank Jack Fletcher, who
wanted to convert the Guadalcanal operation into a hit-and-run
raid and who took off after forty-eight hours, directing RAdm.
Richmond K. Turner to depart, too—taking with him much of
the Marines' supplies and equipment.

Twining tells those bitter stories without emotion. He paints
an eloquent picture of Marines—on half-rations (much of
which were captured from the Japanese), emaciated, and
plagued by malaria—taking on the best the emperor had to
offer as they defended precious Henderson Field. And he
describes with unrestrained admiration the heroism of the
Marine, army, and navy pilots who, flying patched-up planes,
took to the air daily and triumphed against fearful odds.

Here is war—real war—in all its nakedness, chronicled in
the words of a wise and perceptive observer. Thanks to Bill

Twining's diligence and persistence, nobody will ever again be able to lament that Guadalcanal has not been given its deserved place in the pages of history.

Every book has weaknesses, of course. This one's chief shortcoming can be found in the very brief, almost misleading, autobiographical remarks the author makes at the beginning. Modest, self-effacing almost to the point of deception, Twining seeks to portray himself as just another in a long line of unremarkable Marines, but he was much more than that. In truth, Twining was marked from the outset of his career as a leader with courage and initiative, a steel-trap mind, and a renown for getting things done—no matter how difficult. His modesty also became legend. His self-deprecatory behavior is best portrayed in his comment herein that "after the war, I served as head of the Marine Corps Board at Quantico, charged with the development of specific postwar planning and legislative duties connected with unification of the armed forces."

What an immense understatement! It would be more accurate to say that after the war Twining perceived, as did few others, the bone-deep hostility to the Marine Corps entertained by the army as well as that service's determination to engineer the elimination of the Corps. Despite the vigorous antagonism of the army, apathy on the part of the navy—which had problems of its own—and opposition in his own branch, often from officers much senior to him, Twining courageously pursued the legislative preservation of the Marine Corps and its mission. He had a little help from a small group of loyal younger officers who believed in him and who were prepared to risk the opprobrium of their seniors in the Corps, but it was Twining—his resolution, his vision, and his wisdom—who won the day. It is his precise words, written with the stub of a lead pencil and recorded in the National Security Act of 1947 (later Title X, United States Code), that protect the Marine Corps to this day.

It is for all these things that Marines past, present, and future are in Bill Twining's debt.

—Lt. Gen. Victor H. Krulak, USMC (Ret.)

Preface

I have tried to portray herein a little-known aspect of the war: the role and responsibilities of the professional staff officer in converting the plans and decisions of the high command into ordered and responsive actions in the forward area of battle. This is the purpose of the military staff.

In the Marine Corps divisional staff there are four staff section chiefs and their functional sections: personnel (D-1), intelligence (D-2), operations (D-3), and logistics (D-4), all headed by a chief of staff reporting directly to the commander. It is not a council of war, as I found out early on, although the head of a section may be questioned freely about those matters pertaining to his particular subdivision because of his presumed detailed knowledge.

During my service in the 1st Marine Division these staff officers were never assembled as a group. Confederate Gen. Stonewall Jackson, early in his career, lost a battle. He is reputed to have said, "I have held a council of war, and I have lost a battle. As God is my witness I will never hold another." General Vandegrift must have read that, too.

The rivalry and discord between line and staff have spanned the decades from the time of Lord St. Vincent, who wrote, "The futile employment ycleped *Staff* should be totally done away, and all the frippery of the Army sent to the devil," to the era of Chesty Puller, who proclaimed in 1942, "Them potted palms up at division, they get promoted because they can write a good letter."

This view is a case of "first, kill all the lawyers" transferred to a military setting. The staff is there because it serves a vital

purpose. Recognition is rare, medals are few, but the successful staff officer can at least take pride in having served as mid-
wife at the birth of great events.

General Vandegrift returned to Melbourne, Australia, from
Washington, D.C., in late March 1943. Then, in addition to
my planning for the Cape Gloucester operation, he designated me to prepare a detailed action report covering operations of the 1st Marine Division on Guadalcanal. An officer
had been attached to the division by the Public Relations Section of Headquarters Marine Corps for this express purpose
but had failed to comply.

Writing the report seemed an insurmountable problem, as
our operations section records had been burned on Guadalcanal in November at the general's specific direction. Consequently, the report had to be based mostly on memory. I wrote
the narrative part of the final report on an additional duty basis, largely at night or when sick in quarters with malaria, and
the time allotted was totally unrealistic due to General Vandegrift's imminent departure to assume command of I Marine
Amphibious Corps (IMAC) with headquarters in Noumea,
New Caledonia.

Memory might have been sufficient for a report covering a
brief operation of two days—even two weeks—but not for a
prolonged campaign like Guadalcanal, which for such purposes extended from 24 June to 9 December 1942. There
were no records to which to refer except the sparse entries in
our operations journal (communications log) and sketchy reports and diaries from organic units of the division in Australia. From remote Melbourne it was impossible for us to
locate and then communicate with the now-scattered elements of the reinforcing air and ground and U.S. Army forces
involved. The result was that the division commanders' final
report included inadequate detail as to the vital services and
contributions of these separate units. It became in reality a report inordinately focused on operations participated in by
units of the 1st Marine Division to the exclusion of Marine

Air, 2d Marine Division, 1st and 2d Marine Raider battalions, and 1st Marine Parachute Battalion.

Consequently, our division commander's final report stank, but at least it stank of the battlefield. The official Guadalcanal monograph, not issued until 1949, also stank, but not of the battlefield. It is largely a rehash of our inadequate final report without a serious effort to fill in the gaps referred to above.

The Guadalcanal Campaign was the decisive battle of the Pacific war, won by the effective joint action of all the arms and services of the United States. In this effort the Marine Corps played a vital and defining part, yet the Corps has never seen fit to produce a first-rate account of its participation in this most important battle in its long and honorable history.

Therefore, as the senior survivor of the battle for Guadalcanal, I am recording my own memories of those momentous events of more than a half century ago.

I was born in Wisconsin and grew up in Oregon, where I learned to hunt, fish, and shoot in company with my five older brothers. Our childhood was greatly influenced by Grandfather Twining, an old soldier who had fought throughout what he always referred to as "the War of the Great Rebellion" and who told us how our family had served in all the nation's wars, beginning with the Plymouth Colonies War against the Narragansett Indians in 1645. In time each of us brothers served in his own war, four of us in two wars. One became chairman of the Joint Chiefs of Staff.

During World War I, at the age of fifteen, I won a competitive appointment to Annapolis, due in large part to my grandfather's tutoring. As an educator, preparing young men for the service academies was his lifelong hobby. I was his last student. His first was George Barnett, who served as major general commandant of the Marine Corps during World War I.

Upon graduating from the U.S. Naval Academy in 1923, I was commissioned a second lieutenant in the Marines. During peacetime I served in a number of assignments that brought me into working contact with the wartime leaders of the Corps.

I participated actively, although in a minor role, in all aspects of the development of amphibious warfare, which was to play such a prominent—yet unforeseen—role in the Atlantic, the Mediterranean, and the Pacific theaters.

My great interest in the Marine Corps became the area of amphibious operations, particularly the defense of advance bases—the business of holding advance bases seized in the island-hopping campaign of a Pacific war, which our Marine Corps leaders had visualized in detail as early as 1921.

Before Pearl Harbor I became the assistant operations officer of the 1st Marine Division. One month after the landing on Guadalcanal, I succeeded my boss, Col. Gerald C. Thomas, USMC, as D-3 (operations) when he became chief of staff of the 1st Division in September 1942. At that time I became responsible for conducting the defense of the Lunga Perimeter until 9 December, when the division was relieved. My duties included preparation and execution of all division-level plans for attack and defense on an hour-to-hour basis—twenty-four hours a day—throughout this period. These activities included the offensive battles along the Matanikau River, the counterattacks at Koli Point, and the successful defenses against the reinforced Sendai Division in October and the simultaneous rout of Japanese forces attempting to break our forward battle position at the mouth of the Matanikau River.

After the war I served as head of the Marine Corps Board at Quantico, Virginia, charged with the development of specific postwar planning and legislation connected with unification of the armed forces.

At the outset of the Korean War I was sent to Camp Pendleton to assist in the embarkation and loading out of the 1st Marine Division for Inchon; and thereafter, the organization of a troop training unit for supplying replacements for units engaged in Korea, and establishment of cold weather training camps in the Sierra Mountains of California.

In 1952 I went to Korea and became assistant division commander of the 1st Marine Division, then holding an active sector in the Punch Bowl area near Korea's east coast. In 1953 I returned to Korea as a major general to command the

1st Marine Division, now on the DMZ near Munsani. Attached to the division were the ROK Marine Division and a Turkish brigade, giving me a corps-size command.

My last tour of duty was in the rank of lieutenant general at Quantico, Virginia, as head of all Marine Corps schools. I retired from the service on 30 October 1959 at Quantico with the rank of general.

Acknowledgments

I thank the following individuals for their cooperation, assistance, and belief in this project:

Capt. James A. Barber, Jr., USN (Ret.), publisher, *U.S. Naval Institute Proceedings,* Annapolis, Maryland, for reassignment of article rights and years of correspondence.

Patrick Carney, chief librarian, base libraries, and Deanna Herrman, library technician, Camp Pendleton, California, for their professionalism and courtesy whenever I needed a book, a reference, or other information.

George B. Clark, the "Brass Hat,"* of Pike, New Hampshire, for his encouragement and always ready supply of names and phone numbers of who to contact for information and photos.

Benis M. Frank, chief historian, History and Museums Division, Marine Corps Historical Center, Washington, D.C., for supplying photos and maps.

Col. John E. Greenwood, USMC (Ret.), editor, *Marine Corps Gazette,* Quantico, Virginia, for reassigning rights to an article of mine and supplying photos and maps.

Lt. Gen. Victor H. Krulak, USMC (Ret.), of San Diego, California, for graciously writing the foreword and for our many years of serving together in the Corps.

Maj. Walter R. Schuette, USMC (Ret.), the "Village Wordsmith," Fallbrook, California, for transcribing much of my handwritten text into computer copy.

Kerry Strong, director of archives, Marine Corps Research

*Clark's Book Sales Business

Center, Quantico, Virginia, for her can-do response to requests for photographs.

Dale Wilson, former executive editor of Presidio Press, for his interest and helpful suggestions.

And those others, too numerous to mention by name, who gave encouragement, time, and information to make this project possible.

CHAPTER I

Amphibious Warfare

Major General J. F. C. Fuller, a distinguished historian of
World War II, was of the opinion that "in all probability amphibious operations were the most far-reaching tactical innovation of the War."[1] They were more than far reaching. They
were decisive. Most certainly they were not "innovations."
The Siege of Troy, the first battle of any sort in recorded history (1194–1184 B.C.), was a majestic example of the amphibious assault involving 1,000 ships and ten years of bitter
warfare on the mainland of Asia Minor. Thereafter the Persians made frequent use of amphibious operations during
their centuries of unrelenting effort to destroy the civilization
of the Greeks.

In 55 B.C. Julius Caesar displayed a surprising grasp of the
art of amphibious warfare in his conquest of Britain. He sent
an advance man to examine beaches secretly along the British coast to determine their suitability for landing. During the
landing itself Caesar used his warships to provide a rudimentary form of naval gunfire support, protecting the unarmed
transports with great flights of arrows and projectiles, the latter hurled ashore by catapults mounted on the warships' decks.
However, he or his advance man made a mistake destined to
be repeated by army generals worldwide over the ensuing
centuries—he chose a gently shelving beach instead of one
steep-to beach. As all Marines and sailors would have known,
this caused his transports to ground at a considerable distance

1. J. F. C. Fuller, *The Second World War* (New York: Duell, Sloan & Pearce,
1949), p. 207.

from the beach itself, requiring the troops to struggle ashore, almost helpless under constant attack by Britons driving their chariots through the surf. Nevertheless, the valor of the 10th Legion eventually prevailed, the landing succeeded, and Britain became Roman.

An embarked landing force possesses unlimited mobility, dependable logistics, and, above all, the ability to achieve surprise in overwhelming strength. No one as yet has found a sure way to oppose this form of attack. In 490 B.C. Miltiades allowed the Persians to land unopposed on the beaches at Marathon before he destroyed them. A century later SunTzu wrote in his *The Art of War*, "When an advancing enemy crosses water do not meet him at the water's edge. It is advantageous to allow half his force to cross and then strike."

The argument has continued over the intervening centuries. In World War II the Japanese employed a water's-edge defense at Tarawa but allowed our forces to land unopposed on Okinawa. The Japanese lost both these islands, although Tarawa was a close call. The Marines were employing the water's-edge defense effectively at both Wake Island and Corregidor before they unwillingly surrendered by the express direction of higher authority.

At the instigation of Marine Corps Commandant John A. Lejeune during the period between the world wars, the Marine Corps made a major effort to develop the doctrine, techniques, and equipment required for the successful conduct of amphibious warfare and to design a method of defense against it. The reasons were twofold. First and foremost was the realization that the British reverse at Gallipoli, with its attendant heavy losses, was largely due to a series of avoidable mistakes arising from a total lack of expertise and doctrine covering the planning and execution of this most difficult of all military operations. Second was the realization that the Orange Plan against Japan would in all probability require the successive seizure of a series of islands extending across the Pacific from Hawaii to Japan, including Guam and the Philippines.

(For ease of conversational reference and informal communications, families of plans were designated by a color. Plans against Japan were named "orange." However, each war plan developed over the years was assigned a separate number for use in formal communications. For example, the ALNAV [All Navy] message mentioned elsewhere in this book mandated execution of one of the series of orange plans in effect on 7 December 1941.)

The requirements of the Orange Plan were clearly envisioned in *Marine Corps Operations Plan 712, Advanced Base Operations in Micronesia,* of 1921. This remarkable document was the work of Lt. Col. Earl H. "Pete" Ellis, USMC, a skilled and experienced war planner. In it he predicted, with uncanny accuracy, the objectives we would need for a successful return to the Western Pacific and, in some cases, precisely the size of the force that would be required. He also forecast the overall nature of future oceanic combat, including the use of carrier aviation as a major weapon. Unfortunately, Ellis did not live to see the enactment of his plan. He died in 1923 under mysterious circumstances while on an intelligence mission in the Japanese-mandated Palau Islands. In a very real sense he was the first casualty of World War II.

The development of an amphibious doctrine was assigned to the Marine Corps schools at Quantico, Virginia, where two small committees of experienced officers were established, one for landing operations and the other for advanced base defense. Their tentative doctrines were tested in fleet maneuvers in the Caribbean from 1922 to 1941 by the East Coast Expeditionary Force, except for those years when this force was engaged in Nicaragua and China.

I participated in several of these operations. In 1924 as a newly commissioned second lieutenant I commanded a rifle platoon assigned to the defense of Firewood Bay on Culebra Island and received my first letter of commendation for repulsing a landing by the 18th Company, 2d Battalion, 5th Marines. This experience roused my intense interest in defensive tactics, which continued throughout my thirty-six years' service in the Corps. In 1937 I commanded a machine gun company in fleet maneuvers at Vieques, Puerto Rico, and the following year during the Puerto Rican maneuvers I served as brigade intelligence officer (B-2). Our maneuver "enemy" was the U.S. Army garrison of Puerto Rico, commanded by Gen. Walter C. Short, who was destined to command the U.S. Army Forces in Hawaii at the time of Pearl Harbor. We surprised him in Puerto Rico by landing at night and moving by covered approaches to seize our objective overlooking the city of Ponce.

Strangely enough, the development of amphibious operations never received the full backing and approval of all senior officers of the Corps. Its successful accomplishment was the work of a minority element directed by Maj. Gen. John H. Russell, sixteenth commandant of the Corps. A strong leader, he faced down opposition that in some cases bordered on outright insubordination. This professional schism remained a factor until after Pearl Harbor.

During these years I served as a Fleet Marine Force officer and also as an instructor in the Marine Corps schools. Forward-looking seniors such as Maj. Gen. Holland M. Smith and Col. Graves B. Erskine encouraged us to broaden our efforts and reach out for new solutions. I served as a member of the Landing Craft Continuation Board, composed of navy and Marine officers, which developed the Higgins boat, the first successful landing craft. Among other things, we conducted experiments using Polaroid-lensed cameras for aerial photography and stereocomparagraphic analysis to determine surf height and underwater contouring of landing beaches. If nothing else, these duties gave me the basics for appreciating the characteristics of beaches and their suitability for landing. I was to find this useful on more than one occasion.

By 1937 the Marine Corps had completed a formal manual for the conduct of landing operations. It was approved by the navy and issued as *Fleet Training Publication 167*, but its circulation was severely limited due to the lack of funds for publication.

Our greatest shortcoming was integrated training in connection with logistics. We lacked training because we had no logistics. Logistics cost money, and we had none. No one had ever seen twenty-five units of fire (ammunition) or sixty days' rations or any other of the weighty allowances needed for combat—bulldozers, cargo trucks, tractors, and construction equipment. The lift capacity (transports and cargo ships) for peacetime maneuvers was less than 1,000 tons overall. (In 1935 the landing force was limited to 258 tons.)[2] Realizing all this in 1941, Maj. Gen. Holland M. "Howling Mad" Smith required us to make up dummy cargo by filling empty ammunition cases with rocks and to bind log segments in bundles of three to simulate 75mm artillery ammunition "clover leaves." But the lift capacity of available amphibious ships imposed a definite ceiling even for these expedients. No one had ever even seen a completely combat-loaded division until we landed in the Solomons on 7 August 1942.

In one category of amphibious warfare development the U.S. Navy had far outstripped the Marine Corps. The U.S. Navy Medical Corps, which also serves the Marine Corps, was responsible for the development of techniques and the procurement of medical equipment meeting the special requirements of a force engaged in landing operations on hostile shores.

Capt. Warwick T. Brown, Medical Corps, U.S. Navy, was for years the senior naval officer serving with the Fleet Marine Force. He heeded this aspect of his duties very seriously, taking sufficient time to think the problems through and then vigorous steps to solve them.

Brown began this activity as early as 1937, when he joined the 1st Marine Brigade of the Fleet Marine Force at Quantico. He stayed on the job with us for eight years. When we entered the war, the medical requirements of amphibious warfare stood close to fulfillment and from the outset met the needs of actual combat in a highly satisfactory manner. This was largely due to the foresight and energy of one man, Captain Brown.

2. Lt. Gen. H. M. Smith, *The Development of Amphibious Tactics in the U.S. Navy* (Washington, DC: History and Museums Division Headquarters, U.S. Marine Corps, 1992), p. 250.

The Marine Corps persevered in this development activity for over two decades. It received some support from the navy, but there was little or no interest on the part of the army. By the midthirties, the Corps, working substantially alone, had produced a remarkable body of doctrine and tactics for the successful conduct of amphibious warfare and had begun the active development of the necessary equipment, such as landing craft, tank lighters, and amphibious vehicles. With the fall of France in June 1940, it became obvious to all that amphibious warfare had suddenly become the key to victory in the war in the Atlantic as well as in the rapidly deteriorating situation in the Pacific. Even the British expressed a reawakened interest in what for years they had dismissed as "the wet stuff."

Our own navy became very active, converting merchant vessels to attack transports and building landing craft in great numbers and in a wide variety of useful types. They also expanded and updated *FTP 167*, distributing it extensively throughout the fleet. I was engaged in this latter effort under the direction of Col. Arch Howard at Marine Corps schools. It was interesting and useful work that gave me a picture of the entire field. My major contribution was a slender chapter covering onshore patrols, based on my experience during recent ventures in this entirely new field while I was with the Fleet Marine Force. After the war and for the rest of my service I headed the Marine Corps panel, which, with the navy, twice rewrote the entire amphibious doctrine: the first time to incorporate wartime lessons and the second to encompass the employment of new weapons, particularly helicopters, to lessen the atomic threat.

The employment of high-speed helicopters as a replacement for the slow moving landing craft of World War II permitted deployment of the ships carrying the landing force over a large area, the dimensions of which were undreamed of in World War II. In 1944 at Iwo Jima a single Hiroshima-size bomb, well placed, would have destroyed both the ships of the attack force and the troops ashore. Today such a force, taking advantage of the helicopter's speed, is able to disperse over an area so large as to render atomic attack indecisive. In addition, there is no congestion of troops and supplies at the beach line because troop units accompanied by their supplies are landed at dispersed locations well inland from the shoreline and in tactical formations rather than as a highly vulnerable mass at the landing beach.

The ability to originate and develop is not a normal attribute of a rigidly disciplined service like the Marine Corps, with its high regard for tradition and precedent, but we were guided and inspired during those formative years by the example and leadership of a remarkable group of men, among them Maj. Gen. Holland M. Smith, Brig. Gen. Charles D. Barrett, and Col. Graves B. Erskine. These men had one trait in common: the ability to elicit willing and enthusiastic participation so that ideas moved in both directions—up as well as down the chain of command.

This startling, almost revolutionary idea had originated in the very sensible mind of Gen. Ulysses S. Grant during the series of bloody struggles following the Battle of the Wilderness. His generals began complaining that the men were using their canteen cups to scrape out shallow depressions in the ground to shelter themselves from the murderous rifle fire of the entrenched Confederates. The generals were discussing ways and means of halting this obnoxious practice when Grant broke in, saying, in effect, "This army has fought and fought well for over three years. If the soldiers now find it necessary to do what you complain of, they must have a reason. We will incorporate what they are doing into our method of attack."

Shovels were issued, and the foxhole—which has saved more lives than armor—was born.

This mind-set in our handful of leaders speeded development of what was needed in every category of the amphibious art. My old friend Sgt. William "Stinky" Davis, who could build anything, had an obsession for bridges, which he built in one form or another from Shanghai to Guantanamo

Bay. Davis persuaded General Smith to let him build a self-propelled amphibian bridge using two LVTs (amphibian tractors). He constructed a supporting framework on each, loaded the hulls with the necessary additional parts—prefabricated for speedy installation—and we had the world's first sea-going bridge. The LVTs swam ashore, crossed the beach, and moved inland to the desired point of erection. The LVTs were anchored in place and served as pontoons to support the floating bridge. All this was developed in an incredibly short time.

Other contraptions, less spectacular but equally useful, competed for attention. The amphibian tractor itself was, in a way, the product of the same outpouring of initiative. For years we had sought a way to land on beaches protected by continuous offshore coral reefs that would not permit passage of landing craft, a hydrographic condition chronic to most Central and South Pacific beaches. One annual school problem, the recapture of Guam, was a case in point. There were no coral-free landing beaches on Guam except a tiny cul-de-sac at a remote spot known as Talafofo Bay. The students howled in disgust. Something had to be done.

Donald Roebling of the famous engineering family had built a swamp buggy for rescue work in the Everglades. This became the amphibian tractor, or LVT, of World War II after an intensive period of development. It was reasonably seaworthy and relied for propulsion on its two tanklike treads rather than a propeller. The same traction system gave it good mobility on land and also afforded a considerable obstacle-crossing capability, including the all-important ability to cross coral reefs.

The appearance of this vehicle in the Pacific completely upset the Japanese calculations of the forces required for island defense. The coral no longer protected them, and they felt it necessary to increase greatly the forces assigned to carry out the task. This was a mistake, of course, because he who attempts to be strong everywhere will find himself weak everywhere. This expansion of Japanese forces imposed a terrific additional requirement for shipping, which in turn provided a multitude of highly vulnerable targets for our submarines.

Just as the secret masses of German artillery in 1914 were heralded as the major strategic surprise of World War I, the LVT may have been the strategic surprise of the Oceanic War.

I served long enough to see the modern navy/Marine Corps doctrine employed by common consent, if not officially, by all the NATO countries and have lived long enough to see amphibious operations grow from the status of a neglected orphan to a naval capability of premier importance.

We Americans are a warlike people, but we are not militarists. Consequently, we have shown little peacetime interest in the art of war and have made few peacetime contributions thereto. The successful and continuing development of the amphibious art by Marines may well rank as the greatest exception to the rule. There is every indication that the form of operation in which we pioneered and excelled will remain one of our nation's principal capabilities in preserving the peace and order of an uncertain world.

CHAPTER 2

Old George

The saying "let George do it" has been with us for a long time. It was used most frequently in the days of travel by Pullman car along the railroads of America, when all porters responded cheerfully to the universal cognomen "George." Currently it seems to be unknown in England, but there is an eighteenth-century English tavern song that begins "Call again for George, boys, call for George again." Presumably "George" was the name for the man who fetched the drinks.

So it was in the 1st Marine Division. Since its designation as a division on 1 February 1941—the first such organization in the history of the Corps—it had been assigned a bewildering array of tasks and subjected to inroads of every description. In addition, it was responsible for developing contingency plans and making preparations for the occupation and defense of sensitive areas in the Atlantic deemed critical to the Allied cause—Martinique, Dakar, and the Azores.

The enlargement from brigade to division size necessitated the formation of two new infantry regiments; the augmentation of the 11th Marines, our artillery regiment; and the creation of new divisional organizations such as the Division Special Weapons Battalion. In addition, there were crippling transfers of valuable, skilled, and experienced personnel to other newly formed organizations such as the 1st and 2d Marine Raider battalions and the 1st Parachute Battalion. These wholesale transfers of key personnel, unavoidable though they were, resulted temporarily in a marked drop in combat efficiency and state of readiness, especially in the case of the 5th Marines, which was hardest hit by all these inroads.

We were the "let George do it" division of the Marine Corps. The 2d Division, already partially committed in Iceland, was necessarily exempted from transferring any of their seasoned noncommissioned officers. Lt. Col. Gerald C. "Jerry" Thomas, then our assistant division operations officer, soon shortened the nickname to "Old George." That name has stuck to the 1st Marine Division, an organization that has probably done more fighting in this century than any similar unit in any of the world's armed forces. World War II, China, Korea, Vietnam, Kuwait City, and Mogadishu—"Old George" was always there and always rose to the occasion.

During this prewar period the division was living under canvas at Camp Lejeune, near Jacksonville, North Carolina. This was a fine training area, and we made the most of it. Amphibious training was conducted simultaneously on a battalion basis by sending one unit at a time to the lower Chesapeake Bay, where transports could operate in protected waters near Solomon's Island—a portentous name, although we were not aware of it at the time. Brig. Gen. Alexander Archer Vandegrift, the assistant division commander, was in charge of all training and I was his operations officer and assistant. It was a rewarding assignment.

One Sunday in December, I had planned to go squirrel hunting with Maj. Lewis "Chesty" Puller, an old friend. Instead I got shafted out of turn with the weekend staff duty. Puller went home to Saluda, Virginia, to be with his family. That afternoon I was doing paperwork in my office when an orderly from communications dropped an ALNAV on my desk. The dispatch read, "Execute WPL 46 against Japan."

That brief message changed a lot of things in the 1st Marine Division. We could abandon the onerous peacetime safety regulations and conduct realistic combat training using ball ammunition for field problems and overhead fire by artillery and machine guns. The men responded with patriotic enthusiasm and intense interest. Progress toward a state of combat readiness was quickly apparent. Despite cold, snowy weather, morale in the tent camps reached a high state. The only exception was one dour old colonel who failed to comply with the wartime relaxations of the rule forbidding the use of ball ammunition in field combat exercises and incurred Vandegrift's undying wrath, leading to the colonel's early replacement. I heard the general muttering under his breath, "Damned old schoolteacher."

After Pearl Harbor I spent a great part of my time at Solomon's Island on Chesapeake Bay conducting amphibious training exercises. Maj. Gen. Holland M. Smith, Commander, Landing Force Atlantic, and his chief of staff, Col. Graves B. Erskine, set up a headquarters ashore. General Vandegrift and I stayed with them. It was particularly interesting and informative to listen to them discuss the background issues of the war against Japan. The loss of most of our battleships would make impossible a quick attack against the Japanese homeland. This had long been the dream of the thrusters, that faction in the navy advocating an immediate response to a Japanese surprise attack. There was now nothing with which to thrust, at least until the giant new battleships of the North Carolina class joined the fleet. Until then, the island-hopper faction must of necessity hold sway.

There was frequent reference to a prominent navy war planner, Rear Adm. Richmond Kelly Turner. He was not supposed to be a thruster. Nevertheless, he had delivered a lecture in 1938 indicating that the fleet would go all the way to Japan "on its own tail" (supported solely by ships, without the necessity of establishing bases en route). Such a course would render our Fleet Marine Force superfluous to the main effort—a matter of deep concern to us all.

The very raison d'etre of the Fleet Marine Force was the seizure and defense of advance bases. The island-hopping plan was firmly tied to Pete Ellis's brilliant strategy of seizing a series of naval bases to support the advance of the fleet across the Central Pacific, including the recovery of Guam and the Philippines. The plan had remained under constant study in our schools, which annually studied and refined in detail the seizure of Kwajalein, Saipan, Guam, and even the Palaus (Babelthuap). Naval officers as well as Marines attended the Marine Corps schools in those days, and their valuable practical input gave the plans added credibility in the eyes of the navy, leading to their eventual acceptance.

One day all the generals went to Washington for a conference. I returned to the transport *Hunter Liggett* (AP-27) to supervise the day's training. After dark, General Vandegrift returned alone and told me he had been appointed to command of the 1st Marine Division, relieving Maj. Gen. Phil Torrey, who was going to Quantico. As division commander he needed to form a new staff and offered me the job of assistant to Lieutenant Colonel Thomas, the new operations officer (D-3).

I was more than happy to accept. It gave me a chance to serve under one of the most highly esteemed and best-liked officers in the Corps. During World War I Thomas had served with distinction in France, where he was wounded and decorated and earned a field commission. In Haiti, following the war, Jerry distinguished himself in a sharp night combat with a superior Caco force. In the years of peace he had held highly responsible positions and acquired a reputation for outstanding leadership, professionalism, and devotion to our small Corps.

Responding to General Vandegrift's constant scrutiny and supervision, the division advanced rapidly toward a state of readiness. We were still armed with the old Springfield rifle and sadly lacking in such new weapons as antitank guns, although we began getting a few, which we put to good use in our training.

New information as to the employment of the division was discouraging. We were told that our 1st Marine Division would probably be used as a source of smaller cadres to garrison Pacific islands because, due to possible army objections, the navy was reluctant to employ Marine units larger than a regiment. This was a severe blow to morale.

Our 7th Marines were the first to go out, bound for garrison duty in Samoa. They were going to war, and the rest of us apparently weren't, so we gave them everything we had—new weapons, scarce equipment, and their choice of officers to bring units up to strength.

After their departure we concentrated on expanding the 1st Marines, which hitherto had existed as only a small cadre. We had plenty of capable and experienced field officers. Company commanders were largely drawn from officers with good service in the peacetime Marine Corps Reserve. I recall particularly officers like Capt. Charles Brush and 1st Lt. Walter McLlhenny, who rapidly developed the fighting quality of their organizations. However, most of the junior officers were young college men who had just completed officer training at Quantico. I had been associated with this group there and reckoned them to be of unusually high caliber. They were to prove me right, both on the battlefield and in their subsequent careers in civilian life.

The senior noncommissioned officers were of an older type, ranging from plank owners in navy yards to skilled personnel from weapons ranges and ship's detachments. Under the leadership of Col. (later Gen.) Clifton B. Cates, they quickly developed into a battle-worthy combat unit that proved its worth at the Tenaru River in mid-August 1942. They progressed rapidly through the basic training cycle, and at least one battalion completed its amphibious training at Solomon's Island.

We had little more than said goodbye to the 7th Marines when, to our great relief, the entire division was alerted for an emergency move to the South Pacific. Wellington, New Zealand, was our destination, and there we would be expected to reach a state of readiness permitting our employment "in minor amphibious operations early in 1943."[1] Again, I suspect that the phrase "minor amphibious operations" was employed as a tactful way of assuaging army sensibilities.

The movement of the 1st Division to New Zealand, although of an emergency nature, was greatly complicated by the unforeseen congestion of wartime traffic that had suddenly overburdened the nation's transportation facilities, hitherto

1. This phrase originated in the Navy War Plans office during the visit of General Vandegrift and his staff. In my orders to New Zealand as advance man I was specifically directed to inform the New Zealand Army authorities of this eventuality. There were no formalities. It was done on a piecemeal, transitory basis.

considered an unlimited resource by military planners. Only one regiment, the 5th Marines (reinforced), plus division headquarters, could be embarked on *Wakefield* (AP-21), a transport that could carry 6,000 men, and then sail directly from Norfolk, Virginia, via the Panama Canal to New Zealand. Their tanks and other heavy equipment would have to be moved by rail to New Orleans for loading aboard *Electra* (AK-21), a navy cargo ship, and SS *del Brazil*, a U.S. merchantman.

The balance of the division, the 1st Marine Regimental Combat Team, would be moved at an unspecified date by rail to San Francisco, where it would load out on SS *Ericsson*, a large Scandinavian passenger liner, also destined for Wellington.

The need for such a complex scheme to move a single division was a sad commentary on the presumably unlimited resources of the greatest and most powerful nation in the world. The situation is even worse today, for we no longer possess the great system of railways that were available to us in 1942. We are now largely dependent on a national system of motor transport that would come to a screeching halt if oil imports were cut off by hostile action, because we no longer possess the vast untapped underground military reserves formerly held back to meet such an emergency. Today's military planners appear blissfully oblivious of this jarring contingency.

CHAPTER 3

Advance Man in
New Zealand

On receiving information of the proposed move to New Zealand, General Vandegrift, accompanied by a small staff group, proceeded to Washington by overnight rail. The general detached himself and conferred with the commandant of the Marine Corps, Lt. Gen. Thomas Holcomb, and with Rear Adm. Richmond Kelly Turner, head of War Plans, and Vice Adm. Robert L. Ghormley, the intended commander, South Pacific Area and South Pacific Force. We in the staff group were briefly introduced and then separated in order to confer with planners at the working level.

I cannot forget our discussion with the navy's logistics planner, a handsome, well-uniformed Harvard School of Business Administration type. Unfortunately, he knew little of logistics beyond the details of ship's supply and nothing at all about the logistics problems confronting a landing force, and he was adamant in his refusal to learn. Lt. Col. Randy Pate, our newly arrived D-4 (logistics), conducted our side of the discussion admirably, but to no avail. The official position was deceptively simple: "The navy will embark sixty days' supply." Period.

Pate explained our recent experiences with navy supply and particularly the matter of troop rations. The navy ration provided fresh meat, eggs, dairy products, and corn flakes in great abundance and in commercial packages. This was satisfactory for ship or supermarket but totally unsuited for the rough trip across a hostile shore in any kind of weather. Furthermore, and of much greater importance, many of these navy components required refrigeration, a service totally unavailable to a landing force. Pate quite reasonably insisted that the rations embarked be modified by the substitution of increased quantities of canned meat, evaporated milk, and other dry stores more suited to the inhospitable landing-force environment ashore.

Our informant's only reply was the single phrase, "the navy will embark sixty days' supply." Pate pressed him sharply, but he clung to his position like a drunk to a lamppost: "The navy will embark sixty days' supply."

And so they did. And so Aotea Quay in Wellington and later Red Beach in Guadalcanal were ankle deep in a mushy melange of corn flakes, Quaker Oats, and Post Toasties as the driving rains of a South Pacific winter dissolved the flimsy cardboard containers dumped ashore. What an unnecessary waste.

In the afternoon it was my turn to shine as we conferred with two members of the Anzac military mission to the United States, a New Zealand lieutenant colonel, retreaded from World War I, and a bright young Australian captain. As the advance man charged with arranging for the construction of our camps and facilities in the Wellington area, I was interested in ascertaining what construction items could be obtained in New Zealand and what items we would have to bring with us. Must we plan for just the movement of the division or, in effect, the removal of its base as well? The logistical impact on a small country would be considerable in the latter case, for we would have to contract for materials locally produced in an isolated nation whose young men had gone to war some two years earlier. The results of our discussions were not altogether satisfactory, but it was a great improvement over the morning's fiasco.

We took the night train back to North Carolina. En route General Vandegrift briefed us on his visit to War Plans. Essentially we would complete our training in New Zealand, attaining a state of readiness sufficient to undertake minor amphibious operations sometime after 1 January 1943.

I was given a one-page letter of instructions and a set of air priority travel orders. The letter directed me to report to the

New Zealand Army authorities at Wellington and secure their assistance in the procurement and construction of facilities suitable for the cantonment and training of a reinforced Marine division—approximately 13,000 men—in the Wellington area. Also, I was to inform the New Zealand authorities that we were to be ready to undertake minor amphibious operations after 1 January 1943.

I was accompanied by Chief Quartermaster Clerk Harry Detwiler, who had been provided with a $50,000 check to cover the costs of the project. Much to my relief, the check was never cashed. A wonderful international mechanism known as Lend-Lease picked up the tab in New Zealand.

We flew on Pan American Airlines' comfortable China Clipper from San Francisco to Pearl Harbor. At Pearl, I was interrogated by two crafty naval officers of Nimitz's staff, who seemed more interested in command politics than in the war. After satisfying themselves that I was just a dumb Marine from North Carolina, they sent me by auto into Honolulu, where Detwiler and I stayed first class at the beachfront Moana Hotel.

The still jittery island was under a military curfew, and people spooked at the strike of a match. Everything was completely blacked out, and the hotel night clerk even objected to Detwiler and me conferring in my room as we tried to plan for what lay ahead of us. Before daylight we were picked up for the ride to NAS Ford Island to catch our plane. The trip to Pearl Harbor was slowed by frequent stops for inspection by the military and civilian police, who apparently were not satisfied with the degree to which our headlights had been blacked out with blue paint.

At Ford Island we boarded a navy PBM, the most beautiful flying boat I have ever seen, although the smaller but more efficient PBY became the flying workhorse of the Pacific War. Our PBM was commanded by Comdr. Bill Rassieur, friend and classmate of Naval Academy days. He ran a ship as taut as any man-o'-war and was ably seconded by Comdr. Sam Pickering, another old friend. Rassieur and Pickering seemed unusually curious about what I was up to. Years later Bill told me that I had been assigned—undoubtedly by mistake—an astronomically high flight priority usually reserved for VIPs of Olympic stature. That also explains the reason for the persistent questioning I got at CinCPac. Undoubtedly the two debriefing officers there believed that my story about camp building in New Zealand was a cover-up for something about which Admiral Nimitz, the commander in chief, Pacific, ought to know.

The trip to Auckland, New Zealand, took five days with overnight stays at Johnston and Canton Islands, Suva, and Noumea. The Marine garrison at Johnston was on its toes getting set for an expected Japanese attack. Morale was high, and they were grimly determined to get even for the loss of Wake.

At Canton we ran into Lt. John D. Bulkeley and the other torpedo boat commander who had recently brought the MacArthur party out of the Philippines. They were headed home. We stayed in adjoining rooms in what had been the old Pan Am guest house. Far into the night the PT boat commanders regaled us with the story of their breakout and perilous journey. They spoke warmly of MacArthur but were more than a little critical of some of the staff officers who accompanied him and who tried to force Bulkeley to abandon the crew of one of the two PT boats when it became disabled. To his credit Bulkeley stoutly asserted his proper authority as commanding officer and determinedly enforced the law of the sea, which from time immemorial has denounced the abandonment of those exposed to its wanton cruelties. Bulkeley appeared modest and reserved. The other skipper—the one who would have been left behind—was far more outgoing and, understandably, somewhat more vehement.

Bulkeley went on to a most distinguished career, winning the Medal of Honor and retiring as a vice admiral after fifty-nine years' service, the longest U.S. naval career on record.

At Suva we stayed in a fine British hotel but found the East Indian staff in a state of near mutiny. They apparently sensed that a Japanese takeover was at hand and that, as members of the new Japanese Greater East Asia Co-prosperity Sphere, they would be able to revenge themselves on the British Raj. They were surly to the point of outright insolence, refused to perform many customary hotel services, but insisted on large tips. The British management, in despair, pleaded with us to put up with their malarkey and were terrified that someone of our party would succumb to the urge toward physical violence, which in their minds is always associated with Americans. I admit the temptation was great. Similar conduct was reported from Singapore before that bastion fell without putting up a fight.

We arrived in Noumea to find that the U.S. Americal Division had taken over after some shadowboxing with the surly and uncooperative Free French. New Caledonia's large nickel deposits were a vital element in our nation's fast-expanding arms production. Canadian resources of that metal proved inadequate for the vast program planned for the immediate future.

Our naval presence appeared very sketchy. The seaplane tender *Tangier* (AV-8) and two squadrons of PBYs appeared to be the only U.S. Navy forces left in the South Pacific area following the Battle of the Coral Sea. We overnighted on board *Tangier*, whose three-stripe exec seemed more interested in collecting our mess bills than in doing anything else, even though this was usually the collateral duty of a very junior officer.

I reported in at the commander, South Pacific, headquarters (ComSoPac) in Auckland, New Zealand, the next day. Admiral Ghormley had not yet reached New Zealand, and his chief of staff, Rear Adm. Dan Callaghan, was in charge, assisted by my old friend Col. DeWitt Peck, USMC, an able staff officer of wide experience. After a short but productive discussion they put me on the night train to Wellington. Upon arrival, I reported to the headquarters of the New Zealand Army, then under the command of Lieutenant General Puttick.

I was asked to report further to Colonel Salmon, a most able and energetic officer recruited from the highest levels of New Zealand's business executives. He was serving in a key position in the logistics branch of their general staff. He knew

I was coming and what my errand would be. I was able to provide him with all information relative to size, organization, and approximate arrival time of the Marine contingents of the division and their peculiar requirements as an amphibious force. He had served with the Anzacs in World War I and, I believe, participated in the 1915 landing at the Dardanelles (Gallipoli). He designated an engineer officer, Captain Shepherd, as my guide and advisor, then sent us out to find locations suitable for the camps and other facilities the division would need.

The next few days were hectic. We prowled the hills and valleys from dawn to dark searching for sites. I'm convinced that New Zealand has only two directions, up and down. Although I was raised in the hills of Oregon and my Marine Corps duty kept me fit, I had to struggle to keep up. Each morning Shepherd would offer the same reassurance for the day's undertakings, "Just a few easy downs today. We'll be back for tea." The downs were not easy, and we never returned in time for tea. Once we waded across a beautiful trout stream. "Any fish?" I asked. "Just a lot of little chaps," he replied, indicating by holding his palms about eighteen to twenty inches apart. Trout must come big in New Zealand. I never had time to find out.

Soon we decided to center the proposed installation around McKay's Crossing, twenty miles north of Wellington. This site provided an unlimited area several miles long by a quarter mile wide of nearly flat beachfront, suitable for the campsite plus necessary drill fields. It was also readily accessible by road and rail. It was backed on the east by an endless expanse of rolling hills, perhaps 300 feet high, given over to grazing sheep. This was the kind of training area the Corps had needed and dreamed of for years, and it was much like the site of our present Camp Pendleton, just north of San Diego, California.

This would give us a fine area for training, firing exercises, and physical conditioning and an extensive beach area for our beach defense and landing operations activities. In addition, there were smaller areas nearby suited to the unique requirements of specialized units such as our amphibian tractor battalion and boat pool, both needing the protected waters afforded by a small harbor. We lacked only an artillery firing range but were offered intermittent use of an existing New Zealand army range situated not too far north of Wellington. Within four days we were able to submit a plan embracing locations and requirements for a main camp at McKay's Crossing, four small additional camps nearby to the south, a proposed airstrip to the north, and nine additional facilities required for logistical purposes in and around Wellington (dumps, storage areas, offices, and so forth). These latter were the special province of my able, energetic, and extremely valuable assistant Harry Detwiler, who quickly established wide personal contacts throughout the Wellington area that proved extremely important as events, foreseen and otherwise, unfolded.

The final step was to receive the approval of the commander of the New Zealand Armed Forces, General Puttick. This fine officer had recently distinguished himself by his brilliant conduct of the withdrawal from Crete following the collapse of Greece. With only a small and greatly outnumbered force, he had inflicted heavy losses on Hitler's airborne elements, drastically limiting their future value to the Axis in North Africa. Naturally Puttick was a hero to the people of New Zealand throughout this dark hour of the war.

The U.S. military attache in New Zealand was Colonel Nankeville, an elderly U.S. Army officer born in New Zealand. He loved the country and was a popular local figure. Learning of my mission, he tried to persuade me to establish the division in the Lower Hutt Valley, a sprawling bedroom community adjoining Wellington on the north.

The proposed site consisted primarily of a severely restricted fairground area surrounded by residences and subjected to urban traffic along the narrow New Zealand roads. It was confining and provided no direct access to the sea or any other suitable training grounds. To move at all would require use of motor transport far in excess of the division's limited organic allowance, thus forcing an additional burden on New Zea-

land's own limited resources. The social aspects of super-
imposing a large military force upon the population of an already developed community were also debatable. I therefore
could not accede to Colonel Nankeville's suggestions, which,
I believe, were made on behalf of Major General Weir, who
exercised immediate command of the New Zealand troops
defending the beaches. To be sure, our presence on the West
Coast would be a factor complicating his defense planning,
but certainly not an overriding one.

As an officer of the Marine Corps, I had enjoyed an unusual amount of experience in the field of beach defense and
the defense of advanced bases, had taught the subject in our
schools, and had contributed to its professional literature. I
had seen no evidence of training or preparation for defense
along the New Zealand coast beyond the erection of a few
concrete dragon's teeth on the coastal highway north of the
capital. I never asked questions, but saw nothing to indicate
that anything more than the most meager of forces existed.
The reason was that with a generosity bordering on nobil-
ity, the New Zealanders had sent their men to the great battles:
North Africa, Tobruk, Crete, and Singapore. In their present
moment of need they stood isolated and alone.

I kept all these things uppermost in my mind when I attended the conference called by Lieutenant General Puttick
at his headquarters. It was a rather large meeting and included most of New Zealand's senior army officers. General
Weir's officers gave a fair and tactful presentation of their
views. They felt our presence on the coast was undesirable
because of our specified and overriding amphibious mission;
that our availability for local defense could not be regarded as
a certainty; and that, because of the murky command relationships, they could not regard us as an absolute in their defense equation. I was not asked to speak, but General Puttick
did ask me, "How well do you know General Vandegrift?" I
replied to the effect that he had personally selected me as his
operations officer when he became assistant division commander of the 1st Marine Division. I said that in 1923 I had

served with him in the 5th Marine Regiment at Quantico, Virginia, and again in the 3d Marine Brigade under Brig. Gen. Smedley Butler in China in 1927–28, and that Vandegrift had selected me to come to New Zealand in my present capacity as advance officer to arrange for arrival and training in the Wellington area. I tried, without saying so, to convey the impression that Archer Vandegrift was not a man who would bring a Marine division halfway around the world to surrender it to the Japanese without a fight and that he would draw a willing sword in the defense of New Zealand's territory if the need arose.

Persuasive speech is not one of my accomplishments, but I must have enjoyed a measure of success on this occasion. Construction of our main camp on the beach at McKay's Crossing began at daylight the next morning. I had been in New Zealand for only a few days. In the United States it would have taken weeks to cut through the barriers of red tape and bureaucracy to achieve the same result.

I went to McKay's Crossing (also known as Paekakariki) each day to observe the construction. I was surprised to see that the work was being done almost entirely by hand. Even the concrete was mixed in small machines turned by hand. There were large numbers of rather elderly laborers, including some women. Noting my surprise, Major Parsons, the New Zealand engineer officer who accompanied me, said sadly, "We sent all our construction equipment to Singapore to work on the fortifications there." The work was performed largely by the New Zealand Department of Public Works in conjunction with the New Zealand Army Engineers. It was all done under the Lend-Lease agreement between the United States and New Zealand.

Through Major Parsons, the New Zealand authorities inquired, somewhat nervously I thought, about what standards of construction we would expect in our camps. He showed me a magazine depicting the rather luxurious semipermanent installations built for our forces already occupying bases in Bermuda and the Bahamas. They were greatly reassured to learn that we expected nothing like that. "Old George" had never known any luxury at home and certainly did not expect it here. We had always lived under our own canvas and needed little beyond sanitary facilities (heads and showers) and screened galleys for preparing rations. Personnel would live in squad tents pitched on wooden decks. We had lived happily this way in the past at Guantanamo and during the snowy winter of 1941–42 in North Carolina. Not quite convinced and feeling that they could do more for us, they insisted on four-man wooden huts they called "baches" instead of the tent decks I had suggested. These were constructed of green lumber from their South Island forests cut from trees in which the birds had been singing the week before.

At the end of the second week the engineers realized that they could not meet the scheduled date of completion at this slow rate of progress and agreed with me on the substitution of wooden tent decks with strongbacks for supporting the tents. I had brought with me construction sketches and the precise measurements used in our North Carolina tent camps. The New Zealand crews immediately shifted to this simplified form of construction. The rate of progress greatly accelerated, and the project was soon back on schedule. No Marine in the New Zealand winter ever was required to live without adequate shelter or under unsanitary conditions. It was a great accomplishment by a country severely handicapped and distraught by war.

Rationing the troops presented no great problem, as New Zealand produced an abundance of food in great variety and of unsurpassed quality. Wartime lack of shipping had isolated both New Zealand and Australia, and exports were reduced to a trickle. Their shelves were full. All they wanted was a statement of our requirements. I had with me a copy of the Marine Corps ration in the form used in subsistence contracts at home. It specified the exact amounts of each item of a proper ration for one Marine for thirty days. It proved of great interest to all the New Zealanders involved. They noted sadly the minuscule allowance of mutton—their great national favorite. No matter, they were up to the rafters in beef and pork. "Ice cream in the ration? Ice cream is not a dessert; it is a sweet. But you can have all you want; we have plenty." It was good, too—better than ours and made with real cream.

One night I answered a phone call from the rationing authority. "You are allowing only one-sixteenth of an ounce of tea per man per month. This is obviously an error." I replied that I could not recall ever having seen a mug of hot tea served in a Marine Corps mess, but once in a blue moon, in extremely hot weather, we had iced tea. They could have it all as far as I was concerned. The New Zealanders were overjoyed. They had little tea for themselves and no way of getting more at this stage of the war. We were promised all the coffee we could use. It was grown on a subtropical island to the north. Good stuff too, but not the way they brewed it.

There was only one other American living at the Waterloo Hotel where I was staying. This was Brig. Gen. Pat Hurley, sent by President Roosevelt to Australia to persuade MacArthur to leave the Philippines. "Easiest job I ever had," Hurley quipped to me more than once.

The Roosevelt administration asked Hurley to remain "down under" as U.S. ambassador to New Zealand's Labor government. A warm, vibrant, fun-loving man, full of grace and irrepressible humor, he enlivened the grim New Zealand scene and found a warm spot in the heart of all the Kiwis in return.

It all started at a parade in Hurley's honor shortly after his arrival. The parade went on as the usual sober affair until Pat spotted a mounted detachment approaching the reviewing stand. As a former Oklahoma cowboy, a cavalryman, and a born showman, he found the situation irresistible. He greeted the approaching horsemen with the first Rebel yell ever heard in New Zealand. It was the wildest whoop since Pickett's Charge. It woke all the dignitaries. The spectators cheered him until the place echoed. It was the Rebel yell heard 'round New Zealand.

New Zealanders are reserved, conservative, and dignified to a degree; but they expect something a little different from Americans. They were not disappointed in Pat Hurley, who brought a message of renewed hope and cheer at the time of

the Singapore surrender, when they found themselves isolated from the mother country and yet not quite sure of the
strength and depth of American support.

Hurley always spoke kindly to me and sometimes invited
me to have dinner at his table. On one such night it was raining hard, a real toad choker. We were the only guests in the
large dining room with five gracious waitresses to assist us.
General Hurley scanned the typical British menu. One allit-
erative item always intrigued him, and he would read it aloud:
"Pickled pork and parsnips." After dinner he herded the ma-
tronly waitresses and me out of the hotel, insisting we all go
to a movie. We crowded into the ambassador's large limou-
sine. Then, after the fine show, with rain still pouring, we de-
posited each lady on her own doorstep and returned to the
hotel in triumph.

With camp construction properly under way I directed my
attention to the Wellington harbor area, which I knew would
soon be the center of much activity. The shoreside facilities
consisted of a number of small piers built long ago and incon-
venient for modern operation, particularly in connection with
military cargoes and equipment.

However, one large modern and commodious installation
was available to us: Aotea Quay. It would accommodate three
to five ships, depending upon their size, moored bow to stern
along the harbor side. Construction was of reinforced concrete with broad, unobstructed areas for cargo storage and
unimpeded movement of heavy trucks. It was a beautiful facility in which the New Zealanders took great and justifiable
pride. I saw nothing to equal it in any of the other ports of the
South or Southwest Pacific: Auckland, Sydney, Melbourne,
Brisbane, or Noumea. Without it we could not have met the
swift movement demands that would be placed upon us by
events then unforeseen.

Construction of the camp was now well under way, and I
had time to begin preparations for the arrival of the division
itself.

Navy ships began assembling in the harbor. Two transport divisions—*McCawley* (AP-10), *Neville* (AP-16), *Fuller*

(AP-14), and *American Legion* (AP-35), together with their auxiliaries—were first. The vessels had just disembarked the 7th Marines (reinforced) in Samoa, where they were deployed in defense of those islands and consequently had passed out of the division's control. Then these ships were unexpectedly diverted to New Zealand to take part in amphibious training exercises with the remainder of the division, numbering 13,000 men, and consisting of two reinforced regiments, an artillery regiment, and division troops, all proceeding to Wellington in two echelons. Neither had yet arrived.

The commodore of this first unit was Capt. Lawrence Reifsnider, USN, commanding the *American Legion*. It was a lucky break for the Marines and the military fortunes of the United States that Captain Reifsnider was the senior officer present afloat (SOPA). Many of the transport captains were disgruntled, passed-over officers who regarded their present jobs as bottom-of-the-barrel, end-of-the-road assignments. They refused to take seriously the role that amphibious warfare would play in the South Pacific and could not realize the opportunity it offered them to redeem their professional careers.

The one exception was Captain Reifsnider, who must have failed of selection to flag rank only because of some minor indiscretion in junior officer days. He embraced a positive view of the role of amphibious operations during the forthcoming phase of the war and the importance of the part he could play in it. The captain placed great faith in and reliance upon his military staff officer, Maj. William B. McKean, an officer well versed in every phase of amphibious warfare. McKean was a close friend of mine and had been a fellow instructor in the Marine Corps schools at Quantico.

Reifsnider cooperated closely with the Marines throughout the war, was highly regarded by Admiral Turner, received increasingly responsible assignments in the amphibious forces, and attained the rank of rear admiral. Most of the other captains were soon replaced by younger and more aggressive officers.

The *Ericsson* and the *Wakefield* were huge transports used only for the administrative movement of large units and not for landing operations. They were not designed or equipped to perform the mission of attack transports. Hence the criticism popular along the Washington Beltway that they should have been sent out combat loaded is based on a faulty concept of amphibious warfare and amphibious ships. These large ships would have to be unloaded in Wellington and their troops reembarked on smaller, combat-loaded attack transports, designed, armed, and equipped to go in harm's way with a reasonable chance of survival.

Furthermore, at the time of embarkation—May 1942—the Battle of Midway had not yet been fought, and there was nothing to indicate that this unforeseen and brilliant victory would give Admiral King—who instinctively knew what the navy and Marines should do and where they should do it—a fleeting opportunity to take the offensive. Hence this administrative movement was an entirely sound and economical procedure at a moment when our maritime shipping was at a wartime low.

Even with the economies of administrative loading it was necessary to augment the movement with additional ships able to accommodate the heavy equipment and weapons of a Marine division: tanks, construction equipment, tracked landing vehicles, and medium artillery. The first of these freighters to arrive in Wellington Harbour were the *Electra* (AK-21) and *del Brazil*.

My New Zealand army mentor, Colonel Salmon, had called me to his office and informed me of the impending arrival of these two vessels, which had been traveling independently. He apprised me that the New Zealand waterfront was a "different world" and that he and the other authorities could do nothing for me down there. I would be on my own.

I soon found out that "down there" was a tightly organized, communist-oriented community controlled by Captain Peterson—the Harry Bridges of New Zealand. Port Director Peterson ruled with an iron hand. This nondescript person claimed to be a Dane but spoke totally unaccented "American" suggestive of a background and origin somewhere in our mid-Atlantic states. He talked like an archetypical communist sleeper who had somehow failed to get the word that the United States was now allied with Russia in the war against the Axis Powers.

The wharfies over whom Peterson exercised absolute authority were a likable, manly group, but they necessarily maintained an unbroken allegiance to their leader, just as our own longshoremen supported Harry Bridges. There was a constant series of strikes, or work stoppages, as they called them. None were serious or of long duration, but in total they had the effect of slowing unloading operations to a snail's pace. "Raining" and "they hadn't got their mackintoshes" were favorite reasons for ceasing operations. The ships furnished refreshments to the night shift. They enjoyed the way we made our coffee. Then came the night I was notified, "They're off the job again. They want tea instead of coffee." We had none. More time lost. The highest daily record was fourteen strikes in twenty-four hours.

The arrival of the *del Brazil* brought matters to a head. She had been loaded out of New Orleans with equipment for the division tank battalion. Several of these heavy vehicles were loaded on top of the hatch covers providing access to the holds. It was necessary to offload the tanks first, and *del Brazil* carried a special jumbo boom for this purpose. The New Zealand crane operator, one of Peterson's minions, swung the boom outboard—then let it go on the run. It crashed to the deck, with the end protruding over the side-bent into a useless dogleg. Qualified noncommissioned officers and others who witnessed the incident were unanimous in condemning it as an act of deliberate sabotage.

There was in Wellington Harbour a fifty-ton crane ship, the *Hikitia*, that could handle the loads involved. But it operated under the control of Port Director Peterson, whose refusal to assist was positive and point blank.

Accompanied by Lt. Col. John D. Macklin, who was the officer in charge of Marines embarked in *del Brazil*, I went to the ship's agents in the city of Wellington and asked for assistance. At the mere mention of Peterson's name the agents went into a state of shock and threw up their hands in dismay. No help here, although the U.S. government was paying them a handsome fee for looking after the ships' interests in Wellington Harbour. I am afraid I became a bit exercised in my denunciation of their discreditable conduct.

John walked me back to the Waterloo Hotel, where we tried to figure out our next move. We called John the "Old Fox." An officer in the First World War, he had been active in the Marine Corps Reserve for many years. In civilian life he was a superintendent of public schools in an Ohio city and a Shakespearean scholar who could quote the Bard in endless but apt dissertations. He also played poker. On this occasion, spiced with a few quotations from Hamlet, he let me know that he was not enthusiastic about my proposal, which was to make a back door approach to Pat Hurley at breakfast the next morning. I thought the idea was somewhat chicken myself, but I was just that desperate.

About 2100 I received a call. It was the Old Fox down on *del Brazil*. He said, "We've just got the last of those tanks off the hatch covers." Then followed an illogical and disjointed account. Something about "a working party of sergeants . . . and four bottles of whiskey . . . got themselves invited aboard the *Hikitia* . . . you owe me two bottles of whiskey!"

I didn't press him for details. I never want to know what happened down there. The Marine Corps has the finest sergeants in the world, but they *don't* go on working parties. Over the centuries we have found that some things in the Corps, such as the care and training of recruits, are best left to sergeants. To this list, I now add the hijacking of friendly ships in a friendly port. I am sure the Old Fox would agree.

The unloading of the two ships continued uneventfully until we reached the ammunition tonnage, usually stowed in the bottom of holds due to the effects its great weight has on the stability of the ship. All work ceased when the first cargo net loaded with ammunition was lowered to the dock. This time the wharfies won, due to New Zealand's port regulations prohibiting the unloading of explosives within the environs of a city.

Local authorities waived enforcement of the rule, and we proceeded with the task using Marine working parties instead of the union stevedores, who refused to touch the stuff. We had few men available for this hard work and were extremely grateful to receive help from one of the local American oil companies in the form of roller trays, long ladder-like frames with rollers instead of rungs, allowing the men to push heavy loads and thus avert the backbreaking task of lifting and carrying. The New Zealand army assisted us with heavy motor transport to carry the ammunition to an impromptu magazine in a canyon outside the city. We never did return the trays. I told Detwiler to take them back and thank the company. He overruled me, saying, "We'll need these for the rest of the war." We did. If I could remember the name of that oil company, I would never buy a gallon of gas from anybody else.

June is late autumn in New Zealand, and the weather was beginning to change. We were concerned about sheltering our supplies and equipment, a problem that would be greatly multiplied when the division arrived. Warehouses in New Zealand are numerous but small. Detwiler had leased everything available, but their capacity was totally inadequate for our needs. Most of the warehouses were full of wool, accumulated since the war began. Few ships came to the Antipodes, and fewer wanted to load wool. The skipper of *del Brazil* told me that as soon as he unloaded in Wellington he would pick up a cargo of wool from the warehouses in Christchurch on the South Island and take it back to the United States. Suddenly I had a great idea. Why not load *del Brazil* from Wellington warehouses instead of sending her to Christchurch and turn the resulting vacant storage space over to us?

But I had failed to include one vital factor, the New Zealand national psyche, in an otherwise logical equation. In New Zealand the words "wool," "sheep," and "mutton" are a trinity never to be taken lightly. It is a pastoral country where a person who fails to close a gate, thus permitting the "boxing" of different strains of sheep, sinks to the social status of a horse thief in our Old West. Agreements concerning these matters in New Zealand are as solemn and sacred as the Magna Carta. So my sensible proposal was rejected with amused scorn and mild outrage reverberating from on high. Even the Old Fox refused his sympathy: "After all, Bill, what would we think of a New Zealander who came to Washington and suggested revising the Gettysburg Address, tinkering with the rules of baseball, or, God forbid, even changing the name of Arkansas?"

The whole problem was overtaken by events following in swift succession after the victory at Midway. The essential supplies I sought to protect from the elements would soon become the target of Japanese bombers and battleships, which bounced them around on the shores of a faraway island of which none of us had ever heard.

The Midway victory gave a great boost to the national morale of the New Zealanders. The Singapore surrender had caused them a grievous and irreplaceable loss in men and material. Our surrender in the Philippines was an added blow. They felt isolated, alone, and disarmed, and for the moment they were. To them help from America was just another in a long line of promises, few of which had ever been kept.

On Sunday, 14 June 1942, the *Wakefield* moved into Wellington Harbour. This troop transport carried General Vandegrift and 6,000 members of the 1st Marine Division. There was considerable excitement ashore as the huge vessel tied up to a small dock on the central waterfront. I went aboard and reported to the general, giving him a brief report on the local situation. He was pleasantly surprised to learn that the New Zealand government had already completed camps to accommodate the first echelon and was well on the way to being prepared to receive the second. He was less happy to learn that *del Brazil* and *Electra* were still in port and gave immediate instructions for Marines to take over the unloading of both ships.

Colonel Salmon took the general on a tour of the new camps. I accompanied them and noted the undisguised pleasure with which our old man viewed the spacious camps and their surrounding training areas and his genuine appreciation of what the New Zealand army and Public Works had accomplished in so short a time. Returning to the *Wakefield*, I turned my local duties over to Col. Pate, D-4 (logistics) of the division staff, and departed to report to my regular boss, Col. Jerry Thomas, D-3 (operations). I dropped by the Aotea Quay to tell the Old Fox about our takeover of all unloading. He was delighted. On the way back to the hotel I stepped briefly into the latrine at the end of the quay. There, above the facility (called a u-RY-al in New Zealand) someone had scrawled a classic graffito, "All wharfies is bastards."

CHAPTER 4

Advance Man at Guadalcanal

The transport *Wakefield* arrived in Wellington on Sunday, 14 June. Disembarkation commenced immediately and proceeded briskly and smoothly. All hands were delighted with the newly constructed camp at Paekakariki, with its complete facilities, pleasant surroundings, and nearness to a liberty town. The Engineer Battalion took over camp maintenance and continued making minor improvements. Our boat pool and landing craft units enjoyed a well-sheltered bay for conducting their operations.

The rest of the command embarked on a schedule of rigorous training designed to restore the men to their former level of physical conditioning, lost after long weeks of limited activity aboard a crowded ship. Detailed schedules were established for all phases of military training, including the immediate resumption of amphibious exercises conducted in conjunction with the U.S. Navy amphibious forces in Wellington Harbour. We also established beach defenses north of the city, along a coast rimmed with innumerable handsome sandy beaches.

Command was exercised from Wellington, where General Vandegrift established his headquarters in the old but comfortable Hotel Cecil near Aotea Quay. The hotel's residents had recently departed, leaving these fine facilities for our exclusive use.

On 26 June General Vandegrift was summoned to Auckland by the newly arrived commander, South Pacific Area (ComSoPac), Vice Adm. Robert L. Ghormley. We supposed the purpose was to provide an opportunity for the requisite official calls and an overall discussion and survey of our own and the Japanese military situation in the area. The general was accompanied by three of the heads of his four staff sections, Lieutenant Colonels Thomas, Goettge, and Pate.

That night, we in Wellington received a long coded message as information addressee. It was a warning order from the chief of naval operations (CNO), Adm. Ernest J. King. Subject to approval by the Joint Chiefs of Staff, the South Pacific forces would initiate a major naval campaign on 1 August 1942—only five weeks hence!—with Tulagi Island as the first objective. The plan further stated that after taking Tulagi, we would be relieved by army troops, reembark, and one week later seize positions in northern Bougainville! Not satisfied with all that, it closed gloriously with the Napoleonic injunction: "Be in New Britain, repeat New Britain, by 20 September." They didn't say what year. (The 1st Marine Division eventually fought its way ashore at Cape Gloucester, New Britain, on 26 December 1943.) Marines are good, but even so, none of us had an ego that great.

There was also some padding (extra words, usually gibberish like "send us more Japs,") inserted by the originating station for some arcane reason known only to communicators. I well remember that in this particular dispatch the words were "U.S. Marine Corps, seagoing bellhops, ya, ya, ya." This form of humor was a popular amusement throughout the naval service until, during the battle of Leyte Gulf in 1944, some "little squirt"—a junior officer—added "THE WORLD WONDERS" to a dispatch addressed to commander, Third Fleet, Admiral Halsey, asking, "WHERE IS TASK FORCE THIRTY-FOUR?" Padding of that kind ceased.

The plan did contain one very sound provision. It told ComSoPac in blunt language to get out of his office building in Auckland, hoist his flag on a ship, and proceed to the area of operations, a rudimentary principle for overseeing any campaign. That foreshadowed something we were beginning to suspect.

In addition to being totally unrealistic, the plan was "Blue Water Navy" circa 1907 from start to finish, with little or nothing in the way of specific reference to the role of airpower in this first amphibious campaign of the war. Guadalcanal was not even mentioned. There was a reference to adjacent islands, obviously inclusive of the group of minor islets close to Tulagi, such as Gavutu and Tanambogo. It most certainly did not include the major island of Guadalcanal, some twenty miles to the south of Tulagi. Guadalcanal—ninety miles long and twenty-five miles wide—possessed the only extensive terrain in the area suitable for developing a major air base—an unsinkable aircraft carrier. Therefore, it was the strategic jewel in the Solomon Islands necklace. The Japanese, apparently aware of this, were believed to be constructing a fighter strip there.

General Vandegrift, a man of keen perception and great common sense, recognized the threat of such a base to our position in the South Pacific and insisted that the main effort be made against Guadalcanal rather than Tulagi. In this he was joined by Jerry Thomas, ComSoPac military planner Col. DeWitt Peck, and, I believe, Ghormley's chief of staff, Rear Adm. Dan Callaghan.

"If we're going to do this, why settle for a dinky little frog pond like Tulagi Harbour?" was Jerry's comment.

Admiral Ghormley gave his qualified approval, and planning began for a two-pronged simultaneous attack against Guadalcanal and Tulagi.

Seizure of these two places lay well within the capabilities of our available forces, and together they would provide a firm trielemental base for further operations by land, sea, and air forces in the direction of Rabaul, New Britain, the Japanese base dominating the entire area.

Throughout the planning period, General Vandegrift never referred to the nonsensical part of the plan. He required us to prepare for what he knew we could accomplish with what we had, dismissing the "be in New Britain, repeat New Britain, by 20 September" injunction from his mind as just so much bombast. He insisted on an ironclad execution of our directive from CNO and refused to engage in any chitchat concerning its merits. Those who questioned it were immediately rebuffed. Nevertheless, for the first time I noted the beginnings of the command crisis besetting him until he acted once and for all in mid-September.

Taking no counsel of his fears, Vandegrift rejected all doubts and cavils about what we were ordered to do and regarded those who offered them with condign and unforgiving contempt. In this regard I was reminded of another general from Virginia of like mind-set. It was after midday at First Manassas, and the Union troops were advancing victoriously. On Henry Hill a staff officer approached his general and said, "Sir, I fear the day is going against us." Without turning his head the general replied, "If you think so, you had better not say anything about it." Within the hour that same general, there on that same spot, would earn his immortal title, "Stonewall."

I do not know, but I believe that the growing irrelevance of General Vandegrift's chief of staff, Col. Capers James, stemmed from similar feelings of misplaced confidence.

I am sure the general was just as appalled as the rest of us—an untrained division, made up largely of patriotic young men who had enlisted immediately after Pearl Harbor, rushed through a few weeks of abbreviated recruit training, joined the 1st Marine Division in North Carolina, and spent most of their time since then on board ships en route to New Zealand. Now, on short notice, we were ordered to take on a battlewise major opponent even before all of our half-trained division had reached the area.

Security also was a matter of deep concern. Embarkation at a large seaport such as Wellington is not conducive to operational secrecy. There was no alternative, but since we had already publicized our forthcoming amphibious training exercises, we decided to continue this as our best form of deception. The ruse was only partially successful. The old hands were not taken in when they saw what was going aboard the ships. They had been through all of this before, some in World War I, others in China, Haiti, Nicaragua, or the Dominican Republic. The youngsters were excited to be going on an amphibious training exercise, and, in a way, it was the truth. What we didn't tell them was that they would hit the beach firing ball ammunition instead of blanks. The Old Breed would quickly spread that scuttlebutt.

The reembarkation went smoothly, thanks in large part to the efforts of a young officer, Maj. Victor Krulak, who wasn't even there. Two years before, while on the staff of Maj. Gen. Holland M. Smith, commander, First Amphibious Corps, Krulak was assigned the onerous task of formulating detailed logistical and operational procedures for joint use by the navy and Marine Corps in pursuance of our amphibious doctrine. Heretofore these critical procedures had been an area of much confusion and sometimes violent disagreement. This astute and dedicated officer produced a remarkable series of documents covering embarkation, loading, ship-to-shore movement, and shore party operations.

These procedures—some innovative—were all tested operationally during the summer of 1941 by Amphibious Forces Atlantic, the overall naval command. Highly successful, they were approved by commander, Amphibious Force Atlantic, and placed in effect for that force, which was then contemplating a movement into the Azores.

I had brought copies with me, just in case. Working with Maj. William B. McKean of Commodore Reifsnider's staff, we were able to gain agreement between General Vandegrift and the commodore to employ these documents in anticipation of their eventual acceptance by Rear Adm. Kelly Turner, commander, Amphibious Forces South Pacific (ComPhibForSoPac), when he reached the area.

This singular treaty-like arrangement provided the working basis for the smoothest, most trouble-free embarkation I ever participated in. There were a minimum of confusion and rancor and a maximum of cooperation and efficiency. One ship was combat loaded, buttoned up, and in the stream within a record forty-eight hours. The other vessels were not far behind. The young officer behind it all, Major Krulak, went on to a brilliant and productive career culminating as a lieutenant general commanding Fleet Marine Force Pacific during the Vietnam War—the most effective officer I have ever known.

During this period, to regularize my position and authority, I was designated commander, First Base Depot, an organization providing rear area support for an engaged Marine division. Such an assignment was regarded by all good Marines as a fate worse than death. I had become a quartermaster, a bean counter, at least for the time being. I made a point of never going to my office. I refused even to find out where it was located. But this assignment did bring me back in touch with my old friends Colonel Salmon and Harry Detwiler. Both contacts proved exceedingly helpful throughout our time in New Zealand.

Amphibious shipping was in extremely short supply, and it was necessary to impose draconian restrictions. General Vandegrift's order was brief: "Take only that which is necessary to fight and to live." This meant bullets, beans, and blankets. No tents, no cots for officers, no luxuries of any sort. The only exception made was in the case of accoutrements for the Division Field Hospital. Even these proved to be unnecessary as we captured a suitable building near Kukum and used stretchers instead of cots to facilitate evacuation from the hospital to nearby stretcher-size foxholes during the frequent periods of bombardment from sea or air. As the operation progressed, most casualties were quickly evacuated by air to Noumea.

As part of my new job, I inherited all the problems involved in rationing the landing force that Colonel Pate had vainly tried to solve with Navy Supply in Washington. The weather was still fine, but even so Aotea Quay was littered with corn flakes as the flimsy cardboard shipping cartons came apart, scattering their contents. This was a continuing reminder that our rationing problems were still with us. For example, the supply of meat available to us was totally useless because we lacked refrigeration. I explained our meat problem to Colonel Salmon. His immediate reply was, "We will give you every tin of meat in New Zealand." And they did, along with coffee, dehydrated milk, and powdered eggs. The canned meat included a considerable quantity of lambs' tongues, considered a delicacy down there. The response of my Marine Corps friends was predictable: "Twining has gone and bought up every lamb tongue in New Zealand and now we'll have to eat the goddamned things." Later on, however, they proved a welcome alternative to the smelly mountain of dried fish we inherited from the emperor, or the eternal Spam of the U.S. ration.

I had left New Zealand on a new assignment before the second echelon, 1st Marines (reinforced), arrived on the *Ericsson*. They had suffered a stormy trip and were forced to endure a 1,500-calorie daily diet of bad food. Though not in good physical condition, they had to immediately unload *Ericsson*, combat load its cargo on three separate attack transports and one AKA, and reembark. The weather turned unusually foul (it was now winter here, south of the equator), and the working details labored in three shifts around the clock in the chilly, wind-driven rain. It was utterly impossible to meet the deadline for making an attack on 1 August. A delay of one week was granted by the Joint Chiefs.

In the meantime, I left Wellington in company with Major McKean of Commodore Reifsnider's staff. We were to make an aerial beach reconnaissance of the objective area, Guadalcanal and Tulagi. General Vandegrift was particularly concerned about the nature of the beaches selected for the landings, especially those on Guadalcanal, about which we had no information, no pictures, and only an ancient German chart to guide us. He became singularly uneasy when he noted that the beaches on Koro Island in the Fiji Islands, chosen by the Navy Department in Washington and designated for our rehearsal landings, appeared to be totally unsuitable for the purpose. He wanted the beaches and their approaches that we intended to use on Guadalcanal and Tulagi to be sighted by someone qualified to pass judgment on their suitability. Both McKean and I had had good recent experience along these lines during the Fleet Landing Exercises of the late 1930s. As B-2 (intelligence) of the old 1st Brigade, I had personally reconnoitered the beaches used in the St. Croix, Vieques, and Puerto Rico landings, some at night using rubber boats and some by air, and felt I had attained a fair degree of competence in assessing a beach's suitability for troop landings.

At Auckland we reported to Admiral Ghormley's headquarters and were told that we would be flown to the objective area from Noumea. We arrived in Noumea by PBY the next day and were billeted in *Argonne* (AG-31), an ex-submarine tender that had relieved *Curtiss* (AV-4), a seaplane tender, and flew the flag of Rear Adm. John S. McCain, commander, Air Force, South Pacific Area (ComAirSoPac). The admiral's air force was composed primarily of two hard working squadrons of PBYs and some Marine fighters.

McCain sent for me the next morning. He knew there was a war going on and intended to do something about winning it. Just talking with that man gave me a good feeling. He told me he couldn't send us into the Solomons from Noumea, his planes being too short-legged. The Army Air Corps officer there could but wouldn't. "No use asking him," said Admiral McCain. I had known the AAC officer in Hawaii when we were both second lieutenants and privately agreed with the admiral's assessment. He said that he had a good friend, General Scanlon, commanding the Army Air Corps in Port Moresby, New Guinea, who he knew would get us in there. McCain sent a personal dispatch to Scanlon asking for his help. As I started to leave he snapped, "What do you know about aerial reconnaissance anyway?" I was formulating a modest reply when he cut me off with, "Well, you got to go anyway. Even if they burn you up. Good luck."

We flew to Brisbane, Australia, on a Qantas Air commercial plane. There, the U.S. naval representative, Commander Slawson, arranged for our flight to Port Moresby via Townsville, Australia, on Army Air Corps planes. At Port Moresby everything had been arranged for our reconnaissance the following day. We enjoyed a good dinner at the Australian Officers' Mess and afterward were summoned to General Scanlon's living quarters, where he spoke very freely with us. He felt his force was getting inadequate support from Australia. His pilots, some of whom had been stationed at Clark Field in the Philippines and had been fighting since the start of the war, were exhausted, and their equipment was in bad condition. Tomorrow he would send out his largest strike of the war, twenty-four B-17s. He doubted if over half would reach the target. Less than half did. Scanlon was of Old Army origin; he had known my brother Nate in the old days and, like him, had a West Pointer's keen interest in close air support for soldiers engaged in battle on the ground. This apostasy eventually led to his professional undoing in the air force.

It was 17 July. McKean and I turned out before daylight and were taken to Twenty Mile Field to enplane for the trip to Guadalcanal. At the field our flight faced a long delay while the heavily loaded B-17s made their takeoffs for Rabaul. We had left Moresby before breakfast and were thoughtfully invited by the Australians to a place they termed their *pie shack*. It consisted of four rough wood posts covered with a roof of thatched palm. Inside was a ruddy-faced, bare-waisted Australian soldier making something he called coffee in a huge aluminum kettle over an open fire. He dumped several pounds of ground coffee into his copper, as all kettles are called down there even if they are made of cast iron. Next, he opened can after can of evaporated milk and poured the contents over the dry coffee already in the pot, tossed in a few pounds of sugar, and finally added water to the brim, stirring it with a two-by-four stud, saying, "Let 'er rip." What a brew!

There were reputed to be small cans of fruit available to sustain us during our long flight, but these had long since disappeared into the pockets of the Air Corps crews who preceded us. This too had been the fate of the hardtack, but a few bits and pieces of crumbs were still left in the bottom of the metal container. McKean and I filled our pockets, providing against the necessities of the day.

We met our pilot and copilot, a major and captain. Both were obviously capable, experienced, squared-away types. I felt we were in good hands. They explained that our flight would be made in a B-17P, a plane adapted to long-range photographic flights by the conversion of the bomb bay space into fuel tanks. Our flight would be a long one—stretching the maximum range of the aircraft.

We taxied to the runway but were again delayed by the return of planes with rough engines or other mechanical difficulties developed during the early part of their Rabaul strike. Once in the air our troubles seemed over. The plane performed perfectly, the weather was fine, and the visibility was unlimited.

McKean and I were assigned places in the nacelle at the nose of the plane, where the clear plastic gave limitless forward vision. I was assigned the bow machine gunner's position, which covered the sector dead ahead and also allowed optimum observation of our objective.

As an old machine gunner, I was entranced by my weapon. A new development and product of vibration science research and engineering, it could fire over 1,000 rounds per minute, as opposed to the 150-round output of the ancient 1917 Browning our ground forces still used, a crosseyed old bitch that kicked, jerked, and jolted like a jackhammer gone mad.

McKean and the plane's navigator were situated behind my left shoulder on the port side of the nacelle. Our "map" was a reprint of a prewar illustration from the *National Geographic* covering the islands of the Southwest Pacific north of Australia. There was not much detail—Guadalcanal was about half an inch long—but nothing better was to be had.

Celestial navigation was apparently new to the Army Air Corps, and our youthful navigator was certainly not overly conversant with its techniques. He took an occasional sun line, then resumed reading a comic book, in which he was completely absorbed. I recalled vividly the trip to New Zealand in Bill Rassieur's PBM. There the navigator was a young ensign just out of Annapolis. Sam Pickering rode herd on him all the way and kept him at the onerous sun line task as long as we were in the air.

About 1400 we spotted Guadalcanal and Tulagi on our port bow and altered course to the north to make a first run over Tulagi. I had expected to make the first run over Guadalcanal but soon understood the reason for the pilot's decision. Recent reports of enemy planes based in the area had not been confirmed, but if any were present they would undoubtedly be Rufes—Zeros on floats—operating out of Tulagi Harbour. Their presence or absence would be the controlling factor governing the length of our visit. We flew at low altitude— between 2,000 and 3,000 feet—taking pictures as we passed over the Tulagi beaches. My visual inspection confirmed what the old German chart of Tulagi Island had indicated: coral reefs offshore almost everywhere, making landings impracticable for any except light forces. As McKean and I studied the inhospitable beaches, the intercom came alive with excited shouts of "float planes taking off from Tulagi Harbour!" No one was certain of their number.

We headed south across Lunga Channel to Guadalcanal. The pilot calmly passed the word: "Clear all guns." I turned loose a few short bursts in the general direction of Red Beach on Guadalcanal—probably the first shots fired by a member of the 1st Marine Division at an enemy target in World War II. The machine gun fired beautifully with no more vibration than a water pistol. I couldn't believe it.

Over Koli Point on Guadalcanal, our pilot turned right and headed west over the shoreline to give the cameraman a chance to run a photographic strip of the sandy beaches bordering Lunga Point, our proposed landing area. I was overjoyed to see that the beaches were totally unlike those we had just seen on the Tulagi side of the channel. Amazingly, there was no evidence of coral on either the beaches or the approaches thereto. The deep blue color of the water indicated good depth extending up to the shoreline itself. These were undoubtedly steep-to beaches, perfect for landing both men and supplies—ideal in every way for our purposes. On the left there was unmistakable evidence of an airfield. There was a large gap in the center but the project had plainly reached an advanced stage of construction.

Over Lunga Point the plane was turning for another run to photograph a strip further inland from the beach when the intercom came to life with shouts of "Here they are!" and "Here they come!" All hell broke loose. Our plane shook from the fire of its several guns, punctuated all too frequently by the heavy jolt of an enemy 20mm projectile exploding inside the fuselage. Our pilot maneuvered violently to evade their firing runs and give our own guns a favorable firing opportunity. There was a triumphant howl—"You got that son of a bitch!"—as one Zero came apart in a burst of fire. Then a cry of "There goes a smoker!" as another of our little friends dropped out of the fight.

By this time our pilot, still closely pursued, had reached cloud cover and sought to stay within it by twists and turns of a sort never found in any flight manual. As the plane continued its violent gyrations in the clouds, I could not escape the fantasy that it had become a huge antediluvian monster twisting and turning, fighting for its life, in some misty primordial swamp against the savage onslaughts of a pack of predators.

Things quieted down. Our pilot moved away from cloud cover, hoping for the best. We had completely lost our orientation but knew too well that our altitude was less than that of the surrounding peaks. Fuel consumption during the fight was unavoidably high, and the remainder was insufficient to take us home unless we were favored by a tail wind. We had taken several hits. Miraculously, all of the plane's mechanical functions were operating perfectly. We had lost our radio reception capability, although we could transmit.

McKean kept a wary eye on the map and our young navigator. Since we did not know our point of departure from the target area, it would be difficult, if not impossible, to assess our location accurately until we made a landfall on some island recognizable from the air. On the way out, D'Entrecasteaux Island, with its unmistakable outline, had been our point of departure for Guadalcanal. Now we scanned the horizon for it as our landfall on the course home to Moresby.

Time went by. The sun was setting. Still no landfall. Finally we passed over an island that appeared in the gathering darkness to be Trobriand, well north of our intended course. This was communicated to the pilot over another phone as ours had suffered battle damage and would not transmit. The pilot misunderstood or ignored our message, for when we reached the New Guinea coast he turned north toward Salamaua—in enemy territory—instead of south to Port Moresby. We had difficulty in persuading him to correct his course.

The pilot had me operate the levers opening the bomb bay so we could make a quick getaway via parachute when the gas ran out. Fortunately, we soon received unexpected aid from Port Moresby. Aware of our plight, they lit up the whole area with every available searchlight and fired a continuous, heavy antiaircraft barrage into the empty sky, creating a welcome beacon on the horizon. Within minutes that seemed like hours, we made a safe landing with dry tanks.

We'd been in the air for thirteen hours and six minutes, and we had burned a lot of gas and fired a lot of ammunition. What had we accomplished? We had taken a few valuable pictures to substantiate what we saw from the air: that the beaches on Tulagi were extremely difficult for a large amphibious landing, while those on Guadalcanal were ideal. We could set to rest General Vandegrift's misgivings that some lotus eater in War Plans was running us into another coral pit like the rehearsal area at Koro Island. Also, we had learned that there was a nearly completed airfield on Guadalcanal and had no evidence that the beaches were defended. Our shot-up plane was proof enough of a Japanese air force presence and that they would shoot at us. Events proved us right on every count.

It was quite late when McKean and I got back to our billet in Port Moresby, and the mess was closed, so we went to bed hungry. Early the next morning—before breakfast—we left for Cairns, Australia. There we were delayed for hours at a small outlying airfield by the nonarrival of the daily plane to Townsville, the advance headquarters of ComSoWesPac's overall command. General MacArthur was still exercising a form of inspirational leadership from Melbourne, well over 1,000 miles to the south. Some mean persons had the temerity to say that at least he didn't go farther south to Tasmania.

We landed at Townsville about 2100 and spotted a mess hall with lights still burning. Inside there was plenty of hot beef stew left over from a late supper prepared for a bomber squadron. I ate five plates of the heavenly stuff.

The next morning we checked in at headquarters to pick up prints of all photographs taken on our reconnaissance. These were released to us only after passing through the hands of the intelligence people at Ferdinand, the code name of the headquarters of the justly famed and highly effective Australian Coast Watchers, a tiny organization that made a huge contribution out of all proportion to its numbers.

We were debriefed at length by Comdr. Eric Feldt, the highly respected head of the organization. The name Ferdinand was derived, I suppose, from the renowned bull with the delicate ego who loved to sniff flowers but never learned how to fight. These men—and, I believe, one woman—did something more than fight. They stayed behind when the Japanese came in and supplied vital information of inestimable value to the Allied cause, accepting the constant risk of death in its ugliest form as just part of the cost of doing business.

Feldt gave us ComSoWesPac's current estimate of enemy strength. We had long considered the high command's figures suspect due to their faulty method of computation. He then gave me, without comment, a slip of paper on which he had penciled the Ferdinand numbers—numbers about half as large.

Feldt informed us that their man on Guadalcanal, Maj. Martin Clemens, an officer of the British Solomon Islands Police, was out of communication at the moment because an injured leg made it impracticable to move his radio equipment and native scouts after each transmission to avoid detection. Feldt had reason to believe Clemens would be transmitting again by 1 August. He told me to tell our communications people to contact Clemens directly using a certain code and code word, which he asked me not to write down but not to forget. I was careful not to forget. I remember them to this day; they were the Playfair code and the code word "Fisherwoman."

We were billeted that night in a small Townsville hotel. News had just arrived of an Australian military success somewhere in North Africa, and people were celebrating for the first time in a long and dismal period. The bar was jammed four deep with rugged characters from the outback who had

made it into town for the great occasion. McKean and I enjoyed it immensely. No one would let us buy a beer. It was a
case of, " 'Ow about another one, Yank, 'taint every dy we
kills a hog."

In the midst of all this I suddenly found myself face to
face with an old friend, Comdr. Mort Mumma, whom I knew
well at Annapolis, where we shot together for years on the
Academy Rifle Team. (He later became a rear admiral and retired to become president of the National Rifle Association.)
It was a pleasant reunion. He volunteered the information
that he had some boats down in the harbor. What kind I did
not ask but assumed they were submarines. (I now know they
were PT boats.)

Mumma obviously knew what McKean and I were up to.
I surmised he was operating his boats in support of Feldt's
Coast Watchers. We walked outside and quickly struck a deal.
If I could get ComSoPac's approval and provide men for a pa-
trol, he would land it at Aola Bay on Guadalcanal to contact
Martin Clemens and get additional fresher information on
Japanese strength and dispositions.

Two days later at nightfall McKean and I reached Noumea
where we tried to find Lt. Col. Merritt Edson, who was supposed to have just arrived with his 1st Raider Battalion. The
town was blacked out. It was difficult to move around and impossible to get information. *Argonne could give us the name
of every ship in port*, but no one had ever heard of Edson's 1st
Raider Battalion. That would soon change.

Next morning we found a Marine officer who told us the
battalion was embarked on three APDs. These ships were
flush-deck, four-stack destroyers of World War I vintage converted to high-speed transports by removing the two forward
boilers and stacks, then changing these spaces into accommodations for 175 men and officers. The addition of davits
and landing craft completed their transformation. We located
Edson aboard *Little* (APD-4). He took us to meet the squadron
commodore, Hugh Hadley from The Dalles, Oregon, whom I
had known at the Naval Academy. Our families were friends
back home. I am sorry to say that I was soon to see him, with

his flagship and its crew, go down after a few seconds of overwhelming fire during night action with a powerful enemy force.

The story of these little ships has never been told. They lived in harm's way from day to day. Few survived. Their casualty rate in KIA and missing was staggering, undoubtedly the highest of any segment of the four services that fought in the Pacific.

Edson enthusiastically accepted Mumma's offer to land a patrol to contact Martin Clemens. He also thought I should call on Maj. Gen. Alexander M. Patch, commanding the U.S. Army's Americal Division, and took me to the headquarters in Noumea. General Patch seemed interested in our activities and pressed us for information. As we left the building, the general's aide overtook us and asked that I alone return to General Patch's office for a moment. The general said, "Twining, I have a message for you to deliver to General Vandegrift. Tell him that my division will be unable to participate in the upcoming operation because we have not yet had any training in amphibious warfare."

I felt this would not be a matter of too great concern to General Vandegrift. From the beginning it had been clear that the army strongly opposed the plan—and not without some justification. We had therefore excluded them from our planning at the very outset. The JCS-approved plan had provided that the army relieve us in time for our attack on Bougainville, but their time-space-distance factors were so incredibly skewed that we had ignored the idea in its entirety from the beginning. It is pertinent to point out that the requirement placed on the Americal Division by the JCS was for an administrative movement for purposes of occupation only. There was no requirement whatsoever for amphibious training of the troops involved.

In compliance with our original orders, we proceeded to Auckland by PBY and reported to ComSoPac Headquarters. Colonel Peck informed us that the 1st Marine Division had left Wellington and reached the rehearsal area at Koro. We told him about the tentative arrangement for the Edson-

Mumma patrol operation. He seemed favorably inclined and left to take the matter up with Admiral Ghormley.

We wandered around trying to locate the Guadalcanal maps that Eric Feldt was positive had been sent to this headquarters. No luck. I have reason to believe they were in the building in the possession of the intelligence officer, a totally inexperienced and untrained person who failed to comprehend their importance.

We met again with Colonel Peck, who informed us that Admiral Ghormley disapproved of the proposed Guadalcanal patrol, saying, "It would be too dangerous." Dangerous? I thought everybody realized that this whole war business was dangerous. After our recent experiences, McKean and I were particularly aware of it.

Over the years our Marine historians have attempted to rationalize this feeble decision by saying that the admiral must have meant dangerous in the sense of loss of operational initiative and surprise if our intentions were revealed. At that time neither McKean nor I entertained any such impression for a moment, and I feel certain that the same was true of Colonel Peck. Onshore patrols were then, and still are, a recognized and approved incident of amphibious warfare and were regularly used in operations beginning with Bougainville in August 1943. There was even a slender chapter devoted to the subject in our amphibious bible, *FTP 167*. This particular patrol would have been a piece of cake for Edson's men. They would have been landed under friendly cover at Aola Bay, miles from the closest Japanese and could have—from unexposed positions and in utmost safety—radioed information gathered by Clemens's native scouts. Even when operating under far more adverse conditions, I know of no case where a patrol member was ever taken prisoner or compromised an operation.

CHAPTER 5

Sour Success

The next day Rear Adm. Daniel J. Callaghan, Admiral Ghormley's chief of staff, was scheduled to leave for Koro, Fiji Islands, our rehearsal area, to represent ComSoPac at a command conference to be held aboard the carrier *Saratoga* (CV-3) prior to the sortie from Koro to our objective in the Solomons. Colonel Peck arranged for us to accompany the admiral's party aboard a PBY to Suva and thence by destroyer to Koro Island.

At Suva we overnighted in the same hotel where I had stayed on my way down from Pearl months before. Nothing had changed. The East Indian staff members were as surly as ever, quite confident that their Japanese "liberators" were just over the horizon and would soon be taking over. The British management was still despairing and apologetic.

Next day we were picked up by the destroyer *Hull* (DD-350) and taken on the short run to Koro, where I reported to General Vandegrift aboard *McCawley* (AP-10), Admiral Turner's flagship, which had also embarked Division Headquarters and the 3d Battalion, 1st Marines, commanded by Lt. Col. William "Spike" McKelvy.

As a rehearsal the Koro Island dry run was a complete fiasco. It was simply impossible to land over those coral beaches. The area had been selected by navy planners in Washington, but one glance at the chart in Wellington convinced us of the site's total unsuitability. Concern over this lapse was basically the reason why McKean and I had been sent on our just-completed reconnaissance.

I don't think the impossibility of landing on Koro mattered

greatly. What we really needed was training in ship-to-shore movement with the boats and boat crews of our attack ships. This enforced change of plans gave us an unexpected opportunity for repeated practice, resulting in greatly improved performance of our ship-to-shore technique. Admiral Turner was shocked at the poor condition of the boats and the performance of their crews. His immediate and forceful steps to correct these deficiencies resulted in our D-day personnel landings on Guadalcanal being the smoothest and best executed of any such operations I have ever participated in before or since, war or peace.

We had tried to find better beaches on Koro when the very able Capt. Ray Schwenke, USMC, departed for Koro at the time McKean and I set out for the Guadalcanal trip. At Koro, Schwenke was confronted with a most parochial U.S. Army general who resented the navy's visit as an unauthorized incursion into his private domain and refused to assist or cooperate in any way.

Things were not going well for us on board *McCawley*. Kelly Turner was a loud, strident, arrogant person who enjoyed settling all matters by simply raising his voice and roaring like a bull captain in the old navy. His peers understood this and accepted it with amused resignation because they valued him for what he was: a good and determined leader with a fine mind—when he chose to use it. Vandegrift was a classic Virginia gentleman. I have heard him harden his voice, but I never heard him raise it—not even at me.

Things had gone well in the beginning. The admiral had reached Wellington without a plan of operations. He and his staff were glad to work backward from our plan as a basis of their own, a reversal of the usual progression. Turner accepted the inclusion of Guadalcanal as an objective after some discussion and seemed genuinely pleased with our scheme of maneuver—the two simultaneous attacks on Guadalcanal and Tulagi. Like Vandegrift, he chose to quietly ignore the manic JCS injunction to "be in New Britain, repeat New Britain, by 20 September." But he insisted on a subsequent objective of his own, occupation of the island of Ndeni, a

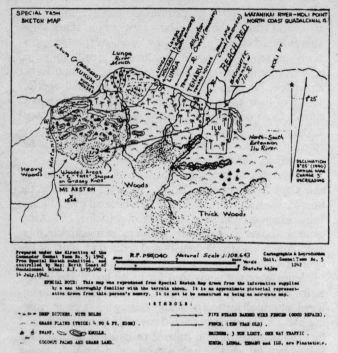

CRUDE SKETCH MAP used in the planning and early operational phases of the Guadalcanal campaign by units of the 5th Combat Team; it is an adaptation of a map prepared by the D-2 Section and typifies the scarcity of reliable terrain information available to the 1st Marine Division when it left New Zealand.

malaria-infested fever hole lying some 300 miles to the east of Guadalcanal, and using our 2d Marines for the purpose. This regular unit had been assigned to us from the 2d Marine Division at San Diego to take the place of our own 7th Marines already deployed in Samoa. The 2d Marines joined us at Koro, combat loaded on attack transports (APAs).

The JCS directive made no mention of Ndeni, and no one has ever explained why it was necessary to go there. Ernie

King, I believe, described it as a place that did you no good if you had it and that you were bound to lose anyway if Guadalcanal folded. However, this was none of our business, and Vandegrift realized it. What was our business was to preserve the viability of our attack plan by retaining operational control of our division reserve, the 2d Marines, throughout the forthcoming battle. If the estimate of enemy strength furnished us was anywhere near correct, we would need a substantial reserve to insure decisive victory without unduly prolonging the operation.

On 26 July the general, accompanied by Lieutenant Colonel Goettge, D-2 (intelligence), Jerry Thomas, and myself, traveled on board the destroyer *Hull* to the *Saratoga* to attend the vital conference of flag officers called by the senior task force commander present, Vice Adm. Frank Jack Fletcher, USN.

The actual designated commander of the operation was Vice Admiral Ghormley, who chose to send his chief of staff, Rear Adm. Dan Callaghan, to represent him. As a very junior rear admiral he had little personal influence, especially since it was becoming increasingly evident that Ghormley himself disapproved of the entire undertaking or at best gave it faint support.

Admiral Fletcher indulged in a few generalities and then dismissed all present except flag and general officers. I tried to play the dumb Marine who didn't get the word and stayed on. I was already alarmed and figured that I could be of assistance later, being probably the best qualified of our group to interpret the precise meaning of the upcoming navy lingo. To no avail. Admiral Fletcher came over to where I was seated, spoke to me by name, and politely suggested I "go down to the wardroom and get myself some coffee or lemonade."

In the wardroom I found Jerry Thomas deep in conversation with Representative Melvin Maas, a World War I Marine and now an officer in the Marine Corps Reserve. Maas was aboard *Saratoga* as a participant in some congressional orientation project and was interested in what we had to say.

When the conference ended we could see that General Vandegrift was deeply disturbed and in no mood to talk. The

sea was making up, and it took a long time for our group
to transfer back to the lively destroyer. I elected to go via
breeches buoy and got thoroughly soaked when *Saratoga* and
the destroyer rolled slightly out of sync.

The *Hull*'s wardroom was full of VIPs, so I decided to stay
on the weather deck. There I met Col. LaVerne "Blondie"
Saunders of the U.S. Army Air Corps, already a highly regarded officer. He was bringing ten to twelve B-17s down
from Hawaii to stage a series of pre-D-day strikes against Tulagi and Guadalcanal and was worried for fear it was a waste
of effort. He said, "We're putting a lot into this. Do you Marines really have anything?"

"Yes, sir. The 1st Marine Division, reinforced."

We returned to *McCawley* before Vandegrift gave us the
bad news. Fletcher insisted on regarding the operation as an
amphibious raid rather than the seizure of a permanent foothold. He doubted that it could succeed in any event and
would not agree to expose his forces for more than forty-
eight hours. Pressed sharply and stoutly by Turner, he refused
to entertain any of the latter's concerns about the fate of our
amphibious forces, especially the fate of the landing force
left ashore.

The stage was rapidly being set up with all the props needed
for a first-class disaster. Admiral King and the others of the
Joint Chiefs had moved correctly and commendably to take
advantage of the Midway victory to seize the initiative. However, the decision to descend in strength at this time on the
Eastern Solomons was not entirely sound. The great overriding and controlling factor that makes such an operation
possible is firm control of the sea in and around the objective
area on a permanent rather than a transitory basis. This *sine
qua non* was entirely absent, and either its absence was disre-
garded or its effect was not understood at the Washington
level.

Whether he realized it or not, Fletcher was responding to
this dictate when he treated the operation as a raid. It was incumbent upon him to exercise control of the sea, as he alone
possessed the means of enforcement. But his initial superior-

ity would diminish rapidly as the Japanese, with more numerous carriers, reached the scene. Their bases were close at hand; Fletcher's base was Pearl Harbor, thousands of miles away. He had seen U.S. carriers sunk in battle and was loath to risk our last carriers in the Pacific in action against a greatly superior force.

This was Fletcher's view on the strategic level, and in a way it was correct. But his somewhat brutal conduct of the *Saratoga* conference was totally incorrect from every point of view, and that damage was compounded by Ghormley's flagrant evasion of his plain duty to be present at and conduct the *Saratoga* conference in person. Had he done so, Fletcher's opposition would have resulted in a standoff, with the inescapable, if painful, necessity of presenting the matter to higher authority for resolution if he, Ghormley, was unwilling to make the decision. This of course, would have involved Nimitz (CinCPac), who somehow had been able to maintain a strange if knowing silence about and avoidance of an obvious command problem.

General Vandegrift accepted Admiral Fletcher's edict with the best grace he could muster and set about the business at hand—the final preparations for the landing. The last two days were devoted to naval gunfire support. Marine officer spotters and pilots operated with and augmented our cruiser planes and adjusted fire on the coastline, a most difficult target, much like shooting at a horizontally stretched string with a pistol: shots were either over or short. Our onshore naval gunfire support teams could not be used effectively because of the terrain. Necessity forced us to use antiaircraft ammunition against terrestrial targets. Bombardment shells were not available, and the cruisers had little or none of the common ammunition we had expected to use. Armor-piercing projectiles would have been almost totally ineffective against earthen beach defenses. The gunfire was rapid and accurate, and it was a morale-building spectacle for our embarked Marines.

I will never forget the Australian cruiser squadron, *Australia*, *Canberra*, and *Hobart*. They made the last firing run of the day, each beautiful ship flying a tremendous white Australian naval ensign from the mainmast, flags at least four times the size of our largest. These firing ships were accompanied by their single spotter plane, an ancient Walrus biplane, a relic of World War I. The old string-bag strutted proudly along at its top speed of about eighty knots. The ships' gunnery was excellent. I wondered if they would fly the big ensigns again on D day; they didn't, but the Walrus came close to being a victim of friendly fire.

We sortied from Koro at sunset and began the long trip to Guadalcanal. I think all hands felt that they had done the best they could with what they had and the outcome was in the hands of God. We were favored by good weather—thick clouds and rain that concealed our movement.

The *McCawley* was not and never had been a particularly happy ship. Like the other transports, she was a dirty ship, something I had never encountered in my previous service in or with the navy. She was commanded by a superannuated hypochondriac who, as a lieutenant commander, had been my battalion officer at the Academy in 1919. He was in no physical condition to command a ship.

As a result, actual command was exercised by his executive officer, Lieutenant Commander Riley, a Marine-hating mustang, a sadist determined to haze Marines. He worked at it twenty-four hours a day. During maneuvers the previous summer he had been able, among other things, to bring about the professional ruin of one of our ablest officers, an embarked battalion commander who was trying to protect his men from extreme abuse at the exec's hands.

Once we embarked on this filthy ship the hassling started immediately. The exec published a ship's order stating that the Marines were littering the decks and therefore would no longer be permitted to purchase items such as candy and cigarettes from the ship's store. Under the draconian stringencies of our embarkation order we had loaded none of these items for ourselves. I had turned the bulk of them over gratis to the ships at Wellington, as their stocks were completely exhausted due to many weeks on station. I felt personally involved and betrayed, but there was nothing we could do without informing General Vandegrift, who was already deeply and unpleasantly entangled with Admiral Turner over the diversion of his division reserve to the Ndeni undertaking.

As we moved toward our objective, the exec began to develop an uncommon interest in blackout precautions, including such minor matters as faint light leakage from portholes having ill-fitting metal covers that screened the thick glass. At the same time a major source of danger, peculiar to *McCawley*, was an intermittently flaming stack; visible for miles around as we charged along for all the world like an old-time horse-drawn steam fire engine. This condition had existed for over a year and was a matter of common knowledge and concern. It had never been corrected, and in consequence the old "Wacky Mac" was definitely not battle worthy. She survived—miraculously—until the evening of 30 June 1943, during the Rendova operation, when she took three torpedoes, one Japanese and two U.S.

The exec liked to check our portholes. It gave him a pretext to prowl around Marine country at will, looking for trouble. He was constantly annoying us in the division staff area, an enclosed compartment beneath the signal bridge. There all staff sections were crowded together busily engaged in revising and rewriting our attack orders to conform to minor changes Turner made daily to his own directive.

The production and particularly the distribution of these changes to all ships with embarked Marines were onerous tasks with little profit. When the general finally became aware of the matter he was annoyed and told us to ignore further changes: "The regimental commanders will think I can't make up my mind." This explains minor discrepancies between Turner's and Vandegrift's attack orders published in subsequent official accounts. For example, Turner's order in its final form states enemy strength using the figures McKean and I brought back from Ferdinand headquarters in Townsville, whereas Vandegrift's order shows the initial estimate received from MacArthur's headquarters. He saw no reason to make a formal change, since this particular information was of no real significance to any landing force commander other than himself.

Two days out on the sortie we had a minor flap when Turner announced he was going to accompany us ashore and set up shop on Guadalcanal. We hadn't brought along even a tent or cot for General Vandegrift, but true to the tradition of Lucius Paulus, he felt it incumbent to provide his guest with a tent for his expedition into Macedonia.[1] Turner later flatly denied that he ever had any such intention, but his biographer betrays him by revealing existence of a draft order found in his files.[2] So Spike McKelvy, commanding the embarked Marine Battalion, was assigned the onerous task of going into the holds to find canvas and camp equipment among supplies loaded for the Division Field Hospital.

We began work on a plan of defense, knowing we would face an immediate and terrific reaction from the Japanese. Base defense doctrine had not been developed to the same degree as the doctrine for landing operations because of our limited human resources in the field of military planning. In addition, the basic concept was faulty, at least from the point of view of our requirements for defense of advance naval bases. It was founded on a concept called "sector, subsector defense," developed prior to World War I by the army at Leavenworth for the defense of large coastal areas of the continental United States against a hypothetical large-scale attack of the German army landing on the New Jersey coast and driving northwest to cut off the Philadelphia–Pittsburgh–New England industrial triangle. This problem, probably written about 1907 by then Capt. George Catlett Marshall for Gen. J. Franklin Bell, commandant of the Field Officers School, had been slavishly miniaturized by the Marine Corps to fit the beach situation confronting it in defense of small islands. Work had been suspended on this manual for years in order to concentrate all our efforts on the navy's more important

1. See the epigraph at the beginning of this book.
2. George C. Dyer, *The Amphibians Came to Conquer,* Vol. 1 (Washington, DC: Department of the Navy, 1972), p. 410.

Manual for Landing Operations (FTP 167), but the uncompleted defense manual nevertheless continued as a controlling publication known as the *Tentative Manual for the Defense of Advanced Bases MCS-3*, produced by the Marine Corps Schools.

There had always been wide disagreement about the manual's applicability to Marine Corps requirements. The best chance for a successful base defense by a small force is to fight at the water's edge with a view to destroying the hostile landing force during its moment of greatest weakness, the golden hour between the lifting of the naval bombardment and the establishment of effective landing-force artillery support ashore. The alternative method was to offer no serious resistance until the enemy had landed and advanced inland.

The Japanese were to try both methods. Neither ever worked, but their water's-edge defense came close to success on several occasions; it always inflicted ghastly casualties on our forces, as at Tarawa, Peleliu, and Iwo Jima. At Jerry Thomas's direction I worked up a conventional plan based on *MCS-3*, unworkable from every point of view. Jerry looked at it and said, "Magnificent dispersion." The subject was never mentioned again.

The last days of our approach were made under increasingly thick cloud cover, a gift from on high. We were now well within patrol-plane range of Rabaul and in clear weather most certainly would have been detected. Because of the impenetrable overcast the Japanese had suspended surveillance over the area of our approach. Late in the afternoon of 6 August we ran out of cover. The sky was clear and the sun bright, but it was too late in the day for the Japanese to take advantage of their last chance to intercept us. We had made it.

At sunset I ran into Jerry in the passageway outside our berthing area. He had just left the admiral's mess, where the general and his staff took their meals. He said the ongoing difference over the matter of the division reserve had reached the point of open dispute, with the general grimly and quietly refusing to capitulate. As a closing shot at the general's unshaken argument for release of the reserve, Kelly Turner said,

"Vandegrift, that sounds like something you read in a book."
Jerry paused, then added ruefully, "The old man turned gray
as a cat."

We went up to the hot and crowded little command post in
the compartment under the signal bridge and resumed work.
Night fell, and we proceeded with the details of executing
tomorrow's attack. The exec came prowling around fussing
with the porthole covers and complaining that we should
clear the compartment so the lights could be turned out. His
wind was up. We asked if his engineers had fixed the fiery
stack yet. It was still blazing like a beacon, an attraction for
any Japanese submarine.

About an hour later the exec returned with four seamen
carrying two oil lanterns. Each was about three to four feet
high, one with green lenses, the other with red. I suppose
these monsters were carried as emergency running lights in
case the regular lights near the bridge lost power. Running
lights were almost never used during the war, particularly in a
combat zone. But here was Riley setting up standbys for the
prohibited running lights. The exec had his men light and ad-
just the wicks to a nice smoky flame. His purpose, of course,
was to goad someone into extinguishing them so he would
presumably have an open-and-shut case: "Interference with
the operation of the ship." We went ahead with our work. He
returned in a few minutes, reached into the compartment,
found the light switch, and turned it off, then fled down the
passageway closely pursued by Frank Goettge. Riley dropped
his flashlight clattering on deck and kept on going, followed
by one of the most powerful men I have ever known. Jerry
Thomas threw a partial block on Frank and dissuaded him
from his obvious intent. There was trouble enough on board
McCawley. We finished our work.

McCawley was the last of the Hell Ships. Kelly Turner
must have recognized the problem, for both captain and exec
were replaced after the operation.[3]

When our ships rounded Cape Esperance, Transport Group

3. Ibid., p. 283.

Yoke, carrying the northern attack force, split off and headed toward Tulagi Harbour. The main unit, Transport Group Xray, continued toward Lunga Point. We went to general quarters, though there was no sign that our presence was detected. We almost felt disappointed by our unbelievable good luck. No one likes to be ignored.

Suddenly the classic tropical night ended. The blazing sun came up with a rush. At exactly 0613, 7 August 1942 (6 August in the United States) the heavy cruiser *Quincy* (CA-39) opened the ball. Every gun in the covering force that could be brought to bear joined in a deadly salute to the emperor. Ours was a salute that would bring him into the twentieth century and his prime minister to the gallows. We were announcing that the way back had begun. It was an unforgettable moment of history.

As the sun came up, I was standing on the starboard side of *McCawley* with General Vandegrift and Jerry Thomas. We looked shoreward, eager to orient ourselves with respect to our objective. There was Lunga Point, and in the background, looking for all the world like Mt. Hood, we saw Mt. Austen looming out of the morning's first light. General Vandegrift said, "Jerry, can that thing be Mr. Widdy's Grassy Knoll?"

In preparing the order for the Guadalcanal landing (1st Marine Division Operation Order 7-42), we had directed the 1st Marine Combat Group (Cates) to land and seize as its objective "a grassy knoll four miles south of Lunga Point." This objective had been described to us in those terms by Mr. Widdy, former manager for Lever Brothers Plantation at Lunga Point, in a way that indicated it would be a suitable regimental objective. Lacking both maps and aerial photographs, we had no way of verifying the accuracy of his statements. He had been commissioned in the Australian navy directly from civilian life to accompany the attack force and did give us much valuable information, but unfortunately, lacking military experience, he had given us a totally misleading description. Before our eyes the rising sun disclosed the looming bulk of a massive and almost insurmountable mountain. This was our objective. It was nothing like what had been described to us by Mr. Widdy. As an objective perhaps it would have been suitable for an Army Corps, but not for a regiment. Vandegrift gave immediate instructions for the 1st Marines to stop their advance at the airfield.

The cruisers launched spotter planes. Out of nowhere came the old Walrus from *Australia*, lumbering along at masthead height, keeping extremely close to the ships to avoid misidentification. As I watched from the signal bridge I heard an uproar from the flag bridge. Later I was told by an officer of General Vandegrift's staff that Kelly Turner had ordered, "Shoot down that plane." Instead of passing the order, the talker on the sound-powered phone said, "Admiral, that's the Walrus plane from *Australia* . . . sir." But Turner answered this with silence.

I recalled the old navy yarn that used to delight us as plebes. The skipper of an old predreadnought was shortening chain in New York Harbor prior to weighing anchor. He spotted a bluejacket on the foc'sle out of uniform—no neckerchief— and immediately began bellowing through his megaphone, directing the apprehension of this miserable culprit. Meanwhile the ship, still swallowing, overran the anchor and popped her chain.

Kelly Turner, we were to find out, was quick on the draw but sometimes shot from the lip.

I went below to get breakfast, not because I felt hungry but because I knew it would be a long time before I would have another chance for a hot meal. The *McCawley*'s wardroom mess was excellent thanks to a fine supply officer. Their troop mess was also one of the best. This day they served the traditional D-day breakfast—steak and eggs for all hands. The ship was blacked out below except for a few blue battle lights. Those lights turned my scrambled eggs as green as the Chicago River on St. Patrick's Day. Ditto for the butter on my toast.

At 0650 the landing force was called away. The ships were 11,000 yards off the beach to be beyond the effective range of enemy medium artillery, although we were positive he had none. I took my assigned post observing the embarkation on

the starboard side. Never have I seen a smoother operation.
Landing craft previously lowered and orbiting nearby were
called alongside and loaded with Marines clambering down
the ship's side clinging to cargo nets, their equipment loos-
ened for easy divestiture in case of an accidental fall.

Each coxswain was given identifying number cards to
display on the boat's bow and exact instructions as to his
position in the formation and point of landing. The senior
Marine aboard each boat already had this information on a
separate card.

Boats then took their assigned positions in the proper wave
of the ship-to-shore formation and, after all were present, began the run to the beach, carefully timed to bring them to the
line of departure at H hour.

We had allowed more time than was needed. This miscal-
culation required the Marines to spend an unnecessarily long
wait in the boats wallowing in a choppy sea, so there was a
good deal of seasickness before we got ashore. In subsequent
landings, troops debarked much closer to the hostile beach,
and the assembly process was expedited. Aside from this, the
landing was the best I have ever seen. I attribute our success
to the unfavorable landing conditions at Koro, which gave us
time to perfect ship-to-shore techniques, which were needed
more than maneuvering onshore. Kelly Turner's unrelenting
efforts on boat drill at Koro paid off handsomely.

The boat pool method we used here became the U.S. standard as the war progressed. The Aussies and the Brits would
have none of it, claiming their method of "rile" (rail) loading
was far superior. In their method boats are loaded at the transport's rail and then lowered into the water. Unfortunately, a
percentage of boats always prove to be inoperable after hang-
ing at the davits during a long voyage. Invariably they will be
the boats carrying key officers, important equipment, or vital
armament. "But," the Aussies would say, "it's faster. And besides, that's the way we did it at Gallipoli." Right. And our
Marine Corps post–World War I studies of that operation indicate that "rile" loading was a contributing cause to their

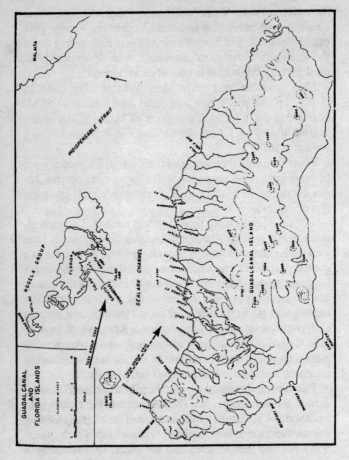

difficulties in securing a lodgment ashore. Of course we were much too polite to tell them that.

At about 1030 I was directed to go ashore with the chief of staff, Col. Capers James, to establish an advanced division command post at Red Beach. As we approached the shore, I heard occasional single shots from our Springfield 1903 rifles. This was puzzling. Our landing craft did not have a bow ramp and I took the precaution of rolling over the gunwale as we grounded on the sand. I felt an immediate stab of sharp pain in my belly and for a fraction of a second thought, "This is it. It's been a short war for me." Then I realized that I had accidentally triggered the CO_2 bottle on my life belt and it had expanded around my waist, gripping it in full force. This attracted all my interest and attention for the next second or two until I found and operated the release.

Our Higgins boat had made a beautiful landing on the steep-to beach, and we stepped ashore almost dry shod. We carried our radios and set them up in an advanced command post established about 100 yards inland. Our first message was to notify division of our arrival and our location ashore.

Immediately, I returned to the beach proper to see what was going on. The scattered firing I'd heard was due to a few Marines shooting down coconuts from the first palm trees that most of them had ever seen. There were others there too. I found the division provost marshal—eating coconut—and told him to arrest anyone firing a weapon and to check all personnel on the beach for stragglers. Reminded of his duties, he did a good job. Order was soon restored.

I was on the beach many times that afternoon and saw no further evidence of disorder. The men on the beach either were forming up prior to moving out or were there for some purpose in connection with artillery, tank, motor transport, engineer, and combat units coming across the beach. These all required guides, equipment operators, radiomen, and a dozen other special qualifications needed to get their parent units under way. The later horror stories about stragglers were without foundation in fact.

About 1320 someone brought me a message from the advanced command post. A Coast Watcher on Bougainville had spotted a large formation of enemy twin-engine bombers "coming yours," as they always put it. The message had gone through a special communications system and reached us from Pearl Harbor less than a minute before the strike began. Word was passed to take cover. It was a waste of effort. No one wanted to miss the show, and it was a good one. Twenty-two twin-engine bombers at 14,000 feet passed over Transport Group Xray and its screening ships. The latter, joined by the transports, put up a highly effective antiaircraft barrage, bringing down at least three bombers. We suffered no damage afloat or ashore.

I walked westward along the government track (an unimproved roadway without bridges or culverts, suitable for foot traffic and in some sections passable for vehicles having four-wheel drive) that skirts the beach in the trace of 1st Battalion, 5th Marines. They had been ashore for two hours and had made little progress. I noticed that a few men had started lightening their packs by throwing away spare articles of clothing. I was alarmed—shades of Bull Run! To my gratification all signs of discard suddenly ceased. Quite obviously sergeants equipped with number twelve USMC field boots had straightened things out in their own way. There would be no more of that nonsense.

I found the battalion a few hundred yards up the beach, halted with its forward elements on the right bank of the Ilu River. The small units along the stream were clamoring to go across. I started back to find the battalion commander. As soon as I left, the troops crossed the stream of their own accord. I found the battalion commander and told him politely—he was far senior to me—to get going before the general got ashore. He made no response, but his battalion was already moving anyway. There were other and larger streams to cross between here and Lunga Point.

Upstream a bridge would be required by the 1st Marines, already coming ashore. We hadn't expected to need a bridge, so the wooden components of Stinky Davis's bridge were buried in the hold of *Bellatrix* (AK-20) under tons of rations. At Koro we learned a bridge would be an indispensable requirement and Davis was told "to get with it." Not one to question an order, he was able to acquire enough timber in some highly irregular manner from the ship's supply of damage control lumber and dunnage to construct a bridge in two sections, each carried athwartships on an LVT.

These horrible contraptions went ashore with the first

wave and moved out ahead of the front lines in the designer's desire to get the job done. Correspondent Dick Tregaskis discovered Davis out there later in the afternoon waiting for customers and complaining loudly about being shot at by both sides.[4]

As a bridge it was a structural monstrosity. The left bank of the stream was six feet higher than the right, resulting in a rakish and totally unbridgelike appearance. The deck was made of an assortment of dunnage, supplemented by palm logs cut on the spot. I always enjoyed confronting Davis with a photograph of it. Over the years his professional pride in finished workmanship caused him to maintain, unconvincingly, that this was not the bridge he built. But it was. And it served us handsomely for moving artillery and vehicles in support of the 1st Marines when they needed it.

I reported the slow progress of 1st Battalion, 5th Marines to the chief of staff, who made no comment but immediately left the CP. I assumed he had gone to confront the battalion commander. Returning to the landing beach, I awaited the arrival of Col. Clifton B. Cates, commanding 1st Marines. I had been instructed to give him a copy of a recently received aerial photograph of Lunga Point and to tell him to disregard that part of the attack order regarding seizing Mt. Austen and limit his advance to seizure of the airfield. This information had been sent to Cates early that morning, but we were not sure he had received it.

While returning to the command post, I encountered the senior colonel ashore, who informed me that if General Vandegrift did not come ashore, he could not be expected to assume command. The colonel considered the situation similar to that contemplated in U.S. Navy Regulations wherein a relieving officer of the deck was justified in declining to take over the watch if, and as long as, he considered the vessel to be in a hazardous situation. I had an idea that the general was already on his way to the beach so did not enter into any

4. Richard Tregaskis, *Guadalcanal Diary* (New York: Random House, 1943), p. 47.

discussion of the matter. I made no mention of this to the general or Jerry when they reached the beach a few minutes later.

We proceeded to the night's command post, which Capt. Jim Murray had established at a covered spot along a branch of the Ilu, not far from Stinky Davis's bridge. The general was dissatisfied with the slow advance. Jerry sent Maj. Bill Buse of our D-3 staff on a reconnaissance of the route ahead, using two LVTs for the purpose. They returned two hours later, having probed as far as the Tenaru River without encountering any real resistance.

Just prior to nightfall the general called a conference of the senior leaders and stressed the need to press on across the Tenaru in the morning. Cates, who really didn't quite know where in the dense rain forest two of his battalions were, covered up by saying that his men were tired and hungry and needed a good night's rest and a hot breakfast before moving out around 1000 next morning. Vandegrift made no comment, but he was a careful listener. He knew as we all did that Cates's men went over the side with three C-ration meals and a brown bag of sandwiches in their haversacks and that nobody was going to get any hot chow for a long time. Cates was a splendid regimental commander with a nonpareil record in France. He was needlessly clutching at straws. His battalions had been ashore only a few hours and had performed flawlessly under great difficulties in fighting the adverse jungle terrain. Cates had nothing whatsoever for which to apologize.

We moved out at first light next morning. The battalions of 1st Marines made rapid progress through the thick jungle and rain forest, emerging on the open country around the airstrip. The 1st Battalion, 5th Marines, continued its overly cautious progress toward the Japanese headquarters camp at Kukum.

At noon a large flight of enemy twin-engine torpedo planes came in from the east and launched an attack against Transport Group Xray and its screening ships. As an air-surface battle it was unique—the surface forces fired downward on the attacking aircraft, not upward as we instinctively think of antiaircraft fire. The enemy torpedo planes skimmed the water in their efforts to sink our ships. Our ships' antiaircraft, Marine shore-based antiaircraft, and carrier planes were all successful. Enemy losses were at least fourteen planes, and the attack was successfully beaten off, but not without loss. *Jarvis* (DD-393) had taken a torpedo just after a flaming plane crashed onto the transport *George F. Elliott* (AP-13), after that ship had been bombed. *Elliott* was abandoned and drifted, burning, throughout the night. Her survivors were rescued by the *Hunter Liggett* (APA-14). *Jarvis* crawled away to the southeast under her own power. She was sunk the following afternoon by Japanese torpedo bombers. There were no survivors.[5]

This attack proved demoralizing to Transport Group Xray. Commodore Reifsnider ordered general unloading to begin before the landing force was in a position to receive the torrent of cargo that immediately descended on the beach. Chaos at Red Beach ensued, and the situation became irretrievable.

Lt. Col. Freddy Wieseman, USMC, who came to know as much about all phases of landing force logistics as anyone, put it this way: "The initiation of general unloading by the Naval (Task Force) Commander is a matter that should be prevented by custom, doctrine, high command, Joint Chiefs of Staff Directive, and force of arms if necessary."[6]

The situation triggering Reifsnider's untoward action was not of his making. Fletcher, Turner, and Vandegrift must all share the blame. Fletcher for his intransigence, the other two for failing to work out a compromise solution as the situation grew serious. Such solutions were available. One would have been to shift the entire beach operation to Lunga Point, where at midafternoon of 8 August ample troop labor could have been made available. Vandegrift was aware of this and for some strange reason ignored the option. Mines? Not a single

5. Theodore Roscoe, *United States Destroyer Operations in World War II* (Annapolis, MD: Naval Institute Press, 1988), p. 174.
6. John L. Zummerman, *The Guadalcanal Campaign* (Washington, DC: Marine Corps Monographs, 1949), p. 46.

Japanese mine was ever found in Lunga Roads. They existed only in the mind of the task force commander along with such other bogeys as PT boats and seaplane tenders.

Reifsnider in his action report noted "a total lack of conception *[sic]* of the number of labor troops required to unload boats and move material off the beach."[7] Vandegrift was more aware of the problem than Reifsnider. Knowing that it was an unsolved problem at the highest levels, Vandegrift had, on or about 27 June, asked for a replacement battalion to serve the purpose. (The Marine Corps has no labor battalions as such.) These personnel were never sent. His remaining source, the division reserve, was taken from him by Turner's insistence on withholding it for the Ndeni project. Vandegrift's only remaining solution was to divert combat troops to the task, but he could do this only if and when they had accomplished their mission ashore. This might have required the transports to remain in the area somewhat longer. At this time they had been in the area only thirty hours before they wanted to go home.

In the governing Force Order the problem had been foreseen clearly but never settled. It had been waffled in true Pentagon style by finding language that each side could interpret in its own way, sometimes a worthwhile subterfuge to secure an agreement of importance that in all other respects is noncontroversial. The magic words were "the shore party commander may call upon unit commanders for additional labor," but they enjoined no specific unit to provide it. Semantics has no place on the battlefield. By midafternoon it became necessary for Vandegrift to ask Turner to cease all unloading operations until Red Beach could be cleared. The breakdown was complete.

Despite this, it had been a highly successful joint operation. Combat loading at Wellington, embarkation, and the ship-to-shore operation on 7 August were successful beyond any precedent. I had participated in four of the seven Fleet Exercises (1924 through 1941) and had never seen things done as well. Success was largely due to the fact that by mutual

7. Ibid., p. 46.

agreement between Vandegrift and Reifsnider, the established procedures prevailing in the Amphibious Forces Atlantic and published in their Force Orders were made governing.

I spent a good deal of the afternoon accompanying Lt. Col. W. E. Maxwell and the 1st Battalion, 5th Marines, in a snail-like advance toward Lunga Point. There was no resistance except for an occasional sniper or a small, bewildered group of construction workers, mostly Okinawans. The battalion commander was still convinced we were walking into a trap. The junior officers and men were disgusted. In midafternoon I broke off and headed for the airfield. On the way I encountered Colonel Hunt with his Headquarters Company of clerks, dog robbers, and MPs and also his Regimental Weapons Company, a first-class combat outfit. Hunt called out, "What's Max doin', still snoopin' and poopin'?" (Marine lingo for scouting and patrolling). I had to agree and moved on toward the strip.

Only minutes later there was a startling outburst of small-arms and mortar fire. I turned around and raced back. Hunt had given up on Max and taken his weapons company, reinforced with the clerks and dog robbers of headquarters, and stormed across the main Lunga bridge. He was proceeding at the head of the column into Kukum when I joined him. There was a moment or two of sporadic firing. I got into the act and emptied a clip at a few Japs fleeing into the palms. It was all over.

We halted momentarily. The sound of heavy firing came to us from Tulagi. We felt left out. No one broke ranks until a scrawny little recruit, with the quartermaster creases still showing in his second suit of herringbone fatigues, ran across the road to a small blackboard nailed on a tree in the center of the Japanese camp. He paused thoughtfully, chalk in hand, then wrote, "Tokyo your full of shit. Pvt. M. Shapiro."

At the same hour that Private Shapiro inscribed his immortal statement, General Hyakutake, commander of the Japanese 17th Army, was at his headquarters in Rabaul receiving his initial briefing on our landing in the Eastern Solomons. Turning to his naval liaison officer, the general asked, "What is a Marine?"[8] To his unmitigated sorrow, he would soon find out.

The camp at Kukum was in great disorder. The occupants had been surprised at breakfast, and the intensity of our bombardment drove them to instant flight. There were large piles of rice in split bamboo matting bags, a small mountain of wooden tubs full of odorous dried fish, and other goodies of mysterious appearance. The paymaster's safe was wide open. On a table was a wooden locker box full of occupation currency, which I turned over to Frank Goettge. I made a quick estimate of the camp's apparent troop capacity—about 2,000 men—and got this word to General Vandegrift, hoping he would revise downward the estimate of enemy strength to a number justifying assignment of additional men to remedy the logistic breakdown at Red Beach.

Colonel Hunt's aggressive action in personally occupying Kukum had produced the desired result in a hurry. But it was no solution to the command problem in his 1st Battalion.

8. Edwin P. Hoyt, *Warlord Tojo* (Lanham, MD: Scarborough House, 1993), p. 124.

CHAPTER 6

Nightmare Battle

On the night of 8 August the division command post was established on the beach in the vicinity of Block Four, a copra-processing shed belonging to Lever Brothers. This site gave us a sweeping view of what was soon to be known as Ironbottom Sound, a broad expanse of water extending across to Savo Island, then north to Tulagi, where deadly fighting was still going on. The flash and smoke of battle was continuous, punctuated at intervals with bursts of heavy gunfire as the light cruiser *San Juan* (CL-54) and its accompanying destroyers responded to calls for naval gunfire to support elements of the 2d Marines landed to reinforce the 1st Parachute Battalion, which had suffered heavy losses in its attack on the adjacent islets, Gavutu and Tanambogo. It was still a dingdong, hammer-and-tongs fight over there, but we were winning.

Frank Goettge, the 1st Division intelligence chief (D-2), and I crossed the beach and took a short swim in the warm water to get rid of two days' accumulated grime. Off to the west we could see the cruisers of the covering force guarding the western approaches to the transport area. One entrance lay north of, the other south of, Savo Island, situated between Guadalcanal and the Florida islands. These entrances were not narrow channels but broad reaches of deep water. Three heavy cruisers with accompanying destroyers were assigned to guard each approach: *Vincennes* (CA-44), *Quincy* (CA-39), and *Astoria* (CA-34) to the north; HMAS *Australia*, HMAS *Canberra*, and *Chicago* (CA-29) to the south.

In the gathering dusk I saw that each group was moving back and forth across its assigned approach, patrolling in column, the northern group employing a rectangular box pattern. As we left the cleansing and refreshing water, Frank stopped for one last look and said, "I guess they're not going to close up for the night." I had almost forgotten that ships in column used to do that. My memory harked back to long night watches spent as a midshipman JOOD on a bridge wing of the old dreadnought *Delaware*, taking continuous stadimeter readings on our next ship ahead. I dismissed his remark with the thought that they probably had some modern electronic recognition device that made closing up unnecessary.

I had also forgotten that the last time a divided U.S. fleet entered battle it was decisively defeated by a single ship, the CSS *Virginia*, the former USS *Merrimac* turned into an ironclad by the Confederates.

It was a soft tropical evening. As we looked across at Tulagi, it seemed utterly incongruous that over there men were fighting and killing each other in the midst of such beauty.

At about 2000 Jerry Thomas told me to take over the command post, stating that General Vandegrift had been summoned aboard the *McCawley* and that he was to accompany the general. There was to be a conference with Admiral Turner and Admiral Crutchley, the British flag officer who commanded the screening force. The general seemed pleased to go; it would probably give him a chance to get to Tulagi for a visit with Brigadier General Rupertus, commanding the diverse small units of Marines, Raiders, and Parachutists, which were especially suited to the close combat encountered on that fortress-like island.

On board *McCawley*, Turner gave his visitors the bad news: Vice Adm. Frank Jack Fletcher had pulled out of the fight, taking with him all the carriers and half the surface forces. This early withdrawal would leave Turner's ships at Guadalcanal without air cover of any sort and would of necessity force him to also pull out in order to save his highly vulnerable transports. Turner had hoped to stay somewhat longer, but his own apprehensions were heightened by receipt of a much delayed dispatch from commander, Southwest Pacific, warning of the approach of a threatening enemy task force. He then treated his listeners to a Naval War College–type lecture, complete with chart and dividers, as to what the Japanese were up to. The enemy task force, consisting of five cruisers and two seaplane tenders, was headed for Rekata Bay to the north, where it would set up and launch another air attack against the U.S. forces here in Lunga Roads tomorrow. Consequently, Turner would have to clear the area by noon tomorrow. From afar he had read the mind of Admiral Mikawa and divined his intentions.

There is a little paragraph in nearly every textbook on military intelligence. In substance it says, "Take note of all enemy capabilities to damage or destroy your own forces. Pursue a course of action that will best enable you to deal with those enemy capabilities most dangerous to you. Do not attempt to discern his intentions."

The Naval War College version, however, is gravely suspect. In part it says: "The enemy's capabilities as well as his intentions must be considered."[1]

I repeat: you cannot know your opponent's intentions, but you can determine with reasonable certainty his capabilities.

The amphibian forces under Turner's command had, in the past two days, turned back repeated strong enemy air attacks and had inflicted great losses while suffering relatively little damage in return. The presence of two "seaplane tenders"— they proved to be destroyers—suggested at worst a last-ditch attack by a handful of PBY-type patrol planes with a limited torpedo capability. This was something Turner's force could have brushed off with ease. The presence of five cruisers, however, indicated a *strong* enemy capability for a night surface attack, a real threat to our dispersed covering forces. Yet Turner opted to evade the minor capability by a withdrawal

1. George C. Dyer, *The Amphibians Came to Conquer,* Vol. 1 (Washington, DC: Department of the Navy, 1972), p. 373.

tomorrow and entirely ignored the major threat, the danger of
a surface attack tonight, failing even to pass the word to his
captains. But many of them had a good idea of what im-
pended anyway.

Information spreads rapidly in the naval service, whether it
be the official word or unofficial scuttlebutt (rumors and gos-
sip exchanged around the ship's drinking fountain and social
center). Sometimes scuttlebutt precedes the official word.
Often, it's "the straight dope."

The people who man the communications system of the
navy are highly intelligent, greatly skilled, and deeply involved in their arcane profession. They understand the ins
and outs of their system better than anyone else. They recognize the "fists" of operators on ships they have never seen.
They can spot an interesting dispatch in a dozen different
ways out of a maze of routine traffic. After all, they want to
know what is going on; their lives are on the line too. By
midafternoon the word was out. The carriers knew it, and
crew chiefs readied their planes. The transport people had it
and passed the word to the Marines at Red Beach. It was
bandied about around every scuttlebutt in the fleet: "The Japs
are coming, and there's going to be a helluva fight." Unofficial, but too true.

That night the captain of one of the cruisers patrolling off
Savo Island wrote in his Night Order Book, "The enemy can
reach this position at any time during the mid-watch." Then
he turned in.[2]

Neither Turner nor Crutchley displayed the slightest apprehension. When the conference ended, Crutchley insisted
on taking Vandegrift to the destroyer minesweeper *Southard*
(DMS-10) for his trip to Tulagi before returning to *Australia*,
his flagship. *Australia* awaited the admiral's return near
McCawley, both ships steaming slowly north of Red Beach,
twenty miles from Savo and the forces under Admiral Crutchley's command. Crutchley had little more than reached his
flagship when all hell broke loose.

2. Information given to Col. Gerald C. Thomas, USMC, and myself in Brisbane, Australia, by an officer of USS *Chicago*, 26 December 1942.

Ashore, at the division command post, the night was passing uneventfully, although our radios could not penetrate the jungle and our wire lines were constantly being cut by our own troops moving along the government track. Ship-to-shore communication was perfect—a mixed blessing.

It had been a clear, muggy tropical evening, but shortly after midnight a high thin mist moved in. About 0100, 9 August we heard the unmistakable sound of aircraft. Maj. Kenny Weir, our air officer, was with me. "Cruiser float planes," he said, "and not ours." A moment later he added, "Where there are cruiser planes, there are cruisers."

The planes, two or three of them, circled overhead and began illuminating the transport area. Their flares lit the entire Lunga Roads with a vivid greenish light of amazing intensity, surpassing anything either of us had ever seen.

At this moment I came face to face with my first hands-on lesson of the war: distinct changes of light intensity produce a plethora of erroneous reports. It happens after every sunset; before every dawn. Familiar offshore rocks or islets suddenly become hostile ships; waving kunai grass takes on the form of advancing infantry. We came to call them "purple shadow reports."

We immediately became the recipients of a series of excited messages from *McCawley*. They came in faster than we could reply: "Japanese attacking Red Beach" and "Enemy landing on Red Beach" are samples of what came from our flagship.

Although we had no communication link with Red Beach at the moment, it was quite apparent that nothing was going on down there. I tried to frame soothing replies. After all, it is difficult for a lieutenant colonel to tell a rear admiral that he is talking through his hat.[3]

What had happened was this: When the Japanese lit up the roadstead, many of our ships' boats plying to and from Red

3. Turner denies sending any such message, according to Dyer, *The Amphibians Came to Conquer*. Nevertheless, at least two were logged in and recorded in full together with our replies in the G-3 journal for the night of 8–9 August 1942 appearing in Phase II of the Final Report of the 1st Marine Division.

Beach in the dark saw each other for the first time. Most boats were armed, and some excited boat crews opened fire, starting an "intramural," as we came to call them in Old George. We were to suffer some of these misencounters ourselves during the next few days, good ones too. They are as old as war itself, a natural phenomenon of growing up on the battlefield, the mumps and measles on the road to military maturity.

Events quickly overtook this minicrisis. The horizon south of Savo Island lit up with gun flashes, searchlights stabbed the darkness, and countless projectiles, from 20mm to 8-inch, arched across the sky, their red and green tracers adding a startling touch of color as they searched for targets. They found them soon enough. Huge fires blazed up momentarily like mammoth boxes of wooden matches ignited by sparks.

"Magazines," I thought aloud.

"No," Weir answered from the darkness. "Those are our own cruiser planes. Still on deck and full of gas. They should have been flown off."

So intense were these flames that on some ships men could not even reach their general quarters stations.

The firing died down. Several minutes later it flared up again, this time north of Savo, where our other cruisers were engaged. The same horrifying spectacle was reenacted. Then silence.

Despite all logic we tried to tell ourselves that we had come out on top. Only Weir was unconvinced. I could tell that he was deeply concerned. As division air officer he had been instrumental in planning and organizing the naval gunfire support for the landing forces. He had obtained the services of Marine aviators trained and experienced in the adjustment and control of naval gunfire against shore-based targets. These officers had been temporally distributed among the cruisers of the covering force. Weir said nothing, but I sensed that he was worried about their fate. Several of these pilots were indeed among those lost that night.

The nightmare Battle of Savo Island was over. Many cheerless hours were to pass before we learned that in less than a half hour an inferior Japanese force had destroyed four of our five cruisers. We had scored only one damaging hit on one enemy cruiser. It had been a disastrous night for us.

It began to rain, a warm rain. I sat down and leaned against a palm, taking such shelter as my helmet afforded, and fell asleep. I was totally exhausted—physically and mentally. I'd had no real rest since before we sighted Guadalcanal. We did not know the results of that brief and furious battle. There was absolutely nothing we could do to aid our friends and ship-mates out on that cruel water, whether they were alive or dead.

We received no more messages from the fleet.

General Vandegrift and Jerry returned shortly after day-break. They said we had lost some ships but were uncertain as to details. There was good news too. Tulagi was now entirely USMC. The fighting was over, and the troops could now turn in full force to clear the Tulagi beaches and expedite unload-ing, which had been going badly due to the intransigence of the commander of Transport Group Yoke.

Someone started a fire. We warmed ourselves. Col. Hawley C. Waterman collected some instant coffee envelopes dis-carded from C rations and made coffee in a metal ammo box for all hands. I drank mine from an empty hash can that had contained my breakfast. Delicious. The rain stopped. Heavy mist hindered our view to seaward. There was intermittent firing by a single heavy gun. The concussion of each explo-sion shook the foliage, showering us with dislodged droplets. Col. Pedro del Valle, commanding the 11th Marines, our ar-tillery regiment, said quietly, "That firing is one of our ships sinking the *Canberra*." Silence engulfed us. The solemn re-quiem for that brave and dying ship continued.

General Vandegrift appeared, and Jerry Thomas gave the oral order for defense, in part as follows:

> Commander, Naval Forces South Pacific reports large enemy forces gathering at Rabaul.[4] We may expect an at-tack on this beachhead within ninety-six hours.

4. The only information we received from ComNavForSoPac during the landing proved false, and ComNavForSoPac apologized. Nevertheless it was

The 1st Marine Division will organize the Lunga Point beaches for defense against an attack from the sea in two sectors.

1st Marines, less 1st Battalion division reserve, plus attached units will on the right organize and defend landing beaches from the Lunga River, exclusive, to the mouth of the Tenaru with its right flank refused for a distance of four hundred yards along the left (west) bank of that river.

5th Marines, less 2d Battalion, plus attached units will on the left organize and defend landing beaches from the Lunga River (inclusive) with its left flank resting on the high ground 1,000 yards south of Kukum.

11th Marines will provide general support from firing positions in rear of the beach areas.

1st Engineer Battalion proceed immediately with completion of the airfield as a matter of highest priority.

All units provide own local security.

No ground will be given up under any circumstances without the express order of the division commander.

It was that simple, and it worked: the first combat order ever issued to a Marine division in the presence of the enemy.

I went over to the new command post located at the airfield only a few yards from the partially completed strip. It abutted an ancient coral reef or finger that provided limited protection against naval gunfire coming from the north. A small adjacent knoll gave restricted observation to the north and west covering part of Ironbottom Sound. Our command post was for all intents and purposes a part of the airfield that obviously would become an inviting target for enemy aircraft and naval forces. Too soon our CP became known as the "impact center."

Just prior to our landing the area had been thoroughly worked over by U.S. Navy dive bombers. Near the east end

---

harmful in that establishment of the defense was given priority over pursuing the remnants of the enemy garrison across the Matanikau, which had been our intention at nightfall on 8 August.

there was what remained of a Japanese blacksmith shop crudely constructed of native materials. Tech. Sgt. Raymond C. "Butch" Morgan, the general's cook, was already inside boiling beans on the blacksmith's forge, which, strangely, was still intact. Butch had inherited the blacksmith's belongings and was already wearing a pair of his pants. The former owner, now deceased, was lying nearby.

Cpl. Walter "Shorty" Mantay, Butch's striker, was busy filling empty bamboo matting rice bags with dirt to build a parapet around the new galley. When I came back several hours later, the boiled beans were done and the blacksmith interred nearby. Mantay was still filling rice bags, and Butch and his pal, Sgt. Hook Moran, were having a coffee in the general's galley. Situation well in hand.

I went down to Red Beach. No ship-to-shore activity was in progress. The beach itself was hopelessly blocked because Reifsnider, the commodore of Transport Group Xray, had on the afternoon of 8 August ordered general unloading to begin. This was the prerogative of the amphibious force commander and then only upon recommendation of the landing force commander based on his ability to receive the increased volume of supply flowing to the beach. No such authorization was ever given, and Reifsnider is largely responsible for the logistical breakdown that followed. Additional manpower was required.

Turner had wrongfully withheld about 1,400 officers and men of the 2d Marines on the ships. He could have put them ashore to assist in the task. Likewise, Reifsnider had available aboard *Hunter Liggett* all the survivors of the *George F. Elliott* (AP-13). Also, he had authority to land some 500 Marines of the 1st Division temporarily detailed as ships' platoons. (One Marine platoon is customarily assigned to each transport and cargo vessel to assist in identifying and selectively unloading cargo needed during the early stages before general unloading begins, at which point their services are no longer required.) The men left behind on each transport would have provided ample manpower. In the disorder of the pullout these men never got ashore to rejoin their combat units. This resulted in a severe loss exceeding in numbers the battle casualties already suffered by the division. These men were never returned to Guadalcanal. Turner had them reorganized as a unit called a "Provisional Raider Battalion." This action was taken totally without authority. By law only the commandant of the Marine Corps acting with the express authority of the Secretary of the Navy can create an organization of the Marine Corps.

At this juncture Vandegrift was confronted with the most critical situation a commander can face—inability to "find, fix, and fight" the large enemy force that Turner had told him was waiting on Guadalcanal. As we now know, Turner's estimate of enemy strength was wide of the mark, since it was based on unrealistic appraisals made at MacArthur's headquarters in Melbourne. But this had not yet been established as a fact at the time Reifsnider gave his devastating order. The torrent of cargo flowing to the beach quickly overwhelmed the resources available to receive it. Confusion ensued, leading to disorder that extended back to the transport group itself. Very little unloading was accomplished after the enemy torpedo plane attack on the afternoon of 8 August, according to Lieutenant Colonel Pate, our D-4 (logistics).

I met General Vandegrift on the beach. He gave me a full account of our losses in the previous night's surface action. I found it almost unbelievable.

We looked out across Red Beach to the transport area. All the ships were under way, maneuvering individually at flank speed. To what end I do not know. They were not dropping depth charges. (Japanese records indicate two submarines reached the area sometime on 9 August but made no attack.)[5] Our transports would not even stop to retrieve their own boats, which pursued them frantically to no avail. The sight reminded me of the Old Mariner's rhyme:

5. Richard F. Newcomb, *Nightmare in Savo Straits* (New York: Bantam), p. 146.

When in danger or in doubt
Steam in circles, scream and shout.

But I pass no judgments, recalling the ancient admonition
of the Roman Gen. Lucius Paulus, "Let him not, on land, assume the office of a pilot."[6]

Gazing out at the scene off Red Beach, General Vandegrift
asked in a soft voice, "Bill, what has happened to your navy?"

I could think of no better reply than "I don't believe the
first team is on the field yet, General."

From his remote observation post on Guadalcanal, Martin
Clemens, Coast Watcher for Ferdinand, described the scene
just as we had observed it at the same hour, noting the absence of one county-class cruiser (Canberra) and some U.S.
cruisers as well (Quincy, Vincennes, and Astoria).[7]

There was scarcely more than a pretext of order after that.
Some ships failed even to retrieve all of their own boats and
crewmen. These men and boats proved a valuable addition to
our small boat pool, operating under command of Lt. Comdr.
Dwight Dexter, USCG, until we were able to return them to
Noumea.

The ships straggled out one by one through Sealark Channel to form on McCawley for the trip back to Noumea. At
nightfall Kelly Turner sent a somewhat misleading dispatch
to Ghormley reporting his departure and our situation ashore.
That brought the operation to a somewhat inglorious end. It
was, to quote Charles I, "an unhandsome quitting."[8]

We were left without exterior communications or support
of any kind and with no assurance that help would be forthcoming. We had no source of information or observation
except what we could derive from a twenty-four-foot observation tower constructed of palm logs inherited from the emperor. We were on half rations, had little ammunition and no

6. See the epigraph at the beginning of this book.
7. Martin Clemens, "A Coastwatcher's Diary," American Heritage (Feb.
1966), p. 109–110.
8. Referring to Rupert's abandonment of Bristol to the forces of Cromwell.

construction equipment or defensive materials whatsoever, and no one would talk to us when we improvised a long-distance transmitter from captured Japanese radio equipment. Outside of that we were in great shape. However, the sorrow of our parting was not too greatly increased by the realization that Kelly Turner would not be here to occupy the tent we had prepared for him when he proposed to come with us into Macedonia and that we would hereafter be forced to depend solely upon "councils but such as shall be framed within our camp."[9]

It is of interest to assess the parts played by certain key figures in the vast drama of our first offensive action. At the Washington level, Adm. Ernest J. King, commander in chief, U.S. Fleet (CinCUSFLT) and chief of naval operations (CNO), was a great leader who sensed and seized the moment. He believed it was better to have "a man, a boy, and a horse pistol" up the slot today than a field army next spring. King rolled the dice, but the risk was not uncalculated. He had good people to work with and good tools at hand. Things went surprisingly well until the Savo disaster. This was certainly no fault of his. Even so, the undertaking was a success. We had taken possession of a strategic area in the major theater of the Pacific. If the Japanese hoped to expand their conquests, we would have to be dislodged. Subsequent history shows that the Japanese laid the foundation of their own ruin in the Solomons. Possession of Guadalcanal meant that henceforth we could call the tune in the Pacific. And we did.

Rear Adm. Richmond Kelly Turner, commander, South Pacific Amphibious Force, alone of the navy leaders, displayed the same type of bold aggressive leadership that characterized King. Unlike King, however, he was possessed of a colossal ego that sometimes led to decisions that ignored the dictates of ordinary common sense. He needed someone to keep him on a short tether. Halsey understood this and did it, but that was later.

Turner's good luck—and ours—ended at 1845 on 8 August

9. See the epigraph at the beginning of this book.

when he received the long-delayed dispatch telling of the sighting of Mikawa's squadron. The message had taken eight hours and nineteen minutes to reach him. From then on things went sadly awry. Turner ordered Vandegrift and Crutchley to come aboard *McCawley*, yet he had no business with either that could not have been handled by the dispatch of a message or a staff officer. In Crutchley's case attendance was highly complicated and dangerous, for it required him to turn over command to Captain Bode of *Chicago*, the next senior officer in the southern group. Crutchley did not inform Captain Riefkohl on *Vincennes* in the northern group of his departure, although actual command of the two groups would devolve upon Riefkohl, not Bode. Nor did he notify Rear Admiral Scott in *San Juan*, screening the eastern flank of the transport area along with HMAS *Hobart*.

Then, in the dark, Crutchley had to close *McCawley*, twenty-four miles away. *Australia*'s absence reduced the firepower of the southern group by one-third. Following the conference *Australia* either would have to attempt the dangerous maneuver of rejoining the southern group in the dark or would have to wait until daybreak. Naval customs and courtesies have their place, to be sure, but not to this extent, particularly in time of war.

Nothing could have been accomplished at such a meeting, and nothing was accomplished. Turner was left uncovered by Fletcher's flight and had to pull out through no fault of his own. Any details to be worked out, such as future communications with the Marines, would have been better handled at the staff level.

The attempts to cover Kelly Turner for his tragic folly range from the grotesque to the frivolous: for example, Crutchley had expressed a desire to "talk things over" with Turner sometime at the latter's convenience. I doubt this was the particular moment either of them would have selected for such a talk. Furthermore, the need for Vandegrift to be present at such a discussion totally escapes me. But there it is in the record.[10]

10. Dyer, *The Amphibians Came to Conquer,* Vol. 1, p. 193.

The unforeseen result of this untoward summons was that an Allied force without a flag officer present was destroyed, ship by ship, in a series of confused single ship versus enemy fleet encounters.

Kelly Turner insists he will accept full responsibility for any mistakes he may have made—and then vehemently insists he never made the slightest error. In his biography there is a particularly illuminating passage of intemperate denials wherein he places blame for the disaster on just about everyone in the world except himself and Mother Teresa.

Particularly exceptionable is Turner's excoriation of Rear Adm. John McCain's patrol aircraft for failure to detect and report the movement of Admiral Mikawa's cruisers during the late afternoon of 8 August. These patrol aircraft were few in number and operated over a vast area at the extreme radius of their endurance.

In this unjust criticism of McCain, Turner lays himself open to the charge that, like so many inexperienced commanders, he failed to employ *all* weapons available to him: specifically, the more than fifteen *scouting* planes of the cruiser force. Had they been sent out to scour the area south of Rekata Bay at sunset, they could not have failed to locate the oncoming enemy force before nightfall, as it was only a comparatively short distance northwest of Savo Island.

Instead, these planes, many with tanks filled with gasoline, remained on their catapults or on deck and became gigantic infernos when ignited by the first enemy projectiles, adding more death and horror to this indescribably dreadful night. In short, Turner had ample means of his own to detect Mikawa's approaching cruisers, but he failed to use them. This is the irrefutable answer to the Battle of Savo Island controversy.

On the landing force side, Vandegrift turned in a competent performance of his assignment. The Marines, as always, had rendered an exact performance of the mission assigned them, the seizure of Tulagi and Guadalcanal: Tulagi with hard fighting and significant losses, Guadalcanal almost by default or, as Col. Jerry Thomas later described the initial landing, with "a blow at a lace curtain."

By sunset on 9 October, Turner's Task Force had cleared the Solomons, and "with this, Alexander Vandegrift and his Marines were left alone to conduct probably the greatest defensive stand in the annals of American Arms."[11]

11. Robert Leckie, *The Wars of America,* Vol. 2 (New York: Harper & Row, 1968), p. 227.

CHAPTER 7

The 1st "Maroon" Division Digs In

The night of 9 August was our first in the permanent division command post adjacent to the western end of the uncompleted airstrip. Butch Morgan was putting out bean soup and bull beef hash, the first hot food anyone had seen since that early breakfast aboard *McCawley* on the seventh. We gorged.

There had been skirmishes with the Japanese down at the Matanikau. We suffered a few casualties. Our small units engaged there had done well.

Our immediate problem was one of establishing exterior communications. Adm. Kelly Turner had failed to provide us with any long-range radio capability when he decided to leave with the surface forces instead of coming ashore. This was one of several problems that should have been settled at the Turner-Crutchley-Vandegrift conference. Lt. Col. Eddy Snedeker, our communications officer, jury-rigged a captured Japanese transmitter to span the distances but could get no response, although we knew Kelly Turner (Task Force 62) had broken radio silence with a message to ComSoPac early in the evening. But neither he nor Admiral Fletcher (TF 61) would respond.

Our command post was primitive. We found some Japanese tarpaulins, one for General Vandegrift and one for the headquarters equipment, consisting of two hand-operated field telephones, a field desk, and a small iron safe for securing classified items. We slept on the ground without blankets. Our other gear, such as it was, lay buried somewhere in the logistical rubble piled up by Reifsnider's minions at Red Beach. We had no bugler. We needed none. Butch Morgan sounded reveille at each sunrise braying for his helper, Mantay, in a voice of brass, "Shorty, Shorty, git hot! Git hot now, Shorty, right away, or I'll run ya up!"

My main occupation during the next few days was checking the development of defenses on the Lunga beaches. These represented a machine gunner's dream. We emplaced our weapons to command long, unbroken tangents of smooth sandy shoreline, ideal for the employment of final protective lines and bands of overlapping and flanking machine-gun fire, capable of mercilessly mowing down anyone attempting to gain the jungle cover on the inland side. Such fire has the great additional advantage of coming from outside the hostile unit's zone of advance. Maneuver against such positions is impossible without securing the assistance or permission of adjacent units, which are usually experiencing similar difficulties of their own.

Such a situation was to confront our 2d Marine Division when it landed at Tarawa in 1944. The landing force was unavoidably exposed for more than twenty-four hours to murderous long-range fire coming from an unopposed area to their left that had escaped destruction by naval gunfire and could not be reached for subjugation except by difficult, costly, and time-consuming movement ashore. This was finally accomplished, and the island was taken, but only after bloody struggles by heroic men.

Lunga Point itself permitted a plan of fires that looked like something out of the textbook, but the jungle positions on the Tenaru River, along the right flank of the 1st Marines, were quite the opposite. The thick jungle growth was an obstacle to observation and fire except frontally, and then only for a few yards. It was not machine-gun country. It required physical occupation of every yard in a defensive cordon, costly in manpower and weapons.

Both types of position were relatively easy to defend in daylight, but both could be effectively attacked at night, and we knew our enemy was particularly adept at this type of warfare.

Meanwhile, the 1st Engineer Battalion was working frantically to complete the essential airstrip. Filling in a 200-foot gap in the center was their first objective. This would provide 2,600 feet of runway, enough for our fighter planes. Even this limited goal required the movement, largely by hand, of more than 7,000 cubic yards of material in the face of continual enemy hindrance.

Sgt. Stinky Davis, the bridge builder of D day, again found himself operating in the bull's-eye of the target. He headed the small group that actually completed the field, placing the fill, grading it with a steel girder dragged by one of our trucks, and compacting it to runway density with the little Japanese road rollers. Japanese cruiser planes, apparently from Rekata Bay, interfered constantly with the work. Stinky's group suffered casualties and was forced to dig foxholes alongside the project every few yards to facilitate taking cover. The Japanese pilots gave special attention to the nine little road rollers we'd captured. Their number was constantly being reduced by the necessity of cannibalizing damaged machines to repair the more serviceable.

On 10 August at 1330, twenty-five twin-engine Bettys escorted by sixteen Zeros circled the area at high altitude. Without bombing us, they disappeared to the east, obviously searching for naval targets. Thereafter hostile air strikes against the field continued on a daily basis or more. We suffered few casualties, primarily due to the effectiveness of antiaircraft fire from our 3d Defense Battalion; this was then our only defense against aerial attack. It forced the enemy to stay at higher altitude during their bombing runs.

The runway was completed on 12 August—just five days after we came ashore—and was extended to 3,800 feet by 18 August. Simultaneously, work started on the task of moving supplies from Red Beach to the Lunga Perimeter. The task was increased with the discovery of large numbers of barrels, crates, and boxes floating in the former transport area. This was probably cargo unavoidably jettisoned by landing craft to lighten them sufficiently to permit their being hoisted aboard the parent ships before they withdrew.

Our division dentist, faced with the prospect of practicing dentistry without his specialized tools, spotted a huge watertight box floating near the beach. It contained his dental chair and complete equipment. He used it throughout our time on Guadalcanal.

Our 100 LVTs proved to be worth their weight in gold as cargo movers. We had embarked only one-third of our heavy trucks at Wellington, and few of these were ever landed. We had captured many Japanese trucks, but only thirty-four could be made operable. These used a cheap grade of fuel not carried in our inventory, but the Japanese had considerately left us a large supply. The LVTs, with their tremendous cargo capacity and ability to travel off-road, on beach, reef, or sea, did the bulk of the work. Movement of our supplies was completed on 11 August.

I believe it was 10 August when the field received its name, Henderson Field, for Maj. Lofton R. "Joe" Henderson, USMC, who had been killed in a bombing run on a Japanese carrier at Midway. Maj. Kenny Weir, the division air officer, set the whole thing up on his own. There was a disabled Higgins boat beached near Block Four that had been abandoned. The boat ensign, a small stars and stripes, was still flying at the stern. Weir took it to Lunga, found a Japanese flagpole, and asked General Vandegrift to come to Pagoda Hill for the flag raising. The general went along with the idea, and the flag was raised over Henderson Field. Weir told me later, "I had to do it, or they would have named it after some potbellied old SOB behind a desk in the Pentagon."

Later in the day, an authenticator message was received from ComSoPac. It did not acknowledge or refer to messages we had already sent but said in part, "Report situation briefly. Authenticate reply by giving names of destroyer and carrier on which you last saw Callaghan."

We were relieved to have established a communications link with the rear area, regardless of how tenuous and uncertain it might be. To Jerry and me it seemed to offer an inviting opportunity for the division to break off its stormy relationship

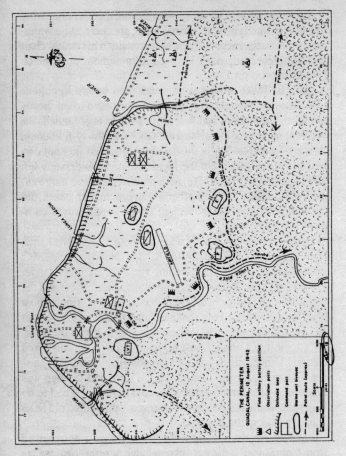

THE PERIMETER
GUADALCANAL, 12 August 1942

■ Field artillery battery position
▲ Observation posts
▢ Defended area
▢ Command post
● Marine unit bivouac
--- Patrol route (approx)

Scale

with Turner and his Task Force 62 and return to our original
status directly under ComSoPac, Vice Admiral Ghormley.
General Vandegrift proved noncommittal. Looking back, I
can see that a greater wisdom than ours had already weighed
the alternatives: either lean on a broken reed for the support
we would need or accept the "warts and all" solution of continuing our present prickly relationship with Kelly Turner,

who had shown character, courage, great energy, and commitment to the business at hand. Our old man had already chosen the latter. Never were we to have any real reason to regret his choice.

Our position on Lunga Point was in the shape of a giant horseshoe facing the sea, with the inland base wide open. This was our back door, covered by an outpost line established by the units operating in the rear of the Lunga beach lines: artillery batteries, the engineer battalion, and the amphibious tractor battalion. This area to the south was still infested by numbers of Okinawan construction troops, cut off from the Japanese main body and now in a starving condition. They would slip through the outpost line at night and into the beachhead in search of food.

For two successive evenings the outposts engaged in noisy "intramurals," precipitated at sunset by minor clashes with these Okinawan "termites," as the men called them. The uproar greatly annoyed General Vandegrift. After the second night the old Trojan in him came to the fore. He took away their ammunition and double manned each post with two Marines armed with only fixed bayonets. There were no more intramurals.

With all projects well under way, the regiments were able to increase patrol activity and regain contact with the enemy forces on both flanks. On the Matanikau River, a few miles west of Lunga Point, a series of small clashes occurred on a daily basis. The former garrison of Kukum had apparently reestablished itself at Kokumbona and was holding positions along the left (west) bank of the river. This force was essentially a battalion of the Japanese Special Landing Force, an organization somewhat similar to our own Fleet Marine Force but composed of navy personnel wearing the naval uniform. They were determined men, like all those we encountered. Their reason for abandoning Kukum on 7 August has never been revealed. They obviously had few resources of any kind and their naval uniforms were unfit for jungle warfare. The Marines began referring to them as the Kokumbona Vagabonds.

The most reasonable surmise as to why they abandoned

their tents at Kukum without a fight is that their commander thought the appearance of our vast task force off Lunga Point heralded only a raid. Accordingly, he took pains to make it easier for us and, in the long run, less dangerous to himself. So he opened his safe, set out the occupation currency, effected other steps to facilitate our easy access, and hoped for our prompt departure, whereupon he could go back to work having suffered little real damage. I believe his conclusion was facilitated and expedited by the volume of eight-, six-, and five-inch naval gunfire that was thunderously pounding on Lunga Point at that moment. No such development occurred on Tulagi, possibly because over there, there was no place to go, so they fought to the finish, as they did throughout the war.

At this time initial contact was made with Sgt. Maj. Jacob Vouza and his small group of native scouts, who were to render such valuable service throughout the operation. I was in the 5th Marines area when they first appeared, bringing in a lieutenant from *Saratoga*'s Fighter Squadron 5 who had been shot down on 7 August. He had multiple bullet wounds in the shoulders, now crawling with maggots. I was alarmed until our division surgeon, Capt. Warwick Brown, USN, assured me that the presence of maggots was quite normal under the circumstances and in fact served a useful purpose in the absence of regular therapy. The natives were rewarded with rice and some Japanese canned fruit. These were better rations than ours.

On the twelfth, the field was operable on a limited basis, and Admiral McCain, ComAirSoPac, lost no time in sending his aide, Lt. William Sampson, USN, in a PBY-5A to check it out. Accompanying him was Capt. Walter Schindler, USN, seeking information from us concerning the Savo battle. We had little to give. The captain brought us ten pounds of frozen strawberries from the admiral's mess. When he left, the general sent for Butch, put him in the two-star jeep, and said, "Take these berries over to the hospital for the wounded people." So ended our first day on half rations.

Patrol reports of 5th Marines over several days indicated

the Japanese were developing a defensive position along the west bank of the Matanikau. There were repeated references to the sighting of white flags in the vicinity of the sandbar at the river's mouth. At that time we lacked detailed knowledge of our enemy's habits. Our intelligence section (D-2) concluded that these flags were signals of a willingness to surrender or at least a desire to talk. We were then unfamiliar with the Japanese soldier's custom of carrying a small white flag in his pack and did not know that these were usually displayed to taunt opponents or to identify their own positions. No one had noticed that these flags always had a red meatball in the center.

A prisoner taken on the previous day, a man in his thirties, powerfully built and of surly demeanor, was interrogated at the command post and seemed to give evidence substantiating our erroneous view. He was a naval enlisted man of some sort, probably from the Special Naval Landing Force unit driven from Kukum. He was tied to a tree at the CP for most of the day with a hawser-size length of manila line around his waist. He wore blue trousers and a white blouse with a blue cape collar like our own navy's old-style dress whites.

Lt. Col. Frank Goettge, our intelligence officer, got permission from General Vandegrift to take a patrol of some twenty-five men to the Matanikau River to establish contact. They left by boat after nightfall, taking the prisoner with them. Landing somewhere near Point Cruz, they moved ashore and were straightaway ambushed near the beach. Frank, leading the patrol, was the first casualty. Only three of our men survived. No bodies were found when Marines investigated the area the following morning, and no significant trace of the patrol was ever located.

This loss was a blow to all hands. Frank, a football player of national renown, was a much respected and admired officer. He had been a decorated member of the old Marine Brigade in France and was wounded in the Argonne. With him on this patrol were the most active and experienced intelligence personnel of both the division and the 5th Marines. It would be hard to replace these men, so qualified in providing contact intelligence at the troop level. General Vandegrift felt the blow keenly in every way. I am sure he blamed himself for not restraining Frank's well-intentioned but ill-advised undertaking. The lesson we learned was that the scope of military intelligence should not be extended to include the conduct of field operations.

The next few days were a period of considerable confusion. None of the records are in agreement on what or when or in what order events occurred—they defy all attempts at reconciliation. Japanese air and surface attacks were continuous and without discernible pattern. The 3d Defense Battalion mounted an extremely and increasingly effective antiaircraft defense. Japanese aircraft losses were forcing the enemy to resort to high-altitude bombing of the airfield instead of the sudden low-level attack method used by their cruiser planes.

There was also a constant enemy naval presence in the immediate area. Boat communication with Tulagi was effectively severed by submarines, which used their deck guns to subject both Guadalcanal and Tulagi to nuisance bombardments at any hour of the day or night.[1] Enemy destroyers were also usually present. However, our losses were not significant in any category.

There was little contact with our own forces during this period. A B-17 would "drag" our field every afternoon. It was a welcome sight. On one occasion I saw the B-17, still at low altitude, score a direct hit on an enemy destroyer south of Florida Island. The destroyer lay dead in the water belching smoke and steam, finally getting under way and proceeding eastward out of Sealark Channel at an impressively slow speed. We had no shore-based artillery, airplanes, or surface craft available to sink this disabled enemy.

Following the ambush of the Goettge patrol and in view of the lessening of the once-imminent threat from Rabaul, there was increased activity by each regiment on its exposed flank.

1. A. J. Watts, *Japanese Warships of World War II* (Garden City, NY: Doubleday, 1966), pp. 161–223. Most Japanese submarines mounted one deck gun of 3 to 5.5 inches.

The first well-organized attack was made by three companies of the 5th Marines, operating independently and at widely separated points. The plan was as follows:

- B Company (Hawkins) would attack straight across the mouth of the Matanikau River.
- L Company (Spurlock) would cross the river at a point 1,000 yards upstream and attack Matanikau Village, situated on the coast, from the south.
- I Company (Hardy), embarked in landing craft, would force a lodgment onshore west of Kokumbona and attack eastward toward the Matanikau River.

It would have been a complex operation even for more experienced troops. It came off surprisingly well, much to our relief at division headquarters. Hawkins, at the river mouth, received heavy enfilading fire from machine guns on the ridge to his left front and reported to his regimental commander that he was "pinned down" on the sandbar. This expression caught the eye of General Vandegrift, who determined to find out for himself. He found Hawkins effectively carrying out his mission and coolly covering the enemy positions with fire. Hawkins showed the general two holes in his helmet and his submachine gun's shot-away wooden stock. The old man later told me: "He was pinned down, all right."

Spurlock's L Company had brushed off light resistance and crossed the river on the eighteenth, the day before the general attack, bivouacking for the night south of Matanikau Village. In the morning they attacked toward the north and fought their way to the outskirts of the village, overrunning a series of well-defended positions. At this point they became the objective of a Japanese banzai charge, the first of the many we experienced on Guadalcanal. However, the element of surprise was lost when the enemy began his assault at too great a distance. There was interval enough to destroy the oncoming Japanese with small-arms fire before they could reach the Marines. It was heartening to know that the enemy could make mistakes too.

Meanwhile, I Company (Hardy) was proceeding via Dexter's landing craft along the coast to its landing point west of Kokumbona. It received rifle and machine-gun fire while still on the water and west of the Matanikau. Opposite the landing point the Marines came under long-range naval gunfire from two enemy destroyers and a submarine patrolling well to seaward. Though ineffective, this fire pursued them to the beach and throughout the brief period of landing.

The Japanese ships did not attempt to close and destroy our small unprotected flotilla. This brings up an inexplicable quirk in the Japanese military mentality that we were to experience again and again. Whether because of lack of initiative or the workings of their strange code of military honor, they often did little or nothing to help their countrymen in an obvious moment of peril.

With Hardy's company ashore blocking the escape route to the west along the government track, the trap was complete. Enemy resistance broke, and the survivors faded into the familiar and unhealthy jungle with their wounded. Losses were incredibly disproportionate. Our dead numbered four; theirs, sixty-six, most killed in the ill-timed banzai charge on L Company. We were happy to see that we had three fine young company commanders: Spurlock, Hawkins, and Hardy. Each would be heard from again.

Good weather continued. In the evenings some of us gathered at the end of the coral finger for a pleasant half-hour bull session. One evening a young officer sardonically suggested that a ribbon might be authorized to commemorate our present activity in the Solomons. Somebody picked up the idea and proposed it be made of the same green herringbone twill as the fatigues we were wearing. All were sure this would be approved by the quartermaster due to the obvious economy involved in providing the material.

This casual project soon became more ambitious—that of a regular medal, something similar to the Marine Corps Expeditionary Medal. We all agreed to the somewhat scatological idea that the "stuff" hitting the fan—our favorite expression—should appear on one side of the medal. There was a difference of opinion concerning what should be portrayed on the other. One school of thought held out for the idea of a Marine grabbing at a hot potato shaped like Guadalcanal; the other, that it should be a transport with a stern on each end so it could "haul ass without turning around."

There was overwhelming approval of the idea that the unofficial motto of the division, *Faciat Georgius* (let George do it), must appear somewhere. No consensus reached, we went our separate ways, and I forgot the whole bit of good-natured foolishness. Months later, in Australia, two young officers from our intelligence section dropped something on my desk—a George Medal, the hot potato version cast in pot metal and suspended by a herringbone ribbon from a bandoleer pin. *Faciat Georgius!* It remains my most prized possession.

We commenced getting information about the enemy along our eastern flank. We knew there was a small detachment near Taivu and were preparing to take it out. Then Coast Watcher Martin Clemens's scouts reported sighting other forces. The latter reports were conflicting and unsubstantiated, so a small patrol under Lt. John J. Jachym, an energetic and capable young officer, was sent out from A Company, 1st Battalion, 1st Marines. His mission was also to provide protection for an engineer reconnaissance group conducting a survey as to the area's suitability for construction of additional airfields. On 13 August the Jachym patrol encountered a Catholic missionary, Father Duhamel, who reported the presence of a large enemy force on the coast to the east. Jachym realized the transcending importance of this information and promptly returned with his patrol to the perimeter. His report confirmed intelligence obtained from other sources. Jerry Thomas decided to send out a strong combat patrol to make solid contact.

Later, we were to receive news that Father Duhamel and the nuns of the mission at Tetere had been murdered by the Japanese. Their blood-soaked vestments were delivered to our command post by the native scouts, who brought us a full account of this bestial act. We had urged these missionaries to accept our protection at Lunga Point until they could be evacuated, but they had decided to remain true to their mission in the most literal sense of the word.

Capt. Charlie Brush, A Company, 1st Marines left with a strong patrol on 19 August moving east along the government track. An approaching enemy group moving carelessly westward along the track was detected shortly after noon near the village of Tetere. Brush, reacting swiftly and correctly, deployed five squads across the road and engaged the surprised Japanese patrol frontally at close range.

At the same time he dispatched Lieutenant Jachym with an enveloping force against the enemy's left flank. Surprise was complete and the patrol was wiped out. Thirty-one Japanese were killed, while only three escaped. Our losses were three killed, three wounded. The matter of the Goettge patrol was evened.

The appearance and uniforms of these troops indicated they were freshly landed members of the regular Japanese Army, the first we had seen. There were four officers, including two of field rank. This was unusual for a small patrol, as was the considerable amount of excellent communication equipment they carried. Brush correctly concluded this was an advance party for a larger force and without delay dispatched all documents found on the enemy dead to Lunga via special messenger. A partial translation hastily made by Capt. Sherwood F. "Pappy" Moran, our senior interpreter, indicated the presence of a special force of about 1,000 men, hurriedly embarked at Truk and sent to Guadalcanal immediately upon learning of our 7 August landing. This was the famous Ichiki Detachment, a commando unit originally intended for the seizure of Midway Island in June.

General Vandegrift made a quick and accurate reassessment of our position. The most dangerous immediate enemy capability had shifted from that of an attack directly from the sea to an overland attack on our right (east) flank along the Tenaru. The river became progressively more difficult to defend as it extended inland, where it was less of an obstacle to the enemy and the coconut plantation area gave way to dense jungle.

Orders were issued to extend the right flank of 1st Marines inland 1,500 yards by the priority construction of hasty defensive positions along the line of the river, in this locality more of a useful control line than an obstacle.

Brush's patrol had captured three or four enemy maps of Lunga Point. We were concerned with the accuracy and detail with which they depicted the location of our defensive positions, the state of their development, and whether or not they were actually occupied. These maps were better than anything we possessed then or at any time during the campaign.

Our preoccupation with the eastern flank was not because we felt any particular threat from an attack by 1,000 Japanese. They could damage us, to be sure. They could strike at any hour or at any point they chose on our thinly held perimeter—they held the attacker's option. But even if such an attack were to be initially successful, we had ample forces deployed elsewhere and the ability to commit them as reinforcements on short notice in overwhelming force. Our real concern lay in the many indications that the unit confronting us was merely an advance element covering the arrival of a much larger force. That could be a real test.

Consideration was given to the idea of moving some of our own forces to the east to bring on a meeting engagement. This would be a logical move in active defense and would protect the airfield from possible artillery bombardment. But our logistical limitations, including shortages in ammunition and motor fuel, precluded expenditure of the amounts required for an all-out attack. (Land forces in attack may expend from four to ten times as much artillery ammunition as those fighting defensively.) Furthermore, the reduction of troops in the perimeter would lower its defensive capability if it were attacked simultaneously from the sea or from the west. Our total lack of reliable information about enemy movements at sea made this a distinct possibility. It was decided to strengthen our security operations at the Matanikau, advance our listening posts eastward to the Ilu River on the front of the 1st Marines, and await developments.

We had not long to wait. The first event marked one of the

great turning points of the Solomons campaign—the arrival
of thirty-one friendly aircraft. They came in late in the after-
noon of 20 August. These aircraft belonged to Marine Bomber
Squadron 232, commanded by Maj. Richard C. Mangrum, and
Marine Fighter Squadron 223, under the command of Capt.
John L. Smith.

The fact that they arrived at all was a minor miracle. Working
against the atmosphere of apathy and indecision that prevailed
at ComSoPac, the always effective and dedicated Admiral
McCain had, with his unlimited initiative, somehow man-
aged to open the gate. The planes were ferried on the escort
carrier *Long Island* (CVE-1) from Espiritu Santo to within
200 miles of Guadalcanal, then catapulted off.

With keen perception McCain had seen the opportunity
and made it a reality. He viewed the island as an unsinkable
aircraft carrier that, used in conjunction with carrier forces,
could destroy the Japanese naval air force. The success of this
interaction turned Guadalcanal from a haunting liability into
an operation of such exponential success that the name itself
became a synonym for death and disaster in the language of
the enemy.

Two destroyer transports—old World War I four-stackers
converted to high-speed transports—sneaked in by night with
CUB-1, one of the navy's self-contained mobile advance base
units. This hastily assembled group of men with a sketchy assortment of bombs, fuel, and ammunition were to fill in as
ground crews to support the newly arrived aircraft.

There was little we could do for our newly arrived friends.
A few tarpaulins, some Japanese blankets, and C rations were
all we had to offer. Engineers and tank battalion personnel
rendered some assistance. (Our tanks had the same aircraft
engines and used the same fuel and starter cartridges.) After a
perilous voyage, the CUB unit had arrived in time to put
planes in the air beginning at dawn next morning.

The Marine squadrons were followed on 22 August by
five P-400s of the Army Air Corps' 67th Fighter Squadron
under the command of Capt. D. D. Brannon. On 24 August
Lt. Turner F. Caldwell, USN, leading a group of dive bombers

from *Enterprise* (CV-6) on an unsuccessful search for a force of Japanese ships, landed after dark on Henderson Field. For over a month the Navy planes reinforced Mangrum's understrength squadron.

These were the first of a group of airmen whose exploits and accomplishments were so remarkable as to beggar description. They founded that invincible brotherhood of the skies, the Cactus Air Force. (Cactus was the code name for Guadalcanal.) Drawn from the army, navy, and Marines, they were the creators of a tradition that yet lives.

Along the Tenaru, the night of 20 August began in the usual way: minor alarms, flares, and scattered firing along the outpost line covering the right bank of the Tenaru toward its mouth. As midnight approached, the sound of firing continued steadily. Fragmentary reports from listening posts on the Ilu and elsewhere indicated a large enemy presence. The division was put on full alert. We were in contact with the Ichiki detachment, numbering about 900 men deployed along the opposite bank of the river.

At 0313, 21 August, a strong force of enemy infantrymen launched a sudden banzai attack at the mouth of the Tenaru. In the then-prevailing dry weather the stream was blocked from the sea by a sandbar. This sandbar was covered by the fire of a small number of Marine riflemen, three heavy machine guns, and one 37mm gun firing canister ammunition and manned by a crew from Division Special Weapons Battalion.

Greatly outnumbered, this small group of defenders took on, with deadly fire, the charging enemy, who attacked with empty chambers and fixed bayonets in closely grouped formation. The enemy officers fell first, and the survivors broke up into confused, leaderless small groups. They killed the occupants of some of our positions and began a firefight. Our men held every position where defenders remained alive until the arrival of reinforcements, who began the process of mopping up. A group of Marines, made up largely of post–Pearl Harbor recruits, had thrown back a superior force of highly trained, battle-experienced, elite enemy. In the best American tradition they had held their ground.

A typical case was that of Cpl. Al Schmid of Philadelphia. Al was a machine gunner, with probably a year or so of time in, so he was the "old man" of the group. With an assistant gunner and two riflemen covering him, Al sent a deadly stream of fire into the ranks of the Japanese as they came across the bar. A Japanese knee mortar shell scored a hit on Al's emplacement, knocking his gun out of action and wounding him and his helper. Al was blinded permanently. Somehow he got the machine gun back into action and continued firing. His assistants coached him from target to target, adjusting fire by watching the flight of the gun's tracer bullets. Al got a medal, and the city of Philadelphia gave him a Chevrolet, but that didn't restore his eyesight.

The firefight spread up the Tenaru; both banks came alive with fire delivered at close range. The enemy opened up with three 70mm landing guns. We responded with close-in fire from our 75mm pack howitzers. The Japanese had flamethrowers but did not use them. We quickly gained fire superiority, and Vandegrift released the division reserve to Colonel Cates with instructions to move it around the enemy's inland flank and come up behind. This would be a difficult maneuver for any battalion, particularly one as inexperienced as ours in the technique of tactical maneuvers. But it worked. A platoon of our light tanks came on and mopped up what was left. This small-size Cannae was over. The Japanese left more than 800 dead along the Tenaru. Thirty-four of our men were killed.

This was our first good look at our opponents. They were all well-developed Japanese youths. Their arms, packs, and equipment were meticulously clean. Their packs contained small amounts of candy and cigarettes but no rations as such. Nearly all carried the inevitable diary and white flag with black inscriptions and the red meatball center that had deceived us earlier at the Matanikau. Some of the packs were said to have contained opium. I did not see any.

While engaged in looking over the field, I was approached by a young navy hospital corpsman checking for wounded among the dead. He was unarmed, in accordance with the Geneva Convention, which we observed at that time. He had spotted a "body" among a group of dead near the river that still had a rifle. Since we had already stripped the field of arms, he suspected the man was a sniper. We approached from the rear. I covered the corpsman while he snatched the rifle and hurled it several feet away. I knew we had a sniper when I saw his ammunition carefully laid out round by round on the ground, not placed in the chamber. This was an old team shot's trick to insure constant weight of the piece as an aid to accuracy. The sniper didn't have a scratch on him. When we started to tie him up, he broke away and ran to recover his rifle. There was only one thing for me to do.

The outcome of the Tenaru battle was a great morale booster for the entire command. Morale was also heightened by the fine performance of the new arrivals at Henderson Field. They had somehow gotten planes in the air by daybreak and knocked their first Zero out of the skies while we were slugging it out down at the river. A few small detachments of Ichiki survivors, on their way east, were intercepted with strafing runs. For the first time in many days there was no Japanese Navy presence in or near Ironbottom Sound.

Jerry and I talked it over. The 1st Marines had done well. But we were lucky. As so often was to happen, our success derived in part from gross enemy mistakes. With ample knowledge of our position, Colonel Ichiki had elected to attack us at our point of greatest strength, the mouth of the Tenaru. Had he moved the point of attack upstream, his troops would have been slowed by the difficult jungle terrain, but the dense cover would have permitted an undetected approach. The Japanese would have been on the field before we could have reacted effectively. With our great superiority in numbers we would have expelled them, but only after a costly struggle and the possible loss of or damage to our newly arrived aircraft.

Why did Ichiki attack at all? His action seems at odds with normal decision making. The main body had been delayed a few days, but its arrival was certain. Why not wait? Was he just an eager beaver who saw a chance to grab the glory? A more reasonable surmise is that, given the history of the war to date, the Japanese regarded themselves as utterly invincible on land regardless of the relative size of the forces engaged.[2] At that point in the war Colonel Ichiki would have been expected to do exactly what he did. There is no record that his ill-timed attack was ever criticized by his superiors. They too suffered from the "victory disease."A pertinent reference can be found in a subsequent attack order leading to the Battle of Edson's Ridge on 13 September in which the Japanese commander, Kawaguchi, exhorted his men to "avenge the spirit of the Ichiki detachment." Colonel Ichiki was not available for comment. After the battle he chose "the honorable death" and left a diary. The final entry sets forth a schedule of events as follows:

> August 19—The approach.
> August 20—The battle.
> August 21—Enjoyment of the fruits of victory.

To me one recollection of the battle was unforgettable. It was the sight of old Gunnery Sgt. Charley Angus, a veteran team shot and one-time national offhand rifle shot champion. Wearing a campaign hat and padded shooting coat and leather lefthand glove, he was calmly blazing away at some Japanese attempting to come through the surf to envelope our left flank. Charley had found his day of greater glory not at Camp Perry but at the mouth of the Tenaru.

---

2. Edwin P. Hoyt, *Warlord Tojo* (Lanham, MD: Scarborough House, 1993), pp. 6, 86. Our forces outnumbered their captors at Bataan by a ratio of more than four to one. At Singapore 100,000 British surrendered, without firing a shot, to a Japanese force one-third its size.

CHAPTER 8

"Come Up on This Hill and Fight"

Following the Tenaru battle Jerry Thomas and I were both of the opinion that our position was facing the wrong way, that our exposed rear was a greater danger than the Lunga beaches. The reasons seemed compelling. The enemy could reach our positions undetected under cover of the jungle. The beaches, now that we had aerial reconnaissance, were less exposed to surprise attack. In addition, the beaches could be quickly reinforced, whereas strengthening the area to the south—the jungle—would be difficult and time consuming. General Vandegrift listened carefully to our arguments but declined to authorize any major changes in the existing dispositions.

We conducted limited operations to the west and east, toward Kokumbona and Tasimboko, to gain information, to keep the enemy off balance, and to comply with Admiral Turner's repeated exhortations to "be more aggressive." He never abandoned his opinion that had we been more aggressive the Japanese would never have tried to reinforce the place. This, of course, is flying in the face of the facts. Preparations for reinforcement were begun by the enemy upon confirmation of our initial landing and were pursued vigorously through mid-November. At that point in the war the idea of giving up positions anywhere in their area of occupation was totally repugnant to the Japanese character and ego, already overinflated by cheap successes elsewhere. Finally, we were lacking in the means needed to mount large scale attacks: we had little transportation, ammunition was in short supply, and, without aircraft, our sources of information were totally inadequate.

The arrival of Marine aircraft on 20 August was the turning point of the operation. Without their continuous support our survival would have been impossible. During daylight hours they kept the Japanese Navy at a respectable distance while covering our support and resupply vessels in the area. These planes also provided fast and effective evacuation of our wounded and a vital capability for emergency logistical support. Their deeds were legendary. They transformed our miserable little strip into an unsinkable aircraft carrier, and from its "flight deck" the Cactus Air Force launched decisive counterattacks. During the 1st Marine Division's stormy sojourn in the Solomons, our aviators—Marine, navy, and Army Air Corps operating from Henderson Field—shot down 416 Japanese planes and sank twenty-one enemy ships in less than four months. We lost seventy-eight planes in combat. The crews of about half were saved.[1]

There was another bonus from the arrival of these planes: the immeasurable upsurge in our morale that greeted their landing never subsided. A great part of their illustrious performance took place directly overhead or immediately in view above Ironbottom Sound. To every Marine this was more than a spectacle; it was a powerful inspiration to "go thou and do likewise" in his own environment. The war overhead was always the great news of the day, written on the billboard at Kukum—the Times Square of Guadalcanal—where Marines who could congregated each evening to read Solomon Islands dope (the term for various bulletins featuring the day's events and posted on the board) and to listen to Tokyo Rose on the bullhorn. The original small Japanese blackboard where Pvt. M. Shapiro had inscribed his immortal message was nailed below our own billboard and was now used to record stateside baseball scores—even baseball became a matter of secondary importance. The advent of our local airpower was, in every way, of incalculable benefit.

1. Final Report, 1st Marine Division, Phase IV, Annex H.

Admiral McCain, ComAirSoPac, was our first visitor. He slept under a Japanese blanket beneath the tarpaulin tent shared with his host, General Vandegrift. McCain was sharp, active, and purposeful. He knew exactly what he wanted to find out and with whom he desired to talk. It was a pleasure to watch him work, talking directly to squadron leaders, pilots, and crew chiefs, explaining what he expected them to do.

The admiral also talked informally to the rest of us, expounding convincingly on something that we had not yet fully appreciated. Guadalcanal was much more than a dirty local donnybrook, a grudge fight between some raggedy-assed Marines and the Japanese. If we prevailed here, we would be saving something more than just our precious butts. In the admiral's view, Guadalcanal was a rampart, not an outpost. Its successful defense could lead to the destruction of Japanese naval power in the Pacific. If the enemy continued on their present ruinous course, the island would become the rat hole down which they funneled all their resources. Their resources were not limitless, and already, McCain believed, they were beginning to suffer from loss of their best pilots—those well-trained naval aviators we had encountered at Pearl Harbor, Coral Sea, and Midway. Those men were irreplaceable.

McCain was on his way to Washington and would tell everybody who'd listen that the retention of Guadalcanal was the key to victory; its loss would forfeit the gains of Coral Sea and Midway and require us to start all over again. This good talk made our ears roar. We began to feel better about ourselves and fully understood the importance of Guadalcanal to winning the war. He assured us that we were doing more than fighting for our lives and enduring the miseries of the Solomon Islands. Even General Vandegrift joined in with words of encouragement and praise.

That night there was a full moon. The Japanese took advantage of it, and destroyers commenced their usual bombardment. Everybody came out of their holes to take a look. McCain and Vandegrift, in their skivvies, stood in front of their tent watching the uproar. After a minute or two the admiral said, "Well, son, this is your war. I'm going back to bed." He called everybody "son," including Vandegrift, possibly three years his junior.

I never saw Admiral McCain again. During the unification scrap in Washington I worked with his son, Captain McCain. He was cut from the same cloth as his father. His grandson, a survivor of the Hanoi Hilton, is a well known and admired U.S. senator.

The admiral also spoke warmly of what we had accomplished on the ground, a welcome change from Kelly Turner's continued carping from Noumea.

Before leaving, McCain pointed out that high trees on the Tenaru approach to Henderson Field endangered operation of heavily armed bombers by necessitating steep angles of ascent. The division engineer was asked to see what could be done. "The trees are too large to be removed," he said. Characteristically, Jerry Thomas was not willing to accept this cop-out and, after thinking it over, sent for Lieutenant Lytz and his platoon sergeant, Stinky Davis. A few hours later Stinky returned to tell us the trees could be removed, but it would take a week.

Four days later I spotted Stinky, all smiles, coming down the road. "The trees are down. One big banyan was twenty feet across the butt. It took 150 pounds of enemy dynamite to knock it over."

The accomplishments of our aircraft began to attract favorable notice, and Guadalcanal was coming to be regarded as something of an asset and not a total liability. Resupply activities picked up, largely devoted to air operations, but demonstrating that they could be done. The first major increment of supplies came with the arrival of *Wm. W. Burrows* (AP-6) and the New Zealand merchantman *Kopara* at Ringbolt (code name for Tulagi) on 29 August, followed at irregular intervals by *Fomalhaut* (AK-22), *Bellatrix* (AK-20), and *Fuller* (AP-14).

Unfortunately, *Burrows* went aground on Tulagi. Valuable supplies and several days were lost jettisoning some of her cargo to facilitate refloating. Refloated on 2 September, she ran aground again, but was able to clear the obstruction and proceeded to unload some cargo at Tulagi. Completely unabashed, the luckless skipper brought his ship to Guadalcanal and "requested" General Vandegrift to come aboard for a conference. (Under an anachronistic U.S. statute passed in 1831, the commanding officer, being the senior officer present afloat [SOPA], could, in theory, exercise command over all naval forces ashore or afloat.) We in operations thought this was funny, but our general was not amused and quickly replied, "If you desire to confer with the commanding general, come ashore." The captain didn't.

During this period *Alhena* (AK-26), *Fomalhaut*, *Betelgeuse* (AK-28), and the New Zealand merchantman *Latakia* brought in supplies and equipment for the Cactus Air Force and, to a limited extent, augmented our supply of rations.

Air cover made it possible to unload at Guadalcanal during daylight and to some extent in Tulagi Harbour at night. It was never possible to unload any of these ships completely due to persistent interference by enemy surface ships and aircraft. Emphasis was always placed on speed of unloading. Cargo intended for Guadalcanal might be discharged in Tulagi, and vice versa. Transfer was effected by use of the utilitarian small craft identified as YPs—yippie boats to those aboard and ashore. Most of these in the Solomons were tuna boats from San Diego, taken over by the navy complete with crew. They were a good lot and could take their lumps with the rest of us. Most of the crewmen held a low opinion of seamanship such as that displayed by *Burrows*.

All of our supplies went into the common dumps administered by the quartermaster, except for organizational equipment and weapons. In return the quartermaster issued from the common source on a per capita or special need basis. Ammunition was the exception. It was in such short supply that it went directly to unit dumps, which never attained full capacity. When an engaged unit went short, the quartermaster levied on others. Lt. Col. Ray Coffman, our division quartermaster, did a splendid job of "distributing the shortages," as we termed it. Usually every ship brought in some of each class of supply.

We continued living on reduced rations, although we attempted to supplement the daily ration going to the very young Marines in the infantry regiments, who out of sheer necessity were required to work hard and long hours with little sleep. A form of Japanese barley, somewhat like oatmeal, served with captured brown sugar—when we had it—was a favorite first meal served daily about midmorning. The evening meal was more conventional but usually involved some form of rice and dried fish or bull beef, even lambs' tongues. Coffee was always plentiful, served sergeant major style: strong, black, and without "side arms" (cream and sugar). The Marines continued to lose weight.

When we went off half rations we still generally adhered to the two-meal-a-day schedule and simply increased the quantities. This fit in better with our situation. Cooking fires drew enemy gunfire during darkness, and noon was the usual time for major raids. A notable exception was Lunga Point during unloading operations; then chow was available around the clock. This popularized to some degree the backbreaking task of lift and carry.

Butch Morgan, the world's finest cook, lived a life of quiet despair. He had replaced the blacksmith's forge with a portable Marine Corps field range called, for some strange reason, a Buzycott. Surrounded by all this splendor, poor Butch had nothing worthwhile to cook. He did manage to console himself by occasionally serving a dish utterly incongruous with our otherwise frugal menu. This was a millionaire's salad, a byproduct of our daily bombardment. Whenever a palm tree was toppled in our vicinity, Butch and Mantay would race to the scene, cut out the large crown buds, and serve hearts of palm, which I understand costs real money down in Florida.

On 27 August the 1st Battalion, 5th Marines, moved into the Kokumbona area in response to increased enemy activity and indications of reinforcement. The battalion, less one company, made a ship-to-shore movement from Kukum to Kokumbona via navy boat pool landing craft. The remaining company proceeded overland by inland trails.

Once ashore, the battalion made unsatisfactory progress, even in the face of only light resistance. One company protecting the inland flank encountered almost impossible terrain and had to be withdrawn. General Vandegrift considered the performance of the command irresolute and directed the regimental commander to intervene on the scene. Command changes were made, and the advance was resumed. Then it was discovered that the enemy had abandoned his strong positions and moved inland. The operation ended as a complete fiasco. In a complex operation such as this, formal orders are a necessity. None were issued. The very purpose of the operation was obscure. The battalion commander was not aggressive, but that fact was well known to all his superiors. This characteristic had previously led to recommendations that he not accompany the division overseas. These recommendations had been overruled. Now it would be difficult to find a suitable relief.

Betelgeuse now brought us more than rations. On 1 September she landed a large group of men with their supplies and equipment at Lunga Point. These men were unarmed, but they brought with them something more valuable than weapons. They were Seabees, men who could do anything and do it right, as they quickly demonstrated when they turned to our primitive airstrip and speedily upgraded it to an acceptable operational status.

These Seabees, organized as members of a naval construction battalion, were serving in a unique organization, one of the true innovations of World War II and one of the most important. Hitherto and traditionally the army and Marines had relied solely on combat engineers, organizations made up of young men who were taught elementary engineering skills in addition to basic infantry training. Such units are sufficiently competent to construct and repair roads and bridges, operate water purification systems, and perform other works that sufficed the needs of armies of the past. But this capability fell short of meeting the sophisticated requirements of mid-twentieth-century warfare, with its ever-increasing demand for construction of airfields, railways, and electric power–generating stations plus bases, docks, and repair facilities for naval vessels. The military requirements by mid-century spanned almost the entire spectrum of the nation's trades and services. Such disciplines cannot be acquired overnight by new recruits. However, America is rich with millions of able men who already possess these needed skills, acquired during years of civilian pursuits. Tens of thousands of such men, necessarily somewhat older than most servicemen, were only too glad to serve their country by enlisting in the navy's construction battalion program. These Seabees furnished almost unlimited high-tech support for all the armed forces. It was one of the most successful and well-received innovations of the war. It was so sensible that no one had ever thought of it before. Its 300 units and 230,000 members gave valuable support to the services in all areas where we were engaged. Most of the credit for this noteworthy contribution is due the chief of the navy's Bureau of Yards and Docks, Rear Adm. Ben Moreell.

During the next few days, advantage was taken of the availability of the APDs of Transport Division 12 to move the Raider and Parachute battalions, commanded by Lt. Col. Merritt "Red Mike" Edson, from Tulagi to Lunga Point.

TransDiv 12 had lost *Colhoun* (APD-2) to a Japanese bomber on 30 August. Later, on the night of 5 September, *Gregory* (APD-3) and *Little* (APD-4) were mistakenly illuminated by one of our PBYs and quickly sunk by overwhelming gunfire from a Japanese destroyer force. *McKean* (APD-5) and *Manley* (APD-1) were the only ones left.

McKean was lost later at Bougainville. Curiously, the APDs went down in numerical order, 2, 3, 4, then 5. *Manley* alone survived the war. Due to our close association with them before and during the war, we Marines felt keenly the loss of these brave little ships. To my mind, no group in the Pacific accomplished so much with so little.

We began receiving reports of a new Japanese force assembling in the Tasimboko area twenty miles to the east. It was first estimated at 300 men. Plans were begun for Edson's Raider Battalion to make a strike in that area. As arrangements progressed, further reports indicated a much larger force had landed—possibly as many as 3,000. There was no separate confirmation, so it was assumed that the count by Martin Clemens's native scouts was a gross overestimate, and we proceeded with the original plan.

The plan was put into execution on 8 September, when the Raider and Parachute battalions embarked in *Manley* and *McKean*. Our APDs—now reduced to two—required two trips each to move Edson's small striking force. At dawn, Edson landed with the advance group at Tasimboko without detection.

It was noted immediately that a large enemy force had landed across the same beach only hours before. Nevertheless, Edson drove ahead to the village and overran it with little resistance. Losses on both sides were small. The village contained quantities of artillery, rations, and stores large enough to suggest the presence of a considerable force.

This overwhelming force of freshly landed Japanese soldiers stood by within view and failed to intervene while, in the short time available, Edson's men destroyed Kawaguchi's base at Tasimboko, broke up his equipment, and urinated on the rice they could not carry off. They then withdrew to the APDs without interference, bringing their dead and wounded and captured rice.

These Marines would meet Kawaguchi again.

This inaction of enemy troops has never been satisfactorily explained. One view is that the code of Japanese military honor precludes voluntarily rendering assistance to a neighboring unit. Assistance must be requested. Another view has it that Edson's attack was ignored as only a diversion that should not have been allowed to disrupt the carefully planned attack schedule aimed at Henderson Field; in other words, the Japanese rigidly adhered to the original plan. Edson said that two large navy ships en route to Tulagi, *Fuller* and *Bellatrix*, appeared off Tasimboko at the critical moment and may have been mistakenly identified as transports with reinforcements for Edson's outnumbered forces. With more facts now available, it would appear that the paralysis of action was due to the fact that General Kawaguchi, the Japanese commander and conqueror of Borneo, had moved inland with the advance units and could not be reached to secure assent for the commitment of the forces at Tasimboko. However, under any view, the incident was illustrative of the frequent lack of initiative by Japanese troop leaders at every level.

Our operation was well executed, with timely and effective gunfire from the APDs and close support from the Army Air Corps P-400s.

Tasimboko will stand as a classic example of the brilliant employment of hit-and-run tactics by a raider. In 1587 Sir Francis Drake led the victorious raid on the Spanish Armada at Cadiz, Spain, and "singed the king's beard" before disappearing, leaving the hapless monarch to contemplate the ruin of his fleet, the loss of his supplies, and the abortion of his plan for an early invasion of the British Isles. Edson's Raiders had "singed Kawaguchi's beard" in much the same way.

After Edson's return to Lunga Point, we held a long and detailed discussion with him in our D-3 (operation) section of the division staff. It seemed apparent that Kawaguchi was moving his forces inland and not along the coast as Ichiki had done. This could bring him opposite the weakly defended and highly vulnerable southern approach to the airfield, which was where an attack would be most dangerous to us. We again sought the general's permission to turn the position around and face to the south, the direction of greatest danger. Vandegrift not only refused but also informed us that he was moving the 1st Marine Division command post to a spot south of the field, where it could operate more effectively than in its present location in the center of the Henderson Field bull's-eye with all its dust, noise, confusion, and bombardment.

The general was certain that Kawaguchi would repeat Ichiki's movement along the coast to the mouth of the Tenaru. Jerry, with his gift for indirection, scored a limited concession. The Raider and Parachute battalions, now presumably awaiting well-deserved evacuation, could be sent to a "rest area" south of the field, where their mere presence would discourage snipers or other minor enemy activity. To this the general agreed, and that is how the Ridge acquired its sardonic second name—Edson's Rest Area. Edson laughed when we told him, but being the man he was, he accepted the dubious assignment without complaint.

Trouble started at once, with small attacks along the open ridge ending at the airstrip and running directly south in a series of low crests, a perfect avenue of attack for a night operation. The tempo and force of these small attacks grew each day and became increasingly dangerous at night.

On the day before the movement of the command post, Maj. Sam Griffith II, Edson's executive officer, sought me out at the CP. The Raider and Parachute battalions had not been able to push the enemy back to the south during the day, so they found it necessary to readjust their own lines to hold what they occupied at daylight. This was alarming news.

I felt obligated to make these facts known to General Vandegrift and did so to avoid further involvement of Jerry Thomas, who had already pressed the point to the very limits of propriety. The general cut me off with a few well chosen words. And that was that.

We closed out the old CP in the afternoon of 10 September and simultaneously opened the new one on the Ridge. Jerry offered to give me a ride in his jeep as soon as he got back from a trip to the wing headquarters at the Pagoda where General Geiger handled the affairs of the Cactus Air Force. After the daily plane came in from Noumea, Jerry returned and gave me a letter to read that someone had tipped him off to pick up at the Pagoda. The letter was a copy of a top-secret dispatch from Ghormley to CinCPac and another addressee. We were not on the distribution list. It summarized in detail our large naval losses during the past month and concluded with a somewhat veiled statement questioning his—ComSoPac's—ability to support further operations in the Solomons area. This could mean anything or nothing, but apparently it meant something to whoever sent us a copy via the scuttlebutt route.

The old man had located his new command post on a heavily wooded spur or shoulder extending eastward from the main ridge. It was a beautiful spot for a dacha in the hills but hardly suitable for a command post. I named it the Robbers' Roost. There was little room. The necessary functions of command direction had to be carried out almost shoulder to shoulder. And there was no place to park vehicles. The engineers had built the general a little screened house with a small bedroom at each end and a larger living space in the middle to serve as an office and reception room.

All this activity caught the attention of the Japanese, who promptly shifted their bombardment to the Ridge and began to soften it up for their forthcoming attack. Snipers moved in at dusk, and small groups of infiltrators made the valleys between the spurs untenable. The engineers dug us in. It was remarkable to see them work; they had real shovels and strong arms. They could foxhole you in a matter of minutes. The engineer galley down in the adjoining ravine was supposed to feed us. They sometimes had to stage a minor counterattack with hand grenades to chase out wandering Japanese who holed up inside the galley. I remember only one meal— a "casserole" of mushy rice and fish served out of a garbage can.

Kelly Turner, elephant hat and all, came up for a visit. He was genuinely interested in our problems and brought along a bottle or two of Dewar's. The admiral was accompanied by his military staffer, Col. Henry D. Linscott, and Congressman Mel Maas. Mel spent the afternoon talking with General Geiger about the air situation. He kept insisting that Geiger ask for more planes. Geiger declined. The field would support forty to sixty but not more without expansion. He did, however, stress the urgent necessity of promptly replacing our losses with planes from Espiritu Santo.

It was another of those beautiful evenings when even the snipers were quiet. Everybody turned in early. I had the first watch on the phones in our blackout tent, contrived from old Japanese tarps and adjacent to the general's screened shack.

General Merrill B. Twining

Interior of sandbagged command post shelter—nerve center of Guadalcanal—and known as "Impact Center." (Left to right) Sgt. Bob Brant, Maj. Bill Buse (on phone), Col. Bill Twining, and Capt. Ray Schwenke. Fifth member of operations section is Sgt. Dick Kuhn.

Going over orders for the 8 September attack across the Matanikau River. (Left to right) Lt. Col. Bill Twining, Col. William Whaling, Maj. Bill Buse (standing), Col. Herman Hanneken. Thomas denounced it as a "council of war" and he never held another.

The Matanikau River laundry and bath.

Front line Marines cleaning their weapons after a rain.

Okinawan construction workers. Marines called them "termites." The Marine sergeant-in-charge has already given them "the word."

Our first visitor, RAdm. John S. McCain, and Maj. Gen. Alexander A. Vandegrift outside the operations section tarpaulin on Guadalcanal. McCain's fighting spirit was welcome.

1st Marine Division Hospital. Wounded were kept on stretchers to expedite evacuation during frequent air raids or bombardments. Building was a former Japanese barracks.

Butch, the world's best cook. D-day plus two and Tech. Sgt. Butch Morgan is boiling beans and coffee on the Japanese blacksmith's forge.

A Japanese tarpaulin spread over rough cut poles served as General Vandegrift's first tent. The furniture came from Mr. Widdy's (Lever Brothers plantation manager) house at Kukum.

Combat post near mouth of Matanikau. Heavily battered by light and medium Japanese artillery, it suffered severe casualties but stood fast under repeated attacks.

Japanese heavy machine-gun position.

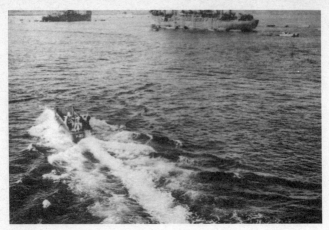

Higgins boat making run from shore to ship.

Arrival of first contingent of Seabees. (Author's collection)

Edson's Ridge after the battle. A four-man fire team is "mopping up" enemy snipers and stragglers under the watchful eye of the lone Marine in the foreground.

Led by native scouts, Carlson's Raiders begin their famous patrol.

Navy plane taking off from Henderson Field.

Japanese building on Henderson Field used as a headquarters by our aviators. The Japanese Navy also used it as an aiming point with results disastrous to us.

Marines landing on Red Beach on D-day, 7 August. The landing craft are Higgins boats. The beach is "steep to," perfect for landing even at low tide as here.

General Vandegrift caught working at his field desk. The "Old Man" glowers at the camera. He despised offices and paperwork.

"Red Mike" Edson briefs General Holcomb, Commandant of the Marine Corps, as to the disposition of his regiment, 5th Marines.

Generals Vandegrift and Rupertus with group of scouts and carriers during operations at Koli Point in November.

1st Marines debarking into landing craft alongside USS McCawley (P10) en route to Red Beach on Guadalcanal, 7 August 1941. (Author's collection)

The huge crater at the edge of the Henderson Field runway was made by a 14-inch shell fired by a Japanese battleship during the night of 13/14 October. (Author's collection)

Possession of the sand bar at the mouth of the Matanikau was vital to the retention of Guadalcanal by our forces. (Author's collection)

The hellish terrain of the Matanikau battlefield. (Author's collection)

One of the "Marus" that participated in the saltwater "banzai" of eleven unprotected transports. Only five made it to the beach west of Kokumbono. (Author's collection)

Tech. Sgt. William A. ("Stinky") Davis checks out the first amphibian bridge at Camp Lejeune, North Carolina. On D-day it proved invaluable. (Author's collection)

Five Japanese tanks, two medium, three light, lie burned out on the sand bar following the climactic night battle with 3d Battalion, 1st Marines. (McKelvy)

Red Beach at 1500 on 8 August (D +1), hopelessly blocked due to the untimely initiation of general unloading of cargo before troops ashore were prepared to receive it.

About 2200 the din of naval gunfire sounded close at hand. Kelly Turner was the first to sound off:

"Vandegrift, what are you shooting at?"

(Reply inaudible.)

"No, those are not Japanese guns. They are U.S. Navy five-inch fifty-ones. I know them well."

(Reply inaudible.)

"I have to bring all this ammunition in here, and I don't want to see it wasted."

By this time I had gotten Maj. Henry H. Crockett down at our five-inch naval gun battery on Lunga on the phone. He informed me the Japanese ships were still out of range and he had not fired a single round. No use to pass the message to the high command. They had just gotten the word. The second salvo straddled us in our CP. Everybody foxholed. I have it on good authority that as the admiral headed for his hole, along with the rest of us, he was still clutching a half bottle of Dewar's. He seemed to enjoy the situation immensely.

The brief naval bombardment set off a series of probes at Edson's forward positions. We responded with artillery and heavy mortars. It was another noisy, sleepless night. We suffered four minor casualties in the command post, resulting from fire of the enemy destroyers.

Turner spent part of the next day looking over our positions and departed safely in the interval between two bombing attacks in the afternoon. Before leaving he told Vandegrift that he did not share Ghormley's extreme views of the situation and thought he saw a way to bring in the 7th Marines. If he did, Vandegrift could land them wherever he felt they were most needed.

This promise was a great relief. Heretofore Turner had insisted on landing them at Aola Bay, forty miles to the east, to cover the building of a second airfield. Better to let the regiment remain in Samoa. At Aola they would just be alligator bait. We could not support them. They could not help us. Even if we could build a field there, the Japanese would eventually be the beneficiaries of our efforts. There was ample room for more fields in the Lunga Point–Koli Point area—land we already held. In July 1943 I counted seven fields we had built there. Nothing was ever built at Aola. It was totally unsuited for any military purpose. Aola simply represented one of Turner's strange obsessions, like Ndeni, enemy PT boats, seaplane tenders, and mines.

Shortly after Admiral Turner left, Jerry Thomas came into the D-3 tent. He was quite upset and produced from his shirt pocket an "eyes only" note from Admiral Ghormley to General Vandegrift, apparently given to the general by Turner just before he departed. It was written by hand on social note paper. It briefly stated the situation confronting him as ComSoPac resulting from heavy losses at sea and went on to say that he could provide no further support for Guadalcanal and that we were on our own. He specifically authorized the general to make any necessary "decisions" or "arrangements." I am not positive which word was used. In either case, the meaning was clear. Jerry was quite annoyed.

In a minute or two General Vandegrift entered, visibly perturbed. The tent was only dimly lit, and I do not believe the general knew I was standing there. His night vision was already failing, the condition aggravated no doubt by our execrable diet. He told Jerry, in effect, "As long as I am here there will be no surrender of this place. We will continue as we are. Tell Bill Twining to prepare a plan of withdrawal up the Lunga using our amphibian tractors if it becomes necessary."

This was the only occasion I ever heard General Vandegrift use the word "surrender." The quite evident emotional state of both indicated to me that they had only moments before read Ghormley's note. There can be no doubt as to what Ghormley's note meant to them. The meaning was all too clear. As far as Ghormley was concerned, we were being cut adrift to shift for ourselves.

There has always been some confusion as to exactly what occurred in this incident. Two documents were involved; not one. The official document was Ghormley's dispatch to CinC-Pac, a copy of which came to us unofficially, as I have described, on 10 September, two days before Turner arrived. Vandegrift was apparently officially informed of its existence by Turner on the twelfth or thirteenth. The longhand "eyes only" note written on social stationery was given to Vandegrift probably on the thirteenth and read after Turner left. Turner's parting statement to Vandegrift was to the effect that he didn't share Ghormley's pessimistic views of our situation and would try to bring in the 7th Marines. Jerry, on more than one occasion, said he was given the document by Vandegrift to keep and had it in his shirt pocket. If it had been an official document, it would have automatically and properly gone to the classified document files, never into Jerry's shirt pocket. The document described by General Vandegrift in his memoirs is not the one Jerry pulled from his shirt pocket and showed me.

The intensity of fighting along the Ridge increased sharply on 12 September and well into the night as Kawaguchi increased the pressure of his attacks by committing additional forces. During the early morning hours a gap developed on the right of Edson's line, but fortunately it was not exploited by the enemy, who was seemingly unaware of its existence. Fighting continued unabated on the thirteenth, although no general attack was launched during daylight hours.

The constant enemy pressure was taking its toll on the hard-pressed Raiders. I went to Edson's command post at midafternoon to assess the situation. Edson seemed terribly fatigued, but he was in far better shape than anyone else up there. Edson commanded a group of exhausted men—men who were nevertheless active and alert, intent on fulfilling their defensive mission; their awareness of the gravity of the situation was obviously far greater than our own.

Alarmed, I returned to the division CP and recommended the immediate commitment of the division reserve, 2d Battalion, 5th Marines, presently commanded by Col. William J. Whaling, who had taken over when Lt. Col. Harold E. Rosecrans, the regular commander, was badly injured by a bomb during an air raid the previous day. The movement was ordered at once, but its execution was delayed by a series of

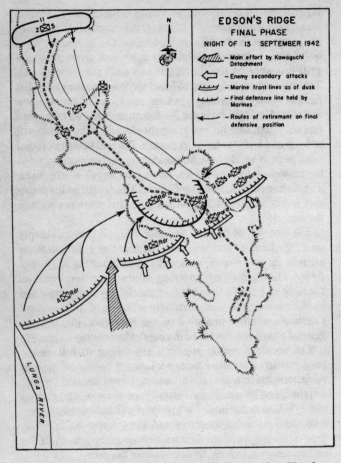

EDSON'S RIDGE
FINAL PHASE
NIGHT OF 13 SEPTEMBER 1942

— Main effort by Kawaguchi Detachment

— Enemy secondary attacks

— Marine front lines as of dusk

— Final defensive line held by Marines

— Routes of retirement on final defensive position

N

LUNGA RIVER

heavy, low-level carrier-based plane strikes against Henderson Field that prevented Whaling's force crossing the open plain surrounding the strip. They did not reach the northern end of the Ridge in time to be committed in an orderly daylight relief. They were posted in partial deployment in position to establish a reserve line in case of a breakthrough.

I remembered that this was the same battalion I had joined

the day after graduating from the Naval Academy, and it was this same battalion that Lt. Col. Frederic M. "Fritz" Wise had deployed across the Paris-Metz highway on 6 June 1918 to stop the German drive into Paris—the closest they ever came. That was when old Fritz told a French staff officer, "Retreat, hell! We just got here!" I think Bill Whaling remembered that day too—he had been among those present.

At dusk the fighting, which had slowed down during the late afternoon, picked up rapidly as Kawaguchi moved ahead at full strength. The understrength parachute companies, utterly lacking the firepower of heavy weapons, were pulled back to the base of Edson's hill, a combination command post, observation post, and final defensive position where Edson and Maj. Ken Bailey personally directed the close-in fighting that characterized this successful last stand. Edson notified me of the movement of the paratroopers with the news that we were now uncovered back at the division CP and warned us that the Japanese, if they saw fit, could come through us "like shit through a tin horn."

Quite apparently Edson felt that we had written him off and that he was very much on his own. He rounded up every man in the area in an effort to augment his dwindling forces. He stood there at the highest point of the Ridge bellowing into the night, "Raiders, parachuters, engineers, artillerymen, I don't give a damn who you are. You're all Marines. Come up on this hill and fight!"

The concluding sentence took on a symbolic life of its own. I even used it once as filler in a message to Ghormley. Jerry Thomas scratched it—fortunately for me. Nevertheless, it has always epitomized the desperation of those days, and that night in particular.

The confused fighting continued along the Ridge, now assailed at several additional points. A friend, Maj. Robert S. Brown of the Raiders, lost a hand trying to intercept a Japanese hand grenade. While sitting in an ambulance near the division command post awaiting evacuation he was wounded a second time, fatally, as close-range enemy machine-gun fire swept the area.

I was reassured to encounter advance elements of the 2d Battalion, 5th Marines, proceeding along the Ridge ready to take over at first light. Lt. Col. Jack Bemis, executive officer of the 11th Marines (artillery), was nearby, busy turning around a few drifters cut off from their parent unit. They went back to fight again. Returning to the command post, I saw the bodies of a Japanese captain and two soldiers at the entrance. Lying nearby was Gunnery Sergeant Beasley, who had headed the command post security unit, killed by the Japanese captain who had hurled his sword like a spear. In turn, Division Sgt. Maj. Sheffield M. Banta had killed the Japanese officer with his pistol. Somebody else shot the two soldiers. Beasley was one of the last of the "Old Breed" Marine NCOs. He literally "died by the sword."

The ferocity of Kawaguchi's onslaughts diminished as daylight approached. Edson held his hill. An enemy force sent down the right bank of the Lunga failed to contact the battalion right wing, where Griffith, in command, was not assailed. At daylight Griffith counterattacked to the south, driving the enemy into difficult terrain, where they offered stout resistance. Prompt support from the Army Air Corps P-400s was effective, and the last of Kawaguchi's organized resistance crumbled.

Isolated groups of enemy were moving aimlessly around down in the ravines. Snipers worked the place over night and day. There were several casualties.

It had been a close thing. Our command post was located in a position where it could ill support the defense. We lost communications almost at once. When a call did go through you might find yourself talking to an English-speaking Japanese. It became necessary to turn the telephones over to the Navajo talkers who transmitted messages in their native tongue, totally secure against Japanese code breakers. These remarkable Navajos had been meticulously trained and could transmit in their ancient language involving messages re-translatable into precise military terminology. "Machine-gun fire," I remember, came out as "constant rain."

After two more days the general returned to the old CP

down at Henderson Field. When we moved I gave Butch Morgan a ride in my jeep. Halfway down the side of Henderson Field a gaggle of low-flying Japanese carrier-based planes came in. They were mean and very personal about it. My driver, Northrup, Butch, and I hit the dirt. I spent the next twenty minutes with Butch in a shared foxhole near the old Japanese hangar, which caught fire. We let it burn. Supper was late.

My most vivid recollection of this period is the failure of the division command to maintain a proper awareness of Edson's situation and to render timely and effective assistance. Our lapse could have led us into a disastrous situation of our own making. There were several contributory causes: the removal of the command post to an exposed point totally unsuited to its requirements; distraction from the performance of our mission by command problems emanating from the rear areas; disregard of the clear indications that Kawaguchi's attack would be a major thrust fully capable of reaching Henderson Field; and, most important of all, not listening more attentively to Edson's views and estimates of the threat confronting him. Before we realized it, the situation had arisen around us, imperceptible as an evening mist, unheeded until the optimum time for action had passed.

Henceforth the Ridge was known as Edson's Ridge in honor of those intrepid men who fought there.

Edson's and Bailey's Medals of Honor were well deserved.

Kawaguchi, who survived the battle, did not seek the "honorable death." He lived to fight and lose again and to author this statement: "Guadalcanal is not the name of an island; it is the name of the graveyard of the Japanese Army."

CHAPTER 9

Abandoned Mission

Immediately following the Battle of Edson's Ridge, sweeping changes were made within the division. Recent promotions had made us overstrength in senior ranks, and the commandant of the Marine Corps directed General Vandegrift to make readjustments. These promotions made the process somewhat less painful. Col. Jerry Thomas, who had been spot promoted, became chief of staff. He had been performing most of those functions for a long time anyway as General Vandegrift had lost confidence in his predecessor. The commanding officer, 5th Marines, and two of his three battalion commanders were also detached. Colonel Edson was given command of the regiment. Maj. Bob Ballance was assigned command of the Pioneer Battalion (Shore Party). Its commander, Col. George Rowan, was considered to have done extremely well, but his age and rank were disproportionate to a small command. Despite his low rank, Capt. Jim Murray was deservedly made D-1 (personnel), a job he had been performing as division adjutant in the absence of Col. Robert C. Kilmartin Jr., who was serving as Rupertus's chief of staff on Tulagi. General Vandegrift called me aside, sternly gave me a little good advice, and told me, somewhat to my surprise, that I would take over as the operations officer (D-3). This unexpected reward reminded me of the story about the dog that bit Frederick the Great. The king not only forgave the offender but also gave him a piece of cheese.

The relief of Col. LeRoy P. Hunt was a sad event, but indicative of Vandegrift's military character and high sense of duty. The general was sending home one of his best friends and our most admired officer of World War I. In 1918 Hunt had been the captain selected to command the company of Marines storming the famed Essen Hook on Mont Blanc, opening the gate for the stalemated French Army.

During this period aviation activity at Henderson Field was augmented by the opening on 9 September of Fighter One, an airstrip parallel to Henderson Field, and the arrival of 24 fighters from the *Saratoga*, which, damaged by a Japanese torpedo, was departing the area for repairs. Still more navy planes came in to bolster the hard-pressed Cactus pilots. Air action climaxed on 13 September, as did the ground action on the Ridge, by a resounding repulse of repeated Japanese aerial and ground threats. Losses of Marine and navy planes were severe, but enemy losses were catastrophic. Throughout this critical period, Geiger, by sheer force of personality and example, maintained effective control of a confused and rapidly changing situation.

Jerry Thomas immediately showed himself to be a highly effective chief of staff. He organized the command post for the first time on a truly functional basis. The general was provided with more suitable accommodations, and the number of personnel in the CP was reduced by transferring nonessential functions to less congested areas.

Butch Morgan moved his galley out of the blacksmith shop and into a screened enclosure at the insistence of our division surgeon, Capt. Warwick T. Brown, Medical Corps, U.S. Navy. Brown had waged a polite, quiet, determined, unrelenting war with Butch over proper sanitation beginning in North Carolina over a year before. The place eventually became almost pleasant, except for the incessant aerial bombings and naval bombardment, which almost totally destroyed the trees and undergrowth that had originally provided considerable cover and concealment.

The first days after our return to the old CP were a time of uneasiness and concern. The air was full of messages, none addressed to us. Those that we intercepted indicated serious fighting at sea, with the loss of the carrier *Wasp* and the destroyer *O'Brien* and damage to the battleship *North Carolina*.

Nevertheless, at dawn on 18 September, Rear Adm. Kelly Turner showed up with his beat-up old transports carrying our reinforced 7th Marines. They were doubly welcome. First, they were a fresh, well-armed, well-equipped, highly trained combat group. Second, they were thoroughly outfitted with a full allowance of supplies covering the entire spectrum of our logistical needs: rations, tools, construction implements, medical supplies, tentage, ammunition, barbed wire, and sandbags.

This was undreamed-of wealth. We made the most of it. All hands turned to. The regiment was disembarked, and all its supplies were unloaded in the record time of twelve hours. Every truck on the island was employed. Even del Valle's prime movers were put to work—a genuine lapse in the eyes of any cannoneer: "Never separate a gun from its prime mover." Don Pedro complained, but his heart was not really in it. Half rations ended. Butch made pie for supper.

Without further ado the general authorized us to turn the position around, facing inland rather than toward the sea. The complete perimeter was divided into ten defensive sectors, each of battalion size. The three beach defense sectors, now less vulnerable to surprise attack from the sea due to the presence of aircraft at Henderson Field, were manned only at night by units normally employed there during the day. These were the Pioneer Battalion (Shore Party), Amphibian Tractor Battalion, and Engineer Battalion.

The remnants of the 1st Parachute Battalion were evacuated to Noumea. They had suffered appalling casualties: only eighty-nine survivors of the original battalion came off Edson's Ridge on their own feet.

The seven sectors facing the jungle to the east, south, and southwest were each assigned to a rifle battalion of the three regiments. Each regiment controlled two sectors. Lt. Col. Robert G. Hunt's detached 3d Battalion of the 2d Marines from Tulagi occupied the remaining sector, with its left flank resting on the left bank of the Lunga River. In moving to its new position, this battalion suffered an extraordinary misfortune when planes from our Cactus Air Force intercepted a flight of enemy bombers and the Japanese pilots jettisoned their bombs and turned back before reaching Henderson Field. By sheer accident the jettisoned bombs struck Hunt's column, moving under cover of the dense jungle canopy, totally unaware of the situation overhead. Serious losses were incurred.

The 1st Raider Battalion, now commanded by Lt. Col. Samuel B. Griffith, was held in division reserve on Lunga Point in a bivouac east of Kukum. This afforded a strong position with all elements capable of mutual support. In addition, it gave each regimental commander a powerful mobile reserve in the form of its third and uncommitted battalion. These uncommitted battalions provided the division commander with a source of troops required for employment outside the Lunga Perimeter as a striking force in the active defense that the general intended to pursue against the enemy.

Its disadvantage was that it entailed the adoption of the cordon defense, abandoned early in World War I in favor of defense in depth. *This was the fundamental tactical decision of the Guadalcanal Campaign and one that was to have a wide effect.* It was not made lightly.

The ancient cordon defense affords initial resistance in its strongest form to enemy assault. It consists essentially of a single line of men and weapons able to bring to bear a sudden and overwhelming fire of all infantry weapons on an approaching force at close range. Only a small mobile reserve is held back out of the firefight for quick movement to repel a breakthrough or reinforce a threatened point.

Perceiving this in the years before World War I, General Von Schlieffen, head of the German Imperial General Staff, secretly created the great strategic surprise of that war: unheard of masses of artillery available in support of the attacking infantry. The massed fires of these unexpected guns literally blasted vast gaps in the French defensive cordons, and the German shock troops poured through into open country. France was saved only because of an irresolute Moltke, Gallieni's taxicab army, and the miracle of the Marne.

These events of World War I created defense in depth more

as an instinctive act of battlefield survival than a studied response. The cordon was abandoned. Units large and small
were distributed in defense of suitable terrain features. Depending upon their size, they were known as combat groups
or strong points. These were established in bands of mutually
supporting posts, sometimes miles in depth, which relied almost entirely on the fire of machine guns and were "wired in"
for all-around defense. As time permitted, they were connected by a labyrinth of communication trenches. This was
the Western Front, and the phrase *defense in depth* became an
article of faith in the minds of those who served there.

According to General Wainwright, MacArthur kept enjoin-
ing the defender of Bataan to "fight in depth, depth, depth." In
his book, General Wainwright does not challenge the injunction and may well have attempted to carry it out.[1] There is no
lucid account of what occurred there or at other places where
the enemy prevailed in the early days. But one thing is certain:
A defense in depth could never have succeeded.

The Japanese had apparently studied our defensive tactics
in great detail. They mastered the process of isolating units
and overwhelming them one by one under cover of darkness
or low visibility.

The terrain of Flanders was ideal for defense in depth; it
was open country with small ground forms and low relief—
optimum country for the employment of barbed wire, machine
guns, and mutual support. On Guadalcanal we were fighting
in the tangled jungle at point-blank range. The small size of
the perimeter provided no room for depth without interference
with our vital installation, Henderson Field. Artillery? We already knew that the Japanese were poor cannoneers. All our
handbooks on the Japanese Army commented on that. Even
our own artillery, largely 75mm pack howitzers with a high
angle of fire, had sometimes, as at the Matanikau River, been
unable to cover certain areas. However, our older officers,
who entered World War I in the Verdun sector, were still sup-

1. Jonathan M. Wainwright, *General Wainwright's Story* (Garden City, NY:
Doubleday, 1946), p. 9.

portive of defense in depth. Colonel Cates was particularly insistent.

One of General Vandegrift's great characteristics was to base decisions on what I believe Winston Churchill once referred to as "the naked event, the event itself"; he had that rare faculty of deciding every case on its own merits. Turning to Edson, Vandegrift asked, "How great a distance do you believe we could leave between separate combat groups and still prevent infiltration at night?"

"Fifteen yards!" Edson replied instantly.

I was instructed to draft the order on the basis of a cordon defense.

This order continued in effect during the remainder of our presence on the island without material change. It also contained another statement: *The defense of Guadalcanal will be primarily by air.* Our tacit tribute to the role of Henderson Field, General Geiger, and the Cactus Air Force, it may well have been a first in the history of the U.S. armed forces.

Our positions were now well dug in, with standing foxholes for the crews of heavy weapons. For the first time, men and weapons were well protected with bands of barbed wire that had come in with the 7th Marines. No longer would we be dependent on a single strand of trip wire salvaged from coconut plantation fences.

But best of all was a massive increase in firepower brought about by the cumulative effect of a fortuitous error in judgment made by some zombie back in Headquarters Marine Corps. Our amphibian tractors (LVTs), at that time not even accorded a combat capability, had each been given an armament of five machine guns: one .50 caliber and four .30 caliber. There were 100 LVTs in the battalion. These 500 machine guns exceeded by many times the division's entire normal allotment. Manna from heaven! These guns were distributed along the front and placed in the hands of gunners extemporized on the spot and taught the rudiments if not the refinements of their new trade. This single increment, I believe, was the decisive element in the unbroken success of our defense, even though we were invariably greatly outnumbered by the Japanese at the point of contact, which was a point they had the option of selecting and attacking in overwhelming initial force. One Japanese officer who had apparently been around the track a few times left us a note in his diary: "Their position is like the hard shell of a giant tortoise, which emits fire and flame wherever it is touched."

General Vandegrift was reassured by the progress of our defenses, but characteristically he was the first to point out the danger of acquiring the barbed wire mentality that had paralyzed the Western Front in 1917. He insisted we take advantage of our increased freedom of action by adopting an active defense aimed essentially at dominating the adjacent outlying area, although we lacked the numbers to occupy and hold it. Quite logically, he felt that this activity would be the most effective safeguard against incurring a siege mentality. I was set to work on a plan for a related series of large-scale sweeps into Indian territory to find out what was going on.

The active defense period was also characterized by the intensification of efforts to improve individual and small-unit standards of independent action. Scout sniper training was made division wide and placed under the able direction of Col. Bill Whaling, a lifelong and highly capable woodsman and one of the finest marksmen in the Corps. He quickly developed a group of operators known as the Scout Sniper Detachment. It was a popular, almost enviable, temporary assignment. Men returning to their regular units spread the warrior gospel. Combat morale and effectiveness rose continually despite losses.

Whaling's assistants were two notable characters. One was our postmaster. Just why Guadalcanal had the slightest need for a postmaster has never been revealed. But this middle-aged man, a skilled deer hunter from the mountains of the south, knew why he was there. He had something to settle with the enemy: His son, Capt. Henry T. Elrod, a Marine fighter pilot, had bombed and sunk the Japanese destroyer *Kisaragi* and won the Medal of Honor, then had been killed while fighting on the ground at Wake Island before the surrender.[2]

The other man, Whaling's unofficial first sergeant known only as Daniel Boone, was a rugged, powerful mountain man with fiery red whiskers. He lived up to his cognomen, spending more time out of the perimeter than in it. Boone would take a patrol out and days later return it to the lines tired and gaunt, then turn around and go back alone on a renewed quest. Later, one such solitary venture was to produce information of immeasurable value at a decisive moment in the defense of the Lunga Perimeter.

The general's plan for active defense also called for successive one-battalion sweeps of the jungle areas outside our lines. This would provide the threefold benefits of offensive action, experience in field maneuver, and the acquisition of more certain information as to enemy location and strength. The latter objective was quickly accomplished, but not in the way we anticipated.

On 25 September, Lt. Col. Lewis B. "Chesty" Puller was sent out on his first foray of the war with his 1st Battalion, 7th Marines. He carried one of our atrocious maps of Guadalcanal based on photographs taken by a rear area photographic airplane during a single flight on a cloudy day. Cloud-covered areas were outlined and blanked out, and the word "cloud" was inserted in the center of each to indicate why no ground detail was shown. Puller's first minor contact occurred in such an area, and he sent me the initial message of his eventful career on Guadalcanal. It read, "Killed Japanese patrol under cloud 6,000 yards south of Lunga Point." Future historians will wonder.

Then proceeding west, across the northern slopes of Mt. Austen, he soon made contact with a much larger enemy force occupying a defensive position barring his advance. A firefight resulted in which significant losses were incurred on both sides. Our casualties were seven killed, twenty-five wounded. The Japanese withdrew during the night.

2. Peter Andrews, "The Defense of Wake," *American Heritage* (July/Aug. 1987).

Two of Puller's companies were sent back with the wounded to carry their stretchers over the difficult and exposed terrain.

As reinforcement, 2d Battalion, 5th Marines (McDougal), was sent out to join Puller for the remainder of the mission. Puller continued west to the upper Matanikau. But in view of the delays already incurred, he decided to come down the river on the east bank instead of the west bank in order to turn over the continuation of the patrol to the 1st Raider Battalion (Griffith), at the time specified in the division order. This was an unfortunate decision. It forfeited the chance to strike the right flank of the main enemy position, established on the high ground along the west bank. Instead, Puller was forced to march across the entire enemy front to reach the mouth of the river. Despite cover provided by the dense jungle along the river, he was subjected to harassing mortar fire all the way to the government track on the coast.

While Puller was slogging through the mud, a round hit within a few feet of him, but its fuse failed to activate in the soft ground. Had it exploded it would have killed him. "Goddamned dud," Puller remarked contemptuously. Always the ultimate Marine, he was disgusted with any professional lapse, even on the part of the enemy.

This would have been a fine time to cease fire and come home. We had been told quite plainly what we wanted to know. But we refused to believe it. We were not confronted with a gaggle of Kokumbona Vagabonds reinforced by a few "stale Japs," survivors of Edson's Ridge who had drifted westward. These were fresh Japanese, full of fight, holding a strong position along the west bank of the river. The decision, to be executed the next day, was to move 1st Raider Battalion up the river to effect a crossing and, enveloping the enemy's south (right) flank, attack in the direction of Matanikau Village. The 3d Battalion, 5th Marines, was to deliver a holding attack across the river at its mouth.

Colonel Edson was placed in overall command. Artillery and air were to support each attack. The 3d Battalion, at the mouth of the Matanikau, was stopped by heavy fire. This was foreseen, as it was essentially a holding attack, and no serious attempt to cross on the sandbar was made because of the certainty of heavy casualties. As a holding attack, it succeeded in pinning down the defenders and occupying their attention. Unfortunately, the enemy position could not be effectively covered by artillery because the trajectory of our fire could not be adjusted to fall into the small area near the river mouth where the Japanese invariably placed their machine guns.

At this point we received a message from 1st Raider Battalion that Maj. Ken Bailey, the executive officer, had been killed, and Lt. Col. Sam Griffith, the battalion commander, had been wounded in the shoulder but was still in command. The message also indicated that the battalion had effected a crossing and was in the position planned for its attack northward toward Matanikau Village. Edson received the same message and interpreted it in the same way. His proposal was to continue the attack at 1330, assisted by a landing near Point Cruz of 1st Battalion, 7th Marine (less one company), recommitted by means of landing craft from Kukum. Puller got on the phone and expressed agreement with the proposal. Edson still did not believe there was a strong enemy presence. I gave qualified approval in order to initiate preparation for the embarkation and movement contingent upon General Vandegrift's authorization. On returning to the command post, the general approved the idea. The partial battalion, under command of Maj. Otho L. Rogers, battalion executive officer, embarked promptly and moved out. *Ballard* (AVD-10), an old four-stacker converted to an aviation support vessel, covered the movement and provided naval gunfire support.

Then things started coming apart.

The improvised landing operation went well, and the troops landed without losses but soon ran into heavy fire. The first casualty was Major Rogers, killed as the troops began to move inland. Upstream, nothing much was happening, as the Raiders were not, as supposed, across the river ready to move against the exposed Japanese flank.

Feeling no pressure or threat from any direction, the Japanese reserves were free to turn their attention to the leaderless 1st Battalion, which had hastily taken up a defensive position on the first hill inland from the beach. The Marines were quickly assailed by two forces at separate points. Their withdrawal became a matter of paramount importance.

We had not suffered a serious air raid for several days, but even before Edson finished giving me his report we were struck by an unexpected low-level attack that almost completely demolished the CP. Everything was knocked down, including most of the trees we relied on for cover. When it ended, I reached for my phone—ten inches of useless wire dangled from the receiver. I tried another phone. The switchboard operator told me all communications were wiped out.

All this with a daylight withdrawal on our hands.

I drove to Kukum, where an artillery battalion was supporting the attack at the river. Over their lines I could talk to their forward observer at the river. He in turn could relay messages to Edson and Puller. *Ballard,* with Puller aboard, was supporting the movements of our endangered troops, ordered by Puller, to cut their way through to the closest beach, where they would be picked up by landing craft sent from the boat pool. Lt. Dale M. Leslie of VMSB-231, piloting a lone SBD, showed great initiative and rendered invaluable support in directing the landing craft to the correct beach and informing them of survivors at other points.

The landing craft flotilla, led by Lieutenant Commander Dexter, U.S. Coast Guard, was heavily involved and fought with the Japanese at close quarters along the beach to protect the embarking troops. Signalman First Class Douglas A. Munro, USCG, won the first Medal of Honor in Coast Guard history for his heroism in this combat. Unfortunately, the award was posthumous.

In addition to its official motto, *"Semper Paratus,"* the Coast Guard adheres resolutely to a less formal one couched in simple one-syllable words: "You have to go out. You don't have to come back." This day they demonstrated that they still lived and died by both mottoes.

To me the real significance of this unlucky operation lay not so much in the fact that the enemy was being strongly reinforced but in the fact that he was in a position to cross the river in force sufficient to threaten the right (west) flank of our perimeter. A foothold at the river mouth would be a serious threat because the key terrain feature there was the sandbar, which provided a crossing over the Matanikau River at its mouth. As long as we held it, our right flank would be secure and the airfield would not become inoperable due to heavy close-range fire from artillery brought across the river. No one had ever heard of a sandbar being a key terrain feature. Mt. Austen was thought by some to be the key terrain feature, and in a way it was. It dominated the scene but was too large, too inaccessible, and too remote to be of any real value to the relatively small forces on either side. We patrolled it frequently and ignored it the rest of the time.

Permanent loss of the river mouth crossing would be a different matter. Jerry didn't think we had strength enough to hold it permanently. I thought we had to take the lesser risk, not accept the incalculable one. I was smart enough not to say anything to the general about it but could see that it was on his mind. The presence of even a small enemy force on our side of the river now gave him great concern.

This was the only thoroughly unsuccessful operation of the entire Guadalcanal campaign. Central cause of failure was abandonment of mission. We had planned this operation carefully to find out what was going on in the area west of the perimeter, an area overlooked due to our preoccupation with the climactic activity on the other flank, including the battles of Tenaru, Tasimboko, and Edson's Ridge.

Native scouts were never able to operate in the area under scrutiny with the same freedom they enjoyed elsewhere. Our primary source of information came from the occasional letters and reports to Clemens from local inhabitants. One such letter, outdated but confirmatory of our own views, described the Japanese in the area as survivors raiding native gardens to keep from starving, malarial, and living in small groups in the jungle. We had no hard evidence to indicate that fresh forces had been landed. We were shaking hands with our answer when Puller made his first contact on the slopes of Mambulo during the afternoon of 25 September. Kokumbona

Vagabonds and stale Japanese don't inflict thirty-two casualties on a Marine battalion.

Our reaction to these losses was an unconscious shift of emphasis from reconnaissance to attack. We began an utterly piecemeal series of reinforcements and attacks that descended to a sour nadir on the afternoon of the twenty-seventh. What began as a sound and sensible reconnaissance operation ended as an improvised, complex, jury-rigged attack for which we had no plan and had made no preparations.

In addition, we had made the same mistake we charged against Rear Adm. Kelly Turner during the Savo Island affair by failing to use all available assets. When we found ourselves stopped at the mouth of the river by machine-gun fire coming from an area unreachable by our artillery, we should have committed our half tracks. These highly mobile self-propelled vehicles could have destroyed or suppressed the fire of the offending enemy weapons by the close-range direct fire of their 75mm guns. In the course of an unplanned encounter we had just neglected to make use of them. Edson agreed.

I am the first to offer my own mea culpa. I should never have gone along with Edson's and Puller's idea of recommitting the 1st Battalion, 7th Marines, in an improvised, off-the-cuff landing near Point Cruz. It was I, not they, who was in a position to exercise a cooler and more detached judgment. They were stung by their reverses and wanted to fight. My conditional acquiescence may well have swayed General Vandegrift's judgment when he gave final approval. In this operation we were unlucky. We let ourselves drift aimlessly into action. Such solace as could be found lay solely in the fact that by timely action we were able to avoid greater losses.

The period immediately following this operation was one of relative quiet except for the continuing bombardment of Henderson Field by enemy aircraft, destroyers, and submarines, almost routine in their deadly sequence. At the command post, the D-3 section continued its round-the-clock routine of providing backup for the front-line sectors—a full-time job for three officers, two sergeants, and two field phones.

The latter were the bane of my existence. In the beginning we were equipped with only the standard Marine Corps field telephone, a magneto-operated, hand-cranked device that Alexander Graham Bell must have created on one of his bad days. I am not mechanically gifted, and my efforts to operate this monstrosity provided the only light moments in the operations tent. Whenever I picked up the phone and grabbed the crank, all work in the section ceased. I would crank and twist and crank again on this fiendish invention, only to put my finger in the wrong place and get an electric shock of enormous voltage. This was the high point of the day for my compatriots, who I suspect deeply regretted it when that diabolic device was replaced by a regular telephone system.

Our D-3 section operated twenty-four hours a day. We never secured for air raids or bombardments when the rest of the command post was routinely evacuated to get people out of the Henderson Field target area. During raids we sheltered in our flimsy homemade dugout, which provided more psychological support than physical shelter. We built up a thriving trade among the smaller units. We never refused a reasonable request. We never told anyone that they should call one of the other sections. We handled that ourselves. A man who needs help doesn't need a lesson in staff functioning at two o'clock in the morning when he has run out of hand grenades. We acquired a decent reputation and much goodwill among the lowly, if not among the bird colonels. During the daily shootouts we shared the CP alone with Doctor Brown and with Butch, if he had something in the oven. With fourteen Japanese bombers circling overhead getting ready to drop, I have actually seen that man crawl out of his hole to retrieve a pan of biscuits from the oven and deposit them with tender protectiveness on the ground beneath his stove.

CHAPTER 10

Buildup to Armageddon

On 30 September we received a visit from Admiral Nimitz. He came to see for himself what life was like at the end of the line. The weather was miserable, but the occasion was pleasant for all of us.

I was called into the general's diggings to brief the admiral on our dispositions, using an aerial mosaic of Lunga Point mounted on a large piece of plywood. After the presentation, I moved to get out of the small enclosure with my unwieldy load but was unable to get through.

As I stood there, Admiral Nimitz asked General Vandegrift to state his views on the Turner relationship. General Vandegrift was extremely circumspect. He spoke slowly, carefully limiting his views to the single statement that without consulting him or the commandant of the Marine Corps, or the secretary of the navy, Turner had organized men belonging to the 1st Marine Division into a totally unauthorized Raider Battalion instead of returning them to Guadalcanal.

Admiral Nimitz seemed relieved and changed the subject. Someone came in, and I got out. I admired the general's good judgment in avoiding the debatable matter of command relationships—to this day a murky area. He had quietly pinned Kelly Turner's shoulders to the mat beyond dispute by relying solely on the unarguable fact that the admiral had ignored the laws governing the U.S. Navy.

Since the beginning of the month it had been obvious that the Japanese were being reinforced nightly, building up large forces west of the Matanikau. And we had information that much larger forces of men and ships were being assembled at

Rabaul. Tanks and heavy equipment were sighted near Kokumbona. There was quite discernible ship movement during the hours of darkness, and signs of great activity along the Tassafaronga beaches were evident.

A prompt response was necessary. The general decided that we should take the offensive at the Matanikau with whatever forces we could muster, even at the risk of being caught off base by a landing at Lunga while our best forces were engaged outside the perimeter.

The third Matanikau operation was carefully planned. It employed six infantry battalions supported fully by artillery and General Geiger's Cactus Air Force.

On 7 October, 3d Battalion, 5th Marines (Bowen), moved out astride the government track. The battalion made contact at midmorning with a significant enemy force already several hundred yards east of the Matanikau River. The advance guard developed its assault and pushed the enemy slowly to the west in an attack continuing until after nightfall.

The 2d Battalion, 5th Marines, moved to the left of the engaged battalion and reached the river without opposition. Meanwhile, the Whaling Group, Lt. Col. Robert G. Hunt's 3d Battalion, 2d Marines, and the Scout Sniper Detachment turned south, crossing upriver at the Nippon bridge, followed by 7th Marines (less 3d Battalion). They reached bivouac areas by nightfall.

Plans for the next day called for the 5th Marines to make a diversionary attack at the mouth of the river. Concurrently, our inland forces would envelop the hostile right flank, attacking successively to the north along the two ridges immediately paralleling the river's left bank: Whaling's Group on the right, 7th Marines on the left.

The resistance encountered by 5th Marines slowed the advance of all following units, making it difficult for them to execute movements at the time planned.

Unfortunately, the next day, 8 October, was one of continuous torrential downpour. Mud in the valley and wet slippery grass on the steep coral ridges slowed the advance of our enveloping force to a snail's pace. It became evident that they

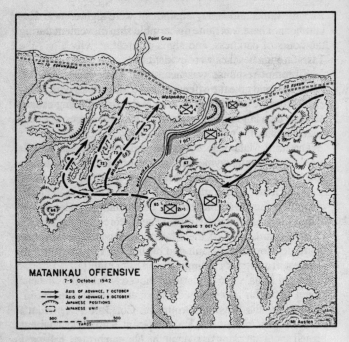

Point Cruz

MATANIKAU OFFENSIVE
7-9 October 1942

→→→→→→ AXIS OF ADVANCE, 7 OCTOBER
➤➤➤➤➤➤ AXIS OF ADVANCE, 9 OCTOBER
︵︵︵︵ JAPANESE POSITIONS
▭ JAPANESE UNIT

500   0   500
YARDS

could not reach their jumpoff position before late afternoon.
The attack had to be postponed.

At daylight, 9 October, the attack was launched under favorable weather conditions. The Whaling Group advanced
rapidly. Brushing aside light resistance, they seized the western approach to the vital river mouth crossing. Hanneken's
2d Battalion, 7th Marines, on Whaling's left, also encountered little opposition and reached the Point Cruz area. Obviously, the enemy had taken advantage of our enforced delay
and pulled back out of the trap.

The general sent for me, saying he had received information and Ultra messages confirming reports that a massive
make-or-break effort was being launched from Rabaul. It
would be necessary to discontinue our ongoing melee with
the Japanese at the river and come home. He concluded with

this imperative: "I want you to keep at least a battalion down there at all times covering that sandbar at the mouth of the river."

Now I knew we had come to the Solomons to stay.

I issued telephonic orders for a daylight withdrawal, covered by a reconnaissance in force by Puller in the direction of Kokumbona. This was a conventional maneuver, since we believed we were not under enemy pressure at any point. Col. Amor L. Sims, commanding 7th Marines, had difficulty in reaching Puller, whose battalion of the 7th Marines was on the extreme left flank. Puller had just encountered a large enemy force moving in for a counterattack and was working it over in great shape when he got Sims's order. He had failed to inform Sims of his situation, a habit common to all old Coconut Warriors, whose credo was "once you clear the camp, tell 'em nothing." Whaling and Hanneken always followed the same pattern. The practice invariably led to serious misunderstandings. Edson and Lt. Col. Evans F. Carlson never engaged in this dubious tactic. Carlson reported in detail every six hours.

Nevertheless, Puller did a fine job of pulverizing the Japanese counterattacking force, trapped in a wooded ravine on his flank, using mortars while at the same time calling in artillery fire to cover his exposed front, held immobile along its zone of advance. As many as 600 Japanese may have been killed in this single minor encounter. Our losses were minimal.

By coincidence, the Japanese had planned to initiate a large scale attack on Henderson Field on 8 October, the day we picked for launching our attack. Had we not been delayed twenty-four hours by bad weather, the enemy would have found himself blocked at the river by the 5th Marines with Whaling, Hanneken, and Puller in perfect position for immediate envelopment of his right flank. In this situation the enemy would have been totally destroyed. We were always unlucky down there.

All this and more became evident a day or two later, when a map and operation order were taken from the body of a

Captain Watanabe, killed while reconnoitering our lines. It confirmed our worst fears. The Japanese intended to seize the river mouth, enabling them to move tanks and artillery to assault our positions west of the Lunga River and pour devastating close-range artillery fire on Henderson Field, totally interdicting its use. From that point on there were no further differences of opinion as to what constituted our "clear and present danger." This was particularly helpful to me in my position as chief of operations (D-3).

The Japanese order had an odd side effect on General Vandegrift, whose acute sense of military honor, decorum, and courtesy in dealing with foreign officers had, no doubt, been enhanced by his experiences as commander of our legation guard in Peking. When one of us spoke out too "realistically" about the Japanese, he was slightly offended. The general never used the term "Japs." It was always politely "the Japanese." Edson, in particular, annoyed him by his persistent use of the cognomen "Nips." However, General Vandegrift's attitude visibly changed after he read General Hyakutake's detailed instructions for the manner of treating Vandegrift as a prisoner, particularly the item about making him remove his shoes before being led into the conqueror's presence.

Our withdrawal to the Lunga Perimeter was completed without enemy interference. They were apparently too stunned by our sudden attack to retaliate. The 5th Marines (less 1st Battalion) had been on the line of the river since 7 October and was left in place until relieved by the McKelvy Group, a temporary task grouping consisting of 3d Battalion, 7th Marines (Williams), and 3d Battalion, 1st Marines (McKelvy), under the command of the latter as senior battalion commander. McKelvy's battalion was assigned the task of holding the vital vehicle crossing of the sandbar at the mouth of the stream. Williams had the onerous task of establishing a tenuous defense of foot crossings up to and including the Nippon Bridge far upstream. Every effort was made to make the sandbar an untenable place for any Japanese venturing a crossing. The artillery was meticulously registered there and in depth along the government track as far as Kokumbona and beyond, with special attention being given to the defile east of Matanikau Village.

Most of our few antitank mines were put in place near the east end of the sandbar, where they could be covered by our fire. Banks of lights, salvaged from broken-down LVTs, were installed and protected by sandbag revetments. These lights brightly illuminated the field of fire extending across the river mouth and enabled our half tracks to deliver aimed 75mm antitank fire by night as well as by day. Enemy artillery was increasingly active but apparently could not reach this critical area and upset our careful preparations.

About this time we began receiving artillery fire within the Lunga Perimeter. Obviously, the Japanese had found a way to land medium artillery (150mm) across their beaches, for we were well out of light-artillery range. This fire was spasmodic, consisting of single rounds registered on the western end of Henderson Field's main runway. We had a splendid view of the runway from the command post and also took all the "overs," as we were totally unprotected on that side. The fire was little more than an annoyance and a source of argument as to whether there was one Pistol Pete or two. Adjustment of fire was probably exercised from some radio-equipped observation post on Mt. Austen. Their radios, like our own, were not too reliable.

When flights of friendly aircraft approached, it became standard practice for the 11th Marines to lay down suppressive fires on suspected Pistol Pete positions prior to and during the landing. The appearance of these medium weapons was ominous. We had none of our own for reply or counterbattery. They had been left behind in Wellington due to inadequate shipping.

I pressed my operational authority to the limit, every day insisting that our artillery must take more active counterbattery measures. Deliberately, I made a pest of myself in headquarters by asking for more and heavier artillery. I knew what should happen—and it did. Several days later two batteries of 155mm guns—one Marine and the other army—showed up in an AKA off Lunga Point, were landed, and within an hour of hitting the beach opened fire on suspected enemy positions well to the west of Kokumbona.

A year later, during my second tour on Guadalcanal, while planning the attack on Bougainville, I prowled around the old Japanese positions and found a gun park where eighteen of their 150mm guns, all intact, were lined up in a row. Nearby was a burned-out ammunition dump containing the remains of thousands of rounds of 150mm ammunition. The only sensible explanation is that we had destroyed their ammo dump early in the game and they were unable to replace it. If so, I believe the credit should go to a U.S. Navy destroyer that had bombarded the area at our request, causing tremendous secondary explosions and fires.

From the very beginning of the Guadalcanal Operation, the lack of purpose and determination by ComSoPac and the highly questionable quality of some of Turner's views were obvious to General Vandegrift, who then derived his own mission from those circumstances confronting him. Vandegrift's forces labored under grave disabilities not of his making and not fully understood in the rear area. Yet, as Admiral McCain had so forcefully pointed out, we were in a position to render a service far surpassing what might reasonably be expected of us. The general understood the supreme value of Henderson Field to the Allied cause and was determined to protect it. He steadfastly refused to devote any significant part of his slender resources to any undertaking that did not in some way contribute to the main purpose of our presence in the Solomons. Turner, with his short span of tactical attention, was constantly pressing for one or another of his schemes, further dispersing our already scarce resources.

The British were the most indefatigable and persistent in wishing to scatter our slim assets. Guadalcanal was not an Australian possession, as so many have presumed. It was British, part of their Solomon Islands Protectorate, one of dozens of widely separated islands and archipelagos of the tropical South Pacific ruled by a British governor general from his capital at Suva in the Fijis, over 1,000 miles away.

Sir Philip Martin, the incumbent official at Suva, paid us a visit. He had two apparent purposes: to have us hoist the Union Jack alongside the Star-Spangled Banner on Pagoda Hill and expand our operations to include physical occupation of the entire area—something the British had never done and we were not about to be drawn into. Underlying all this was an apparent suspicion on their part that we actually had a proprietary interest in this miserable place. General Vandegrift simply pretended not to take the matter seriously. The brief visit was an enjoyable occasion, and when he took his guest to the airfield, his farewell words were: "Well, Sir Philip, maybe we can make a deal. We'll keep the airfield, and you and the Japanese can have the mosquitoes." "Old Glory" continued to fly in solitary splendor on Pagoda Hill.

There were never any important differences as to aims and objectives of the United States and Britain—rid the area of Japanese, regain control of the Solomons, and win the war—but our dissimilar points of view were sometimes apparent. For example, mining for precious metals had been completely suspended in the United States as an activity contributing in no way to the war effort, but here on Guadalcanal we found a small gold-mining operation going on in the mountains to the east of our perimeter. Asked to give support, General Vandegrift offered them help in evacuation but declined on principle to assist them in any other way.

A partial solution to this British problem came about by happenstance. On Tulagi, Brigadier General Rupertus had substantial forces garrisoning the area and maintaining surveillance over Florida Island by constant patrolling. Otherwise there was no active day-to-day contact with the enemy, as was the case on Guadalcanal. The operations of the Marines on Tulagi and the military interests of the people from Ferdinand—the invaluable Australian Coast Watchers organization composed of Australian, British, and native personnel—were combined admirably to provide combat patrols and eradicate small groups of Japanese throughout the Eastern Solomons. This cooperative arrangement for gathering intelligence and eliminating Japanese was effective and mutually advantageous to the British, to us on Guadalcanal, and to

General Vandegrift's subordinate command, the Tulagi Marines, who quickly distinguished themselves as jungle fighters.

I recall one raid in particular. It was made against a twenty-one-man radio installation on Malaita, the most primitive of the islands, where even today a white man is at risk. The raid was conceived and planned by Maj. John Mather of the Australian Army, a graduate of the prestigious Indian Army Staff College at Quetta and, since our landing on Guadalcanal, attached to the 1st Division's Intelligence Section (D-2). Mather's scarred face gave an appearance of fierceness to this huge, powerful man, who was surprisingly soft spoken, well mannered, and gracious. For years he had been a recruiter in the Solomons. The natives swore by him. Even the hostile Malaitamen trusted him.

Accompanied by a native friend, Mather made a trip to Malaita, where they carefully observed the daily routine at the Japanese camp. Soon after returning to Lunga he prepared and gave me a document. We would term it "an estimate of the situation." To John Mather it was "an appreciation." By any name it was one of the best written, most detailed, and most logically presented papers of the kind that I have ever read. It specified step by step in exact detail what must be done, when, and why, to catch the enemy off guard. I went along with the plan but never expected much from it. I was mistaken.

A platoon from Tulagi, I Company, 2d Marines, commanded by 1st Lt. James W. Crain, moved to Malaita in two small sailing vessels. Landing under cover of darkness, they marched to the hostile camp, deployed, and waited for daylight. Just before dawn a Japanese left the enclosure and urinated on a bush under which a Marine was taking cover. The Marine never flinched. At daylight the machine gunner on guard in the watch tower climbed down to join his mates at breakfast, leaving the camp unguarded. This was the preplanned signal for the Marines to open fire. They did. In seconds it was over. One man survived. He was taken prisoner. We suffered no casualties. It was a microcosmic military masterpiece.

The Tulagi Marines performed many such missions, some of them, the largest ones, on Guadalcanal. As a staff officer, I always supported these patrols and raids, feeling that in some measure they were a repayment to the good people of Ferdinand, whose courageous Coast Watchers had done so much for us.

The anticipated attack from Rabaul never materialized, and for good reason. On the night of 11 October, a strong U.S. naval force of cruisers and destroyers commanded by Rear Adm. Norman Scott surprised the Japanese 6th Cruiser Division as it approached Guadalcanal. This was the same enemy division that surprised our ships off Savo Island on the night of 8–9 August. Now, well handled and trained after weeks of night battle practice, our ships closed on the enemy in darkness off Cape Esperance. It was Savo Island in reverse. In thirty minutes the Japanese 6th Cruiser Division was badly beaten. We had paid them back in their own coin.

This victory not only heightened morale among the Guadalcanal defenders but also removed the immediate threat of attack by overwhelming forces. It also permitted the long-planned reinforcement of our division by the 164th Infantry. This fine regiment of the army's Americal Division, commanded by Col. Bryant E. Moore, USA, was composed of National Guard troops from the upper midwest states, the Dakotas and Minnesota.

Disembarkation and unloading were completed late in the afternoon of 13 October. Operational control of the army unit would pass to me the next day. It was decided to have the troops bivouac in the rear of the landing beaches rather than moving to the perimeter, where they were to relieve the 1st Marines for assignment elsewhere.

Their bivouac was in an exposed area, and they took the precaution of digging in for the night. It was well that they did. That night an enemy force of two battleships plus cruisers and destroyers delivered the first of a series of heavy bombardments. For eighty minutes they illuminated Henderson Field and poured in a well-directed fire of fourteen- and twelve-inch shells, which really shook things up. Under their constant pounding, the earth seemed to turn to the consistency of Jell-O, making it difficult to move or even remain upright.

We suffered many casualties. Forty-one were killed, including some of our best pilots. Our wire communications failed immediately. During a momentary lull a radioman in my D-3 dugout—without orders—sent out a call sign to test our communications. The enemy picked up the signal. Response was immediate. Tons of fourteen- and twelve-inch shells began to land in and around the division CP. I thought about the 164th Infantry, out there in center field picking up all the flack in their bivouac area. They suffered casualties but, thankfully, fewer than I feared. What a reception for our new arrivals!

We suffered severe losses in aircraft. Only one of the indispensable SBDs survived the night undamaged. Others were damaged but repairable. Many were completely destroyed. Herculean repair efforts by the line crews made a few of the planes flyable. This small flight took off just before sunset to make a strike on an approaching convoy of seven large transports. The attack was desperately driven home and succeeded in sinking one large transport and damaging another. The five undamaged ships pressed on, and at daylight, 15 October, were observed unloading troops and supplies in the Tassafaronga–Doma Reef area ten miles west of Lunga Point.

Our small force of surviving fighters and dive bombers entered into a frenzied melee, making repeated attacks on the enemy transports after penetrating an intense canopy of antiaircraft fire from shore batteries, transports, and escort vessels. Our planes were under constant attack by Zero fighters coming in relays to cover the transports. By 1100 one transport was sunk and two were beached and burning. The remaining two ceased unloading and fled. As they passed Savo, a formation of B-17s attacked and scored a direct hit on one transport. It burst into flames.

With the departure of the Japanese transports, our aircraft turned to the dangerous but highly important work of destroying enemy cargo piled along the beaches. Great fires and large explosions were observed from Lunga Point. Our pilots had not overlooked the Japanese lack of target perception at Red Beach during the time of our initial landing and did not make the same mistake. Despite all our efforts, the Japanese had brought in a substantial reinforcement of their strong force already ashore. This success would, without doubt, encourage them to repeat the process.

General Geiger was greatly disturbed by the vulnerability of his aircraft in their exposed position and did everything possible to deceive the enemy and reduce losses. The Pagoda was torn down; it provided too convenient a registration point at night for Japanese naval gunfire. Wrecked planes from the bone yard were lined up wing to wing as inviting targets for Japanese pilots to waste their ammunition.

He also established a secret dispersal airfield just outside the perimeter wire on the east flank, where a long grassy expanse provided a clear area of fire for the right battalion of the 1st Marines' sector. I set up a plan for heavily outposting the field when in use. Then I noticed a high pinnacle exactly south of the airstrip and commanding its entire length. This would have to be held at all times, or the field would be unusable. Since the hill was on their front, the 7th Marines were given this outpost chore. They were not too happy about it. Detailed plans existed for their safe withdrawal in case of a general attack—if the field was not in active use.

In order to avoid detection, improvement of the field was limited to the removal of objects considered hazardous to flight operations. Few persons knew of the existence of this "phantom" fighter strip. It appears on no maps and is not mentioned in the official monograph, but it served us well at least once when it was used as a dispersal strip. The heavy rains accompanying the November battles prevented its further use, but the outpost was destined to give us the first alarm and three precious hours to brace for the Sendai Division's assault upon Puller's battalion when it came on the night of 24 October.

The day following their arrival, the 164th Infantry relieved the 1st Marines, who took over the left half of the large sector formerly held by 5th Marines, thus doubling the infantry strength in what was now believed to be the more dangerous approach to the airfield. It was the only open area lending itself to defense in depth and for this reason was assigned to the 1st Marines, commanded by Col. Clifton B. Cates, an outspoken protagonist of this mode of defense. A doctrinaire soldier of World War I, he wanted three days to conduct the relief, but Vandegrift would not hear him out.

Cates then got me on the phone and gave me a thorough lecture on the forty-two consecutive steps taken to effect a proper relief. I, too, had once memorized the three-day forty-two-step routine and with forbearance listened to his scolding lecture. But I kept thinking of a tale told me years before by an officer who took his company of Marines up to the front lines at Verdun in 1918 to relieve a company of French infantry. The French company commander, impatiently awaiting the captain's arrival, took him to the parapet, waved his arm toward the horizon and exclaimed: *"Voila le boche! He weel shoot at you! Au revoir et bon chance."* And was on his way. So much for the forty-two steps!

Despite his minor shortcomings, Cates was a splendid regimental commander. In six months he had turned a bunch of post–Pearl Harbor recruits, a handful of old-time sergeants dragged kicking and screaming off their planks in various navy yards, and a group of green lieutenants just out of Quantico into a fighting machine of the first order. His company commanders were from the peacetime reserve, people like Charlie Brush, who wiped out Colonel Ichiki's advance party at Tetere. They and even some of the young lieutenants would be commanding battalions when the war ended. These officers would leave the Corps, many to embark on remarkable careers: U.S. senators, governors of states, and heads of worldwide corporations such as Bechtel and Merrill Lynch. There would be an assistant managing editor of *Life* magazine, and one of these officers, Lt. John Jachym, who has already been mentioned, would buy a half interest in the Washington Senators—but not, I am sure, by saving his Marine Corps pay.

First Lt. Walter S. "Tabasco Mac" McLlhenny, destined to head the McLlhenny Avery Island interests in Louisiana, was also a highly successful but fiercely independent company commander coming directly from the reserve. I once had occasion to go with General Geiger well out of the perimeter in Cates's sector. He wanted to see for himself whether the open area south and southeast of Red Beach was suitable for airfield construction. Tabasco Mac's company provided security for our movements. The old general, once the finest company commander in the Corps, was obviously delighted to be with a ground outfit for a change and took great interest in everything he saw. McLlhenny put on a fine show.

I asked Lt. Col. Lenard B. Creswell, who commanded 1st Battalion, 1st Marines, "Isn't McLlhenny in your battalion?" His facetious reply, "Well, yes. In a way he does acknowledge a sort of loose relationship."

After the war McLlhenny was active in numerous Marine Corps organizations and ultimately retired as a brigadier general, USMCR.

During this time we began receiving a steady stream of visitors from the rear areas, some from as far away as Washington. None stayed long enough to really understand our situation, but all gave very pessimistic and inaccurate—and unsubstantiated—accounts when they got home. The farther from Guadalcanal one got, the more negative and defeatist the outlook. Some of this got back to the men via the evening bullhorn broadcast at Kukum, where whoever could get away would walk miles to guffaw at Tokyo Rose and her crude attempts at propaganda. Our Marines were astounded to learn that there was "grave doubt in the nation's capital" as to whether we could hold out. They hadn't heard about that—and didn't like what they heard. Marines got mad and booed the bullhorn, particularly the night of 19 October, when Secretary of the Navy Knox feebly told a news conference, "I certainly hope so," when asked if we would be able to make it. Uncomplimentary things were said.

I often wondered why some visitors were permitted to

come. There seemed to be no specific reason beyond casual curiosity.

One visitor that I recall vividly was an officer of a type Australians call a Pommy. His ancestors may have lived in the Antipodes for a century and a half, but he still talked about "going home" to England for Christmas. They are not greatly admired and fortunately are few in number. This one walked into our miserable dugout near the end of a very bad day. He was a handsome young major wearing a beautifully cut uniform and a splendid Digger hat, appearing as if he had just come off the parade ground at Sandhurst. After looking us over disdainfully, he spoke to my assistant, Maj. Bill Buse: "I say, what do you chaps do to keep fit?"

Good question that. We hadn't thought much about it lately. Like everybody else, we were just trying to keep alive from one day to the next.

Fresh from a tour of duty in England, he was a survivor of the "lunnon blitz," as he described it. He glanced over our situation map and shook his head in disapproval. We then entered into a spirited war-gaming exercise in which he defeated me with an endless number of Japanese battalions maneuvering at lightning speed across mountain ranges to thwart our every effort. We were done for. No doubt about that. He even told us so.

Just then the third air attack of the afternoon, a mean low-level affair, hit the command post. We all "assumed the position" and hunched up as we sat on the ground with our backs to the coral wall to reduce the effect of concussion from a near miss. The Pommy looked at us in utter contempt as I told him to get down with the rest of us. Instead he moved to the entrance, screened by only a sandbag blast deflector, and struck a heroic pose. "Get away from there!" I yelled. Too late. I heard it coming. A fragmentation bomb. It made a direct hit on a shelter next door—just a few feet away. Concussion knocked the Pommy flat to the ground with the force of a five-ton truck. The beautiful Digger hat went flying. We were relieved to see him get up, unhurt. He stood there and yelled, "Jesus Christ!" at the top of his voice. After that he dropped all the condescension and talked like a regular guy. He was impressed. I wonder what he said when he got home. There were four casualties next door—all native scouts.

The visitors were nearly forgotten because of another event closer to home and more meaningful. It started to rain at sunset on 18 October and became one of those miserable nights we all dreaded, nights when anything could happen and usually did. About 2100 there was the sound of loud cheering starting in the Signal Company bivouac area and spreading quickly to other units around the command post. Vice Adm. William F. "Bull" Halsey had taken over back at ComSoPac headquarters in Noumea! High command relationships were not matters of discussion around the camps, and I had assumed that there was no general knowledge of or interest in these matters except among senior officers. How wrong I was. Here were men whooping it up and turning cartwheels in the dark at the best news we had heard since Kelly Turner brought in our 7th Marines exactly one month before. Our general made no comment, but I could sense his feeling of great relief at this momentous change occurring in our fortunes.

On the staff we were delighted to read the admiral's first tactical messages. Instead of sending long-winded dispatches involving limitations, reservations, boundaries, and other impediments thought necessary by his predecessor, Halsey gave simple and direct orders. I remember that his first order closed with the words "attack, attack, attack." It was a heartwarming change to us, and I am sure it was even more so to the action addressees.

Admiral Halsey visited us on 8 November, just a few days after taking over as commander, South Pacific. He came to Guadalcanal "to get the feel of the place," something he said he was not getting back in Noumea. His personal magnetism brightened the scene wherever he went, which was about everywhere. He came into our D-3 dugout unannounced and listened carefully to my explanation of our tactical dispositions, then asked some very sensible questions as to why we were doing what we were doing.

Carried away with my own eloquence, I made the mistake of volunteering to say what wonderful things we could do to the enemy "if we had just one more regiment." He cut me down to size by a reply I will never forget: "Hit with what you've got, son. That's what I have to do." As he pronounced the word "hit," he banged his fist into a sandbag, which split and scattered sand along his sleeve. There was a certain symbolism in that rotting sandbag that did not escape either of us.

Nobody who was present ever forgot the dinner in the general's mess on the eve of the admiral's departure. I noted that Butch Morgan and his striker, Shorty Mantray, were somehow both immaculately clad and groomed for the occasion. The dinner itself was fit for the gods, including steaks and the finest apple pie I have ever tasted. Where Butch got the makings for such a feast he would never reveal. Either the admiral brought them with him from his mess in Noumea in a conspiracy with Butch, or the latter somehow had made an under-the-counter deal with one of the ships in a souvenirs-for-goodies exchange. Those steaks alone were well worth a Samurai sword.

At the conclusion of dinner the admiral announced that he wanted to meet the world's greatest cook. My heart sank as General Vandegrift told me to escort Admiral Halsey into Butch's adjoining galley and meet the founder of the feast. Butch, for once in his lifetime, was overwhelmed. He hung his head, his powerful tattooed arms at his side, rough hands twisting his apron. When the admiral concluded his complimentary appreciation for "the finest meal I've ever had," it was Butch's turn: "Aw, shit, Admiral, you didn't have to say that."

The next morning, as Halsey got into the plane to leave, he turned to Vandegrift and admonished, "And don't you do anything to that sergeant of yours."

CHAPTER 11

October Dogfall

October 1942 was a rainy month in the Solomons. Uncertain visibility and downpour-flooded airstrips handicapped the Cactus Air Force in its effort to maintain continuous operations. Fortunately for us the island soil was quick drying. A soggy field could dry out and become usable, even slightly dusty, in a few hours. The Japanese were aware of this too and pressed their advantage at every opportunity to strike us while Henderson Field was wet. It was always their golden chance to inflict severe losses on us at the field itself or to cover the landing of troops and supplies on the beaches west of Kokumbona.

Our people up in Pearl were reading the Japanese's mail pretty thoroughly by now, and they kept us informed. This communications intelligence was called Ultra but sometimes referred to as Magic. Much of this top-secret information was gained by our cryptographers at headquarters, commander in chief, Pacific Fleet, who had broken some of the Japanese codes.[1] A very limited portion of this information was distributed, and that only to those whose responsibilities required it. From this intelligence we knew that the Japanese Seventeenth Army, commanded by Lt. Gen. Harukichi Hyakutake—an officer of known ability based at Rabaul—had assumed the task of regaining Guadalcanal.

Their major unit, the 2d Division, had landed near Kokumbona and was reinforced with the Kawaguchi Detachment and

1. W. J. Holmes, *Double-Edged Secrets* (Annapolis, MD: Naval Institute Press, 1979), p. 23.

other units, including tanks, heavy artillery, and engineers. The 2d, also known as the Sendai Division, was an elite outfit comparable professionally in every respect to our own 1st Marine Division. In addition, it enjoyed a semisacred status due to its historic origin.

One of its regiments, the 29th, was considered to be the premier unit of the Imperial Japanese Army. This regiment prided itself on its physical conditioning and ability to endure under the worst conditions of climate, fatigue, and short rations. One of its annual exploits was a December night ascent of Fujiyama, with the soldiers under arms, with full packs, and in their underwear. For years we had read about this regiment, but none of us expected ever to see it.

Hyakutake agreed to send the Sendai to the Solomons only on condition that the Imperial Navy would give specific assurance of its safe arrival. It was flattering that the Japanese now took us seriously enough to send their best, not just a bunch of banzai bayonetmen fresh out of the rice paddies. Any damage we could inflict on them would be doubly effective so far as their prestige was concerned.

Immediate command of the force was exercised by Lt. Gen. Masao Maruyama, although General Hyakutake issued the written orders and was on Guadalcanal at least part of the time.

We were privy to information that Hyakutake was considering a three-pronged attack on the Lunga Perimeter: one assault from the west, one from the east, and one from the south. This was the same scheme of maneuver Kawaguchi had hoped to employ when he attacked Edson's Ridge on 13 September. His was the main blow from the south. On the same night a battalion had assaulted the 1st Marines' sector from the east and was repulsed by Cates's 3d Battalion, commanded by Lt. Col. William N. McKelvy. The following night another force had delivered a half-hearted attack from the west against the left flank of 5th Marines, then employed on beach defense. That was thrown back by Captain Spurlock's Company of 3d Battalion, 5th Marines. These latter two attacks in no way assisted the main effort, being on too

small a scale and badly coordinated with respect to the principal thrust against Edson's position on the ridge. They were
also, in effect, "off the battlefield," as so frequently happens
when excessively wide envelopments are attempted at points
too remote from the principal objective to be tactically significant. Furthermore, we did not attempt to "divine" the
enemy's intentions, as the Naval War College puts it. We had
seen enough of that during the run-up to the naval fiasco at
Savo, and we had all agreed that the "divine" business should
be left solely to the Navy Corps of Chaplains.

We did assess in great detail the enemy's major capabilities, including some not mentioned heretofore. We decided
the one most dangerous to us would be a quick thrust across
the Matanikau at its mouth (attack from the west), seizing the
sandbar and bringing their heavy stuff across to knock out the
airfield with massed short-range artillery and mortar fire
from the ridge west of the Lunga River. This could be quick
and decisive.

Next most dangerous was a thrust directly at the airfield
from the south along the ridge where Edson had made his
successful stand against Kawaguchi on 13 September. Under
cover of the jungle, it would be possible to reach our perimeter undetected. If the enemy broke through to the field, it
would be messy and damaging but not decisive, as we could
expel or destroy the intruding force in short order. At this
time there was nothing to indicate an attack from the east, but
it was certainly a dangerous capability and one we would
have to face extemporaneously when, wherever, and if it occurred. All or any combination of these moves would have to
be anticipated in our preparations and distribution of forces.

There were extreme differences of availability and use of
interior lines of movement and communications existing between our two forces. Assume that a battalion of Marines and
a battalion of Sendai face each other across the Matanikau
River. It would take us only three hours to move that Marine
battalion to Edson's Ridge. However, if the enemy battalion
across the river had to go to the same spot on the ridge and
face us, it would require at least five days of arduous travel

through the near impenetrable jungle. They would arrive exhausted, understrength, and short of food, heavy weapons, and ammunition. This disparity gave us an extremely important advantage in terms of maneuver, which seems to have been entirely overlooked by our adversaries.

We felt confident that our dispositions were good and our defenses well developed. McKelvy's force holding the line along the Matanikau River was not strong enough for all-around defense, but it could hold the main crossing. If an attempt at envelopment was made, McKelvy could be quickly reinforced. The sectors of the main perimeter facing west were strongly held, protected with wire barriers, and covered by preregistered artillery barrages by 11th Marines. This represented the strongest single position we had ever held.

There seemed to be no movement across the Matanikau River. What was Maruyama doing? Where was Hyakutake? No one had any idea. Day after day we sent out patrols. Their reports continued to be negative. The native scouts went farther afield than ever before. Nothing. They explored the native trail almost to Kokumbona. Nothing along there but small bands of badly armed, dispirited, stale Japanese, which they "fairly dealt with." Air photos were taken daily. Nothing but the endless, unbroken jungle canopy. We were stumped.

Meanwhile business was picking up down at the river. All signs indicated that we might expect a strong attack from the west. Ground probes at our lines increased. Artillery fire increased, the forward battle position being the favored target. The enemy was using 150mm howitzers and plenty of ammunition. We responded with our two batteries of recently arrived 155mm guns: one army battery, one Marine. Their effective fire caused quick shifts in the Japanese firing positions and resulted in the destruction of some enemy guns.

Lt. Gen. Thomas Holcomb, commandant, U.S. Marine Corps, and members of his staff landed at Henderson Field late in the afternoon of 21 October. The Japanese put on a good show for our guests. Commencing at sunset they launched an attack across the sandbar by nine tanks supported by infantry.

This strong probe was broken up by the intense fire of infantry weapons. The Japanese lost one tank.

Next day, enemy bombardment was renewed with increasing intensity. Although well dug in, McKelvy's battalion suffered six killed and twenty-five wounded, indicating an artillery bombardment of World War I intensity, something we had never before experienced, with the exception of the terrific night naval gunfire pounding we had taken at Lunga many days earlier.

At 1800 on the twenty-second, the bombardment was renewed with increased ferocity when the heaviest artillery concentration of the entire campaign was placed on McKelvy's positions at the mouth of the river and along the government track and on the rear-area installations of the forward battle positions. The Marines had spent the day improving their positions and held fast.

"After all," as one youngster modestly explained to me, "where the hell could you go?"

When the artillery lifted, a company of Japanese tanks supported by infantry attempted to storm the sandspit as a prelude to their well-known "filleting attack." They intended to send the tanks straight down the government track to disrupt our only line of communications while their massed infantry followed in great depth on a narrow front. This had to be stopped at the outset. It was. Antitank fire from our half tracks swept the bar. Carefully prearranged and precisely registered artillery concentrations commenced on signal and laid death-dealing barrages on the government track across the river, along which we knew their columns of supporting infantry had to be moving.

One tank made it across the sandspit and crashed through our wire. PFC Joseph D. R. Champagne reached out of his foxhole and placed a hand grenade on the tread as the tank stopped beside him. The explosion partially disabled the tank. It was destroyed by 75mm fire from a nearby half track. The sandspit was littered with the wreckage of nine hostile tanks and numerous enemy dead. Patrols later reported hundreds of bodies lying along the government track leading to

Kokumbona. These dead Japanese had been caught in the meticulously planned and carefully executed fires of 11th Marines artillery. The hulks of three additional burned-out tanks were also discovered.

The fighting along the front of McKelvy's 3d Battalion, 1st Marines, ended by midnight with the repulse of a small force attempting to cross the river at a point a few hundred yards upstream. The left battalion of the McKelvy group, 3d Battalion, 7th Marines (Williams), passed a quiet night, not having been engaged.

It had been a long night. Brigadier General Rupertus, over from Tulagi to take command while General Vandegrift was in Noumea for a conference with Vice Admiral Halsey, was following the battle with us. He had Butch Morgan make coffee, which Mantay brought to us in the dugout. It was early morning when I finished work.

At first light, 23 October, when I was just about to get some sleep, Lieutenant Colonel Williams, commanding 3d Battalion, 7th Marines—unengaged on McKelvy's left—called to tell me that they had just spotted a strong enemy column on our side of the river. The Japanese were out of range, traveling in hellish terrain and making slow progress, but moving to a position threatening Williams's exposed left flank and rear. They had found a crossing well upstream from the Nippon Bridge and crossed under cover of darkness while we were preoccupied with the brawl at the river mouth.

This column was probably the hard-luck Oka detachment. There has to be a clown in every circus, and that apparently was Colonel Oka's unhappy role in the Seventeenth Army. He ran into bad luck wherever he went. Oka had brought his command to Guadalcanal as the guinea pig outfit in an ill-fated attempt to reinforce their garrison, using a fleet of small boats and lighters to avoid exposing larger ships to the tender mercies of our scout bombers, the Douglas SBDs. Our fighters and Army Air Corps P-400s also gave Oka's troops a bad time all the way down from Rekata Bay. They arrived in bad shape on 5 September. From then on they could do nothing right. Captured diaries and intercepted messages bad-mouthed poor old Oka. At daylight Oka, on this occasion, had set up his CP near the river and sent his troops on by themselves. As in any army, this did not wear well with the people upstairs. We almost felt sorry for the guy, but it was fun to read his mail.

General del Valle's artillery and General Geiger's planes worked Oka's troops over all day before they made it to a heavily wooded ravine providing good cover and room for dispersion. The enemy was now located within striking distance of the left flank and rear of 3d Battalion, 7th Marines. They were in a position that threatened to cut off our forward battle position from the perimeter.

That day we had planned to regularize the situation by pulling McKelvy's battalion out and replacing it with 7th Marines (less 1st Battalion—Puller). This would in effect be turning the position over to 7th Marines, with Sims exercising command. Puller was to stay in position on the perimeter, singling up his lines in order to cover the entire regimental front until the return of the relieved McKelvy battalion on the river. This was a standard practice to compensate for our lack of strength. This would restore tactical unity and provide headquarters and service support necessary for a permanent stay on the river, but it required Puller to hold the entire regimental sector for one night. It did involve a worrisome risk.

The new situation called for a quick revision of plans. The relief at the river was called off, and Sims and his 2d Battalion were diverted to the task of protecting the left flank and rear of the exposed forward battle position from an attack by the Oka detachment. The 2d Battalion was commanded by Lt. Col. Herman H. Hanneken, proud wearer of the only Medal of Honor in the division at that time. In 1919 Hanneken had made an incredible night penetration into the mountain headquarters of Charlemagne Peralte, killing this Haitian leader of the Caco guerrillas in a gun battle illuminated only by a flickering campfire. For this, he won the Medal of Honor and a commission as second lieutenant. Later, in Nicaragua, he captured Gen. Jiron Sandino's second in command. Hanneken was quite a soldier, well able to deal with the likes of Colonel Oka.

In accordance with division directives, Sims had Hanneken take up a position extending the left of the existing forward battle position, refusing it sharply to the north in the direction of the main perimeter along a precipitous ridge. The position was much too long for an understrength, malaria-ridden battalion, but it had to be held even though it was so attenuated as to amount to little more than a strong line of outposts. The steep slope would in itself be a considerable obstacle to Japanese assault. The day of the twenty-fourth was spent in hastily fortifying the Ridge. Our artillery and aircraft worked over the area occupied by the Japanese incessantly, with unknown results. At sunset the troops on both sides engaged in the usual vituperative shouted colloquy involving the empress, Eleanor, Babe Ruth, and the strange dietary preferences of the Mikado. The night passed quietly—why, I cannot imagine. It was not exactly quiet back in the perimeter, where Puller's battalion was singled up along a full regimental front.

For days we had scouted the area along the upper Lunga, but despite entirely negative results I was filled with a strange foreboding. The flabby attack at the sandbar was certainly not the work of the Sendai. But where were they? Recalling their predilection for dramatic and challenging feats of physical endurance, they might now be right out there in front of Puller. But they weren't.

On the twenty-fourth we made an all-out patrol effort during the day. Near sunset Daniel Boone's Scout Sniper Patrol came in. They had gone far and wide and found nothing. Boone sent his patrol on ahead to be home in time for chow. Sharing apprehensions like my own, he had gone back alone to take another look. Just after dark he came to the command post. Near the big bend of the Lunga he had spotted something. "It could have been a patch of evening mist, or it might be the smoke of many rice fires." I thanked him, never saw him again, and never knew his real name. But I will always remember him. In war it is still the man—not men—that makes the difference.

I called 7th Marines at their old CP on the perimeter. They had left a skeleton regimental headquarters behind when they took off that morning. Lt. Col. Julian Frisbie, the regimental executive officer, was in charge. I told him what I had just learned from Boone. He replied that a straggler from a regimental patrol had reported seeing a Japanese officer scanning our positions with binoculars that afternoon. He had suspected the boy of telling a yarn to cover his embarrassment about getting lost and hadn't passed it on. He would pass the word to Puller, who was busy getting ready for the night with his men sprinkled across a regimental front. Frisbie asked about withdrawing the strong outpost on the pinnacle covering Geiger's secret dispersion strip. We decided to leave it in place with renewed instructions about withdrawing to the north—all the way to the beach before trying to reenter our lines. We would notify the people down there.

It was quiet for a while; then it started to rain heavily. At exactly 2130 on the twenty-fourth there was an abrupt outburst of intense firing coming from the area of the pinnacle outpost. In a minute or two it ceased. Suddenly I knew: The Sendai Division was knocking on our door.

Immediately, I gave orders for the closest division reserve battalion to start moving to Puller's assistance. This was far beyond the limits of my authority as operations officer. I quickly reported my actions to General Rupertus and Jerry Thomas, who confirmed them without hesitation. The reserve battalion in that area was from the newly arrived 164th Infantry of the army's Americal Division. Lt. Col. Robert K. Hall, USA, commanded the battalion. They were good people and, as Fletcher Pratt later described them, "an organization of stubborn Swedes from North Dakota just waiting to get even" for the bombardment they had received at the hands of the Imperial Japanese Navy on the night of their landing ten days earlier.

In the rain and darkness it would be a time-consuming process to effect the reinforcement. Meanwhile, Puller was on his own. I never had a moment of doubt. I did not feel we were outnumbered that night. To me, Puller's presence alone represented the equivalent of two battalions. I had known him since 1926, when we were second lieutenants in the same company at Pearl Harbor. We were lifelong friends. I spent my last day in the Marine Corps visiting the Pullers at their home in Saluda, Virginia, with my wife, Vivian, who was a close friend of Chesty's wife, Virginia.

The forty-one men at the outpost on the pinnacle held their fire and evacuated their position, moving northward to the beach. They reentered our lines at the government track examining post. Their casualties were one man missing, later presumed KIA. They had rendered a great service in the culminating moments of their hazardous assignment.

The Sendai reached our lines three hours later. It was a wild fight. They came through the tangled jungle in successive waves. There were nine battalions of them, led by the famed 29th Regiment, against one of ours. They had intended to come down the open ridge on the right of the regimental sector, just as Kawaguchi had done in September, but lost direction and came at us through the jungle north of the ridge. Our artillery performed in great style. Close-in artillery support in thick jungle is not practicable, but our artillery played a hunch they'd used down at the river. A rough road led to the center of our position, one we had built on 7 August, the day of our landing, and had then forgotten. Inevitably, and to their great sorrow, small units and individual soldiers drifted to this road as the best means of traversing the unfriendly jungle. Our murderous artillery concentrations laddered along this approach and inflicted shocking casualties on our unseen opponents. Their famed 29th Infantry Regiment was destroyed.

Hand-to-hand fighting continued throughout the night. At 0500 the Sendai killed all the defenders in one locality and punched a small salient in our front. It looked ominous for a while, and we called on the "Old Reliables," our 1st Combat Engineer Battalion, to set up a last-ditch defense on Pagoda Hill at the airstrip as insurance against a further breakthrough. It proved unnecessary. The salient was reduced later in the day.

By 0630 Hall's battalion of the 164th had been completely inserted—and in the worst possible way, that is, in small groups sent in to plug holes in the weakening line. Under the extreme conditions of weather and visibility no other method was practicable. It was a matter of thickening a thin firing line. A navy chaplain proved a valuable guide in getting the newcomers into the front lines. He had learned his way around during his constant visits to the troops.

These troops were sorted out the next day. Hall's battalion took over the left battalion sector, Puller's the right. Both braced for a renewed attack.

Peculiar flaws in our organization had developed, simple things no one had ever thought of. We had experienced no difficulty in moving up ammunition and grenades in great abundance. The Old Fox, John Macklin, now division ordnance officer, saw to that. But there was a shortage of water—not to drink, but to cool the heavy Browning machine guns upon which we relied so greatly. If a water jacket ran dry, the barrel would become red hot and warp. Then it could not be withdrawn from the jacket for replacement and the gun became useless. Machine gunners were using their own urine as a means of keeping the guns operational. No one had ever thought of the water problem until we came face to face with it in the middle of the night. Of course we had water cans at the guns, but their numbers were totally inadequate for the unanticipated quantities of ammunition we were firing—thousands of rounds per gun. Gunners replaced shot-out barrels at frequent intervals during the night. It cost the taxpayers a bundle, but they got their money's worth.

The twenty-fifth of October was "Dugout Sunday." It was Condition Red all day, with continuous bombardment from warships, aircraft, and the Pistol Petes over in Indian Country. The word was passed to continue all essential operations regardless of enemy interference until further notice.

Fighting picked up anew that night and reached the same crescendo. The Sendai Infantry struck at the juncture of our two engaged battalions. Once more they were stopped at the

wire by withering fire from both defending units, which inflicted heavy losses. Our losses were not great. Puller and
Hall had the situation under control from the beginning, and
the Sendai Division failed to make anything in the way of a
penetration.

Our old friend Major General Kawaguchi, with two battalions, survivors of the force he had led at Edson's Ridge, also
participated in the attack, making an auxiliary effort in support of the Sendai. It failed, and again he refused to make the
ritualistic self-sacrifice.

In Borneo, where Kawaguchi had first come to fame, he
had achieved an easy success. However, he and his troops had
distinguished themselves by the most bestial and revolting
acts of extreme cruelty, including mass rape and the maiming
and torture of helpless prisoners. If ever a man deserved to
die it was Kawaguchi. The record shows that he was sent
home and placed on the reserve list. It is to be fervently hoped
that he was one of the numerous war criminals sent to the gallows by our forces following the surrender.

Until now no one on our side had even heard of "Maruyama's
road." To keep secret his approach, Maruyama had his engineers cut a new trail far to the south of the existing native
trail, which we had patrolled constantly. The time required
for the road's construction accounted for the days of inac-
tivity before the attack. We should have recognized this as
a possibility and sent patrols much deeper into the jungled
mountains to the south. His ruse was nearly successful, but,
on the verge of achieving complete surprise, Maruyama made
his final bivouac at the big bend within a relatively short
distance of Puller's front and let his men make the rice fires
that Daniel Boone sighted from afar. Puller would never have
made that mistake.

During this same time Colonel Oka had been trying to redeem his fallen fortunes by hammering away at Hanneken's
2d Battalion, 7th Marines, stretched to the utmost limit along
the ridge and blocking Oka from hitting the rear of Williams's
3d Battalion, 7th Marines, which was still in position along
the river. Oka gained several temporary local successes by

massing strong forces against our widely separated groups
manning the ridge. Finally, Oka seemed to have secured a firm
foothold at one point. Then at 0200, the executive officer of
2d Battalion, 7th Marines, Maj. Odell M. Conoley, led a jury-
rigged counterattack composed of headquarters dog robbers,
cooks, and messmen plus some members of the 7th Marines
regimental band who had been laboring all day nearby as
stretcher bearers getting wounded Marines off the ridge.

The counterattack succeeded in driving the Japanese off
our position, and they were unable to get a further foothold as
daylight increased the effectiveness of our fire. Sgt. Mitchell
Paige, for a while the lone defender of the ridge, was awarded
a well-deserved Medal of Honor for maintaining a machine-
gun position and fighting off the enemy until Conoley's counterattacking force reached the scene.

By the morning of the third day the Sendai was destroyed.
Survivors carried the wounded back to Kokumbona over the
Maruyama road. They would never again constitute a serious
threat.

A few days later Colonel Sims came to see me at the command post. Accompanying him was the 7th Marines band
leader, who reported his casualties in the following manner:
"I lost my first trumpet, second trombone, one drum, and second chair in the clarinet," or words to that effect. Like all
bandsmen he was a musician at all times and in all places.

Sgt. John Basilone, of Puller's battalion, received the
Medal of Honor for his heroic performance as a machine
gunner during that first night of fighting. He was later to lose
his life on Iwo Jima. I recommended that Lieutenant Colonel
Puller also receive this award but was overruled. Why, I cannot imagine.

Hyakutake had planned a three-pronged attack against us.
The attack from the west, potentially the most dangerous, was
stopped initially at the sandspit, and finally when Oka was
thrown off the long ridge by Conoley's counterattack. The attack from the south by the Sendai was stopped by Puller and
Hall before it could reach Henderson Field. But there was no
simultaneous attack from the east. We hoped it would never

come but soon received a message from Pearl to the effect that Admiral Yamamoto and General Hyakutake would land advance elements of the 38th Division east of Koli Point beginning at midnight of the following day.

One thing we did not want was to have Japanese forces astride the government track on both east and west flanks. I obtained grudging permission to send Hanneken's 2d Battalion, 7th Marines—with one battery of field artillery attached—east to the Koli Point area. Brig. Gen. Pedro del Valle went into a tantrum when I asked for artillery support. He put on a real act. To hear him tell it, we had already used up all his ammunition, and he didn't have enough left to fire the cannon salute for one rendition of Tchaikovsky's 1812 Symphony. I dared not carry the matter up to higher authority. Our Ultra information was sketchy, and also del Valle was not cleared to receive it under the stringent need-to-know restrictions.

We had already launched a new large-scale attack across the Matanikau to exploit our recent successes before what remained of the Sendai could get back to Kokumbona. Apprehensive that permission to move to the east might be cancelled if I persisted in asking for artillery, I chickened out, and Hanneken took his exhausted, understrength battalion on a forced march to Koli Point without artillery. Most of our communications strength was supporting the new attack on the other side of the Matanikau River, and through lack of manpower and phone wire we were unable to maintain telephone communications beyond Red Beach. Preoccupied with the larger operation on the west (right flank) and hearing nothing from Hanneken to the east, I assumed he had made no contact during the night.

Next morning I heard a little gunfire, but a low cloud ceiling distorted the sound and I could not establish its direction. I asked Henderson Field to send a plane to Koli Point to take a look. The pilot reported that there was no sign of enemy activity. We heard no more firing, and I assumed that Hanneken was simply "telling 'em nothing," adhering to the code of the old Coconut Warrior on patrol.

Later, we got a phone call from Red Beach—where we had

landed on D day—not very informative and giving us an in-accurate location. Only one thing was certain: The enemy had made some sort of landing during the night, and Hanneken was in the middle of it but was not in serious trouble. His radios began working and we regularized communications. Air attacks were laid on, but we were hampered by erroneous position reports.

No clear and complete account of what occurred there has ever been written. Several different stories were submitted by agencies all the way back to CinCPac. The more remote the writer, the more certain he was of his "facts": "The Japs landed"; "The Japs did not land; they just landed supplies"; "There were no fresh Japs there, just a small force of stragglers from Kawaguchi's old force"; and so on.

I was there. I was deeply involved. To this day I have never heard a comprehensive and logical account. Inadvertently, I made my own contribution to confuse history. An uncorrected typo in the 1st Division Final Report, where "retrograde" was converted to "rear guard" by the typist, led to an altogether misleading interpretation. Out of the murk and fog characterizing this bizarre encounter, few facts have ever been verified beyond contradiction.

In view of this alarming enemy force buildup to the east, the very promising operation that elements of 5th Marines and 164th Infantry had initiated west of the Matanikau was suspended. The Japanese were not fighting with the same degree of steadfast determination that had heretofore characterized them. In places they were cornered and overcome with relative ease, but we could not afford to exploit these minor successes at the expense of imperiling our eastern flank. It was mandatory that whatever enemy force was there be quickly destroyed.

In these October battles we had defeated some of the finest forces in the Japanese military. Their plan was too elaborate. The three attacks were not coordinated. We were able to concentrate on these efforts one at a time. Had all three struck us at once, we would have been in great difficulty. I can only surmise that the root cause lay in the difficulties arising from inferior radio equipment or that interservice differences prevented unity of action. The Japanese suffered a severe blow to their morale when their blue-ribbon, semisacred Sendai warriors were stopped in their tracks by Puller and his understrength, malaria-ridden battalion. The odds were nine battalions (eleven counting Kawaguchi's force) to one against us when the fight began, but our firepower prevailed over the spiritual armor of their Bushido creed. In one captured diary the deceased had written, "The Imperial Staff must reconsider the matter of firepower."

On 26 October General Vandegrift returned from Noumea after his conference with Admiral Halsey, held only five days after Halsey relieved Ghormley at ComSoPac. We had been on Guadalcanal over ten weeks, and neither Ghormley nor his chief of staff had shown enough interest to visit us or even ask for a personal report from General Vandegrift. Vandegrift brought us the good news that Halsey had promised him "to get you everything I have." At about this same time two favorable but unforeseen developments helped us back in the nation's capital. People were becoming alarmed about the state of affairs in the Solomons, and midterm elections loomed. President Roosevelt addressed individual letters to each member of the Joint Chiefs directing him to furnish immediately all assistance within his power to the defense of our position in the South Pacific regardless of other priorities. This broke the log jam and brought about the ultimate victory.

CHAPTER 12

Carlson "Gung Ho" and a Touch of Genius

With the Japanese now holding coastal positions on both flanks of the Lunga Perimeter, reorganization of our forces became a matter of urgent priority. Brig. Gen. Edmund B. Sebree, U.S. Army, who had come up to supervise the eventual takeover by the relieving U.S. Army forces, was placed in tactical command of all forces along the Matanikau on the right (west) flank. Brig. Gen. William H. Rupertus, USMC, was summoned from Tulagi to take over command of all units operating outside the perimeter on the left (east) flank. These latter forces had been increased to five infantry and two artillery battalions, all employed against the fresh Japanese troops recently landed on Koli Point.

After a series of confused actions, this force, an element of the Japanese 18th Division, was finally surrounded, only to escape inland through a gap in our lines on the night of 11–12 November. It had not been a particularly brilliant affair. Mistakes were made at every level of command. We had employed overwhelming force against a weak opponent—and he had gotten off the hook. But we had accomplished a vital major purpose, that of forestalling a hostile buildup ashore on our left flank. However, the experience brought us to realize for the first time that we had become an exhausted, worn-out division. Even Chesty Puller was down and in the hospital with, as he put it "a fanny full of 'scrapnel.'"

While all this was going on, our old nemesis, Rear Adm. Kelly Turner, still playing soldier, revived his golden dream of an airstrip at Aola Bay and had moved toward its accomplishment by landing a navy construction battalion there.

These Seabees were covered by the 2d Marine Raider Battalion, commanded by Lt. Col. Evans F. Carlson, USMC, plus part of an army infantry battalion and a detachment of Marines of the 9th Defense Battalion. The Seabees found, as had all of their qualified predecessors, that the project was impossible of accomplishment. It was embarrassing. As part of a face-saving solution General Vandegrift agreed to employ the 2d Marine Raiders on a pursuit mission before they were withdrawn from the island. They would take over the job of chasing the remnants of the enemy's badly mauled Koli Point landing force inland over the mountains to Kokumbona.

The 2d Marine Raiders were a splendid organization, meticulously trained and indoctrinated by a most remarkable man, Evans F. Carlson. He was a New England Yankee, the son of a preacher, and the grandson of a Norwegian '49er who had sought gold in California. He had served in the U.S. Army prior to and during World War I, attaining the rank of captain. Resigning his army commission after the war, he enlisted in the Marine Corps and immediately entered the Officer's Training School. Carlson was commissioned a Marine second lieutenant in 1922.

I met Carlson in Quantico in 1923 upon my own entry into the Corps. We took our meals at Mrs. Mountjoy's boarding house in Quantico, there being as yet no officer's mess or club on the base. He was officer in charge of the post stables. Always friendly and helpful, he gave me some much-needed instruction in basic equitation. Carlson was several years older than the rest of us newly commissioned officers and much more mature. After a few days of living with us youngsters in a crowded BOQ, he requested and received other quarters.

That fall, during the Marine Corps East Coast Expeditionary Force maneuvers, Carlson commanded the ambulance train of the Naval Medical Battalion, the last animal-drawn unit in the Marine Corps. We were beset by violent and continuing storms at the outset of our long march from Quantico to Lexington, Virginia. Soon our primitive four-wheel-drive trucks—relics of the Argonne—bogged down completely on the red clay roads of back-country Virginia. The rationing system came to a sudden stop. We went hungry until Carlson's mule-drawn ambulances came undeterred to our rescue and rations were distributed in abundance throughout the storm-bound convoys. Carlson became an instant expeditionary force hero. His initiative also made him a lifelong favorite of Brig. Gen. Smedley Butler, commanding general, who was spared further embarrassment. Carlson modestly deflected all the credit, telling me, " 'Old Ned' " (a familiar name for a mule in those days) "will always do a good job if you just give him a chance."

I did not see Carlson again until the spring of 1937, when I was a student at the Army Infantry School, Fort Benning, Georgia. On a Sunday morning I drove my wife and David, our young son, to Warm Springs to visit the vacation camp of President Franklin Roosevelt. The president was not there, but we encountered Captain Carlson, who had the day's duty. It was here that Carlson first came to the attention of President Roosevelt, who took a particular interest in Marines and the vicissitudes of our small Corps. He was impressed with Carlson's sincerity and uncompromisingly puritanical character.

Carlson's third tour of duty in China—late in 1937—was for the purpose of learning the Chinese language, but as usual he did more than was expected. Carlson obtained permission from Mao Tse-tung to accompany the Communist army on part of the Long March—which covered 6,000 miles and lasted over a year—and went into the field in 1938 with Communists who were fighting the Japanese in remote parts of China.

Carlson was impressed—probably to an undue degree—with the excellence of the discipline, training, and indoctrination of the Chinese troops. He reported what he had seen and done in China to Naval Intelligence and to President Roosevelt, as the president had requested.

Carlson advocated the assignment of leadership positions in our own services solely on a basis of merit rather than fixed military rank. In essence, so do all our military services, and they have tried unceasingly for centuries to develop a system whereby the commissioned officer in charge is in fact the best qualified for command of a given unit. The existing system works well in all the U.S. services. Carlson's system would never be successful on a service-wide scale for the simple reason that there are not enough Carlsons.

Carlson's message was not altogether clear, and it was rejected. He resigned his commission and now had time to write and make speeches about what he had seen and experienced in China.

Lieutenant Colonel Carlson returned to the Marine Corps in April 1941 and took command of the newly formed 2d Marine Raider Battalion with Maj. James Roosevelt, eldest son of the president, as his second in command.

Gung ho! This was the inspirational slogan that Carlson brought from China. He translated it into a war cry and used it to forge these Marines quickly into a cohesive unit with all members zealously and enthusiastically working together. The 2d Marine Raiders conducted their successful Makin Island raid in mid-August 1942.

As a slogan to get persons to unite and work selflessly for the common good, gung ho was admirable and useful. The motto spread throughout the entire Corps, taking on a broader connotation than Carlson ever intended. In this form it has even entered our language.

There is little reason to believe that Carlson carried out his radical leadership philosophy to any extreme degree. The rank structure of his 2d Raiders appears normal, and command seems to have been exercised by the commissioned officers serving under him in much the usual hierarchical manner.

The Roosevelt connection, however, provided Carlson access to the White House and an opportunity to express his views. As one wag remarked, "Second Raiders will never need any artillery support. Carlson's always got twenty-one guns in his hip pocket."

The setup for his Guadalcanal raid was very closely held. I was told only that there would be a raid, that Carlson would report by radio to me at intervals, and that under no circumstances was I to give him anything whatever in the way of orders or instructions. Jerry Thomas told me this several times. The next day General Vandegrift came by the D-3 section and repeated the same injunctions. I was impressed.

Carlson was to be supplied by airdrop every four days. A large number of natives were hired as carriers by Maj. John Mather, Australian army, who was superbly qualified to lead them and who had recently conceived and participated in the successful raid on Malaita Island. The assistance of the natives would be a godsend to Carlson, especially in evacuating casualties. John was a good soldier who knew the bush and its inhabitants, and they in turn trusted him.

The Raiders' rations were extremely sparse. The only items allowed were rice, bacon, raisins, tea, salt, and sugar. Knowing young Marines and their prodigious appetites and love of solid food, I remained unconvinced that these 500 Raiders had suddenly become a bunch of ascetics. Jerry agreed but said Carlson had made a definite point of it. I still shook my head. Over fifty years later I read a book by one of the young participants. He put it like this:

> The awful hunger was a bad dream of its own. . . . For a month it was raisins, tea, bacon, salt, sugar, rice. Oh that rice! That was a worse dream than the running pain in the empty belly.
> Polished rice, unpolished coarse Jap rice, rice boiled, rice fried, rice raw, rice with sugar, rice with bacon, rice with tea, rice with rice! "Goddamn Colonel," we said to him when he came by. "We're hungry."[1]

Thousands of other Marines and soldiers then "sojourning" on the island would have found it hard to disagree. There are limits even to the powers of persuasion of a leader like Carlson.

I monitored the progress of the raid based on Carlson's dispatches. They came in precisely every six hours. They were

1. Michael Blankfort, *The Big Yankee* (Boston: Little, Brown, 1947), p. 298.

informative and clear. His field radios always worked. We encountered none of the annoying nonsense of our own "Banana Warriors" such as Whaling, Puller, and Hanneken, who "hollered" only when they were hurt. The raid—actually a pursuit—was successful from the start despite the difficulty of orientation, as we had no maps of the area, nor did Carlson. We guided on the names of native villages. Even this was only a vague and uncertain business for the natives lived by a form of slash-and-burn agriculture that required the villages to move from time to time when the soil of their present location became worn out. Thus the village names were really the names of areas, each of considerable size. Aerial reconnaissance was our basic resort in the effort to maintain contact. Martin Clemens, the Coast Watcher, also gave us valuable information about the region Carlson was searching and guidance concerning our planned airdrops.

Carlson won victory after victory over the stubbornly resisting Japanese; each contact produced an increased demoralization of the enemy. As a result of this prolonged flight, only a handful of survivors reached the area of Mt. Austen, immediately south of our own position on Lunga Point. By this time the Japanese had lost over 400 of their original 500 men, while only seventeen of Carlson's Marines had been killed in action.

A notable triumph. But how was it accomplished? Based on repeated experience with the Japanese, we had found them reluctant to react to conventional maneuvers. They would simply take up a strong position and stay there till they were killed. This made it a costly way for us to win a fight. To them, their death did not seem to matter. Our usual form of attack was the approved and conventional method adopted by all the world's armies. On making contact with an enemy to our front, we would deploy the main force facing the enemy and feel out his position. Then we would reconnoiter his flanks and send an enveloping force to turn the flank providing the most promise of success from the point of view of favorable approach, ease of fire support, and other considerations. We avoided direct frontal assault except as a last resort. We all remembered what had happened to the Japanese at the Tenaru and Edson's Ridge, and the fate of the Sendai Division, and we wanted for ourselves none of what we saw there.

Too often our enveloping effort was ineffective. Hasty and inadequate reconnaissance and difficult approaches frequently led our flanking force astray, taking it off the battlefield. With our small units, it was difficult to achieve coordination of movement and the timely delivery of supporting fire from heavy weapons and artillery, which were always located in the rear of the main body.

The enemy often felt unthreatened by our small, exhausted, and disorganized enveloping force and so remained in place until taken out the hard and costly way, involving frontal assault and a hand-to-hand struggle of extermination from foxhole to foxhole. This method is known to some as C and A: the nape-of-the-neck, seat-of-the-pants technique of the old-time barroom bouncer. In its full form, C and A translated into collar and ass. Despite its repulsiveness, the phrase describes this mindless form of combat better than sweet euphemisms such as attrition tactics, a term often used by writers but not by participants. We found C and A combat inescapable later on at Tarawa and Peleliu. Fortunately, Marines became better at this than the Japanese.

C and A was a bad way to go, and Carlson had his own method of avoiding it. He used the main body as his enveloping force, striking momentarily at a right angle to his permanent line of advance in what I described in the final report as an eccentric form of attack, "eccentric" being used in the mechanical, not the psychological, sense of the word. Carlson used this maneuver several times during the course of his pursuit, always to good effect. It was clearly recognizable from his dispatches.

Carlson's companies moved separately and fluidly through the jungle. When one of them was confronted with an enemy delaying position, it would maintain contact throughout the remainder of the day and sometimes the entire next day, continuously making a show of great activity all along the hostile front by fire and movement, suggesting but not making an actual attack.

Meanwhile Carlson would deliberately assemble all his uncommitted forces, weapons, and supplies at a point well off the main line of advance but near the enemy flank chosen as the object of his assault. The assault came on the following day, well planned, fully supported, and delivered by an overwhelming force of rested troops. Furthermore, he had not exposed his base; he had simply moved it behind him momentarily.

The Japanese were never able to comprehend what Carlson was doing and at each confrontation showed a steadily diminishing capacity for effective resistance. For the first time in the Guadalcanal campaign, maneuver alone operated to our advantage.

The availability of native carriers gave Carlson the freedom of movement necessary to carry out his king-size envelopments without, at the same time, exposing his base of supply to attack.

Upon completion of this superbly commanded operation the Raiders reassembled at Lunga Point and established their camp outside the main perimeter, where they awaited withdrawal.

I always found John Mather, the Australian army officer who had accompanied Carlson's Raiders, to be a well-educated, thoughtful, and professional soldier, usually hard to impress and faintly skeptical of all things American. During the debriefing, Mather bestowed what for him was lavish praise of Carlson and his responses to the challenging incidents of the raid by frequently interjecting the statement: "He always went by the book. I never saw anything quite like that before."

During this period I saw Carlson only once. It was a strange meeting. The division chief of staff, Col. Jerry Thomas, directed me to go to Block Four, just outside the perimeter, to be present at a meeting between the two Raider Battalion commanders, Col. Merritt Edson and Lt. Col. Evans Carlson. The purpose was to obtain their views on the tactical reorganization of the Marine Corps squad.

At the appointed time I was seated on an old picnic bench

near the Block Four copra shed. The bench faced inland, and I saw Edson's jeep proceeding up the government track from Kukum. It stopped, and as Edson got out I sighted Carlson stalking out of the palm trees across the road. There was no greeting. We all sat on the bench. I was in the middle in more ways than one. Carlson gave his views supporting a division of the squad into three fire teams. Edson then gave his own views, which were essentially the same, except for the addition of one man to act as assistant squad leader. Carlson did not dissent. We sat there for a moment staring into the palm trees across the track. Edson rose and left without another word. Carlson did the same. I returned to the division command post, where I gave Jerry an account of the meeting and offered to write up the necessary dispatch to Headquarters Marine Corps. The offer was refused. To this day I have no idea as to what lay behind this bizarre occurrence.

Following Guadalcanal the four Raider battalions were consolidated into a Raider regiment. This was supposed to be an administrative unit rather than a tactical organization. Its major purpose, I suspect, was to make it more difficult for Rear Adm. Kelly Turner to gain access to individual battalions whenever he felt like playing soldier. If so, it failed its major purpose.

Turner wangled control of the entire regiment for the New Georgia Operation in the summer of 1943 and sent them into the jungle on a vague, ill-conceived, and reckless foray. Known as the Bairoku Operation, it forced the Raiders to pursue the identical tactics that had brought repeated ruin on the Japanese at Guadalcanal—a prolonged and debilitating march through jungle swamps with inadequate rations and supplies and supporting arms, culminating in an unsupported attack on a strong, prepared position. Promised Army Air Corps support was not forthcoming. Like similar efforts of the Japanese on Guadalcanal, logistic shortages (rations, ammunition, and medical) limited the permissible period of contact with the enemy and necessitated immediate attack, which was abortive. Withdrawal was well conducted, and casualties, while severe, were not ruinous.

This superfiasco was Admiral Turner's swan song in the South Pacific. He assumed command of amphibious forces under Admiral Nimitz at Pearl Harbor, where, face to face with Gen. Holland M. "Howling Mad" Smith, USMC, he successfully fulfilled the role of "the navy's foremost landing admiral." In final tribute to Turner, let it be said that he was successful. He was a strong, bold, and daring leader but only as long as he remained within the area of his own competence—the overall naval aspects of an amphibious campaign.

Meanwhile, Carlson had been reorganized out of command of his old battalion. He was sorely missed by his men, who looked upon the organization of a Raider regiment as a device to deprive them of their commanding officer by assigning him upstairs as regimental executive officer on the staff of Col. Harry "The Horse" Liversedge. Liversedge was a giant of a man, a champion of the 1920 Olympic games, and a fine leader in his own way, which was not Carlson's. If this Byzantine maneuver was conducted to relieve Carlson of command, it gives a momentary glimpse of the dark side of the upper levels of the Marine Corps showing its inflexibility of thought and a compulsive suspicion of all things new and untried. Evans Carlson was worthy of more generous treatment than he received.

The advent of the helicopter as a substitute for John Mather's native carriers in the early postwar years gave us an unparalleled opportunity to give speed and muscle to Carlson's method of enveloping attack, an opportunity that we neglected and lost through a series of self-inflicted wounds. It can still be retrieved.

CHAPTER 13

"A Way You'll Never Be"

The threat to the eastern (left) flank of the perimeter was removed, we hoped permanently. But our response had been a stumbling performance from start to finish. Six battalions of infantry supported by aircraft and two battalions of artillery had defeated, but not destroyed, a bewildered, ill-prepared advance unit of a major Japanese landing force by a timely reaction on our part based on exact information provided by the code breakers at Pearl Harbor. Only by the intervention of Carlson's 2d Raider Battalion had the operation been turned into a complete success.

Everybody made mistakes. Orders miscarried. Communications failed. Execution was sluggish. It became apparent that we were running on an empty tank in more ways than one. The rations, never quite sufficient, improved but were always of poor quality. Loss of weight and strength continued through early November. For the first time the number of fall-outs from men unable to shoulder their packs became a significant factor in moving troops. At least 90 percent of the original force to land on Guadalcanal were suffering from malaria, suppressed but not prevented or cured by the Atabrine administered on a daily basis as a substitute for quinine. The secondary symptoms of the disease were apparent on nearly every countenance: yellow jaundice replacing healthy skin color and the same ghastly hue pervading the whites of the eyes. This was accompanied by anemia and frequent recurrence of periods of debilitating fever. Only life-threatening cases were evacuated to rear-area hospitals. The vast majority of cases, those who could stand on their feet and carry on, were treated and returned to duty. These are the medical statistics alone; they do not take into account the hundreds, less severely attacked, who never answered sick call at all but stoically bore their burden as just part of the cost of doing business on "The Canal."

There was little in the way of formal division of duties among the four sections of the division staff. As D-3, I performed certain D-4 (logistics) functions such as distribution of arms, ammunition, and defensive materials. Sometimes we all had a hand in decision making—not according to the book, of course, but it served the purpose of the moment.

On one such occasion I was more than happy to be left out of the loop. General Vandegrift had received a letter from a missionary located in the remote interior of Guadalcanal who had rescued a downed Japanese aviator. Although both injured and wounded, the pilot had somehow survived when his fighter crashed in the jungle. Well cared for by his rescuer, he began to recover. As the pilot gained strength, he became increasingly hostile, until the missionary felt threatened with the loss of his own life. What would the general recommend that he do? I was certainly happy not to take part in that decision. We all agreed that it was strictly a matter for personnel (D-1), Capt. James C. Murray, and the rest of us kept clear.

With the coming of the November rains, the Lunga Perimeter became a singularly unpleasant place to live. There was little shelter. Clothing and equipment molded. Thousands of unburied Japanese dead hidden in the dense jungle filled the air with a cloying, sickening odor, which even spread to our drinking water. The doctors assured us it was entirely free of pollutants, due to added chemicals and the purification process, but even in the heat of the jungle you had to be inordinately thirsty to drink it.

The rats came—big and fat. The ever resourceful Seabees brought in expert exterminators, who surprisingly soon got the upper hand in one of our few victories over nature. Everything possible was done to improve living conditions. And they did improve, although very slowly. The priorities of war had to be served—stocks of aviation gasoline (avgas), ammunition, defensive materials, medicine, and supplies took precedence in ships or planes over such things as tents, cots, and other organizational property, which were limited to occasional driblets. Other common supplies were simply nonexistent. Everybody griped but few complained; there is a difference.

It has been said that the siege is the rudest test of man. I can well believe it. Unlike a single great battle or even a campaign of many battles, there is no compensating interval of respite to recoup body and soul in a return to normalcy. The burden is always there, and its weight increases day by day even though the actual hazard at any given moment may not be particularly acute. It is a burden common to all those engaged, and no one who ever served throughout the lengthy Guadalcanal episode escaped it, at least to some degree or in some form. In many cases it left permanent psychological scars.

During the first days after the landing, our D-3 operations were conducted under the shelter of a Japanese canvas tarpaulin rigged on a frame made of poles cut from nearby trees. This held off the rain, but it was nearly impossible to operate there at night or while under air attack or naval bombardment. When we came back from our foxholes, it was often to find our place of business a shambles.

We got Japanese bamboo matting, rice bags, and shovels and started to build a shelter. All of us worked at it: Maj. Bill Buse, Capt. Ray Schwenke, and Sergeants Brant and Kuhn, assisted by Corporal Northrop, our jeep driver. The men stacked their rifles nearby, and I draped my pistol belt on top. We were joined by a second jeep driver, a new man whose name I never learned. He seemed a little bewildered and insecure but fell to with the rest of us, filling bags and stacking them in a crude revetment braced against the coral wall behind us. Midafternoon came, and we had built up the wall to a height of three feet.

The siren went off announcing Condition Red. A dirty little enemy cruiser plane came in at treetop level, sprayed us with slugs, and dropped a fifty-pound frag bomb within a few feet of our position. There was a heavy concussion, but nobody was hit. Our half-built sandbag wall had saved us. The new man, who had been sitting shoulder to shoulder with me, suddenly pitched forward, toppled to the ground, and started kicking and flailing his arms in spasm. Two navy medical corpsmen carried him away. He had come to us from a forward unit, where they thought he had been "slipping." The near miss pushed him the rest of the way. An act of intended humanity had backfired.

Our rifle stack had been blown to smithereens. We found a few small chunks of Springfield rifle barrels, chopped into two-inch lengths like sausage rounds, but there was not the slightest trace of my Colt .45. In 1935 I had used it to win first gold in the annual Marine Corps pistol match.

Few cases were as dramatic as this. Usually the victim simply became increasingly withdrawn and aloof, inattentive and preoccupied. This invariably resulted in a marked decline in effectiveness and performance of duty.

Combat fatigue was not entirely new to us. Long tours of duty overseas and in the tropics, even in peacetime, took their toll. We called the major symptom "the thousand-yard stare," and the person afflicted was described as "gone Asiatic" or said to have "missed too many boats" and was sent home.

First fully recognized in World War I, combat fatigue was given considerable attention. Sir B. H. Liddell Hart, an authoritative military writer of that conflict and an experienced participant therein, said that it appeared to him that the "sergeant major types" were particularly vulnerable. It did seem to us that what we would describe in the Corps as "squared-away" persons were more frequently hit. These were the exceptionally serious, orderly, self-disciplined individuals who do so much to maintain the standards of a peacetime force. Such men may find a special difficulty in adjusting to the exigencies of battle: the uproar, chaos, waste, destruction, and disorganization accompanying prolonged combat. To them these events ran counter to all the values they had ever known. Less rigid types, freer of the iron restraints of the peacetime military mold, found it easier to adapt. For example, a man like the irrepressible Sgt. William "Stinky" Davis, outgoing, voluble, and enthusiastically contributing to the effort of the moment, would never have to worry about combat fatigue.

Somewhere between these extremes lay the rest of us. Evening was the evil hour. All hands, tired and distraught by the alarms of the day, faced another night of uncertainty. Mistakes were made. Accidents occurred, sired by fatigue and the inability to concentrate.

In the command structure, "purple shadow" decisions were all too frequent. Two highly decorated and able officers, who had faced the enemy unshaken in bloody battles in two wars, committed their reserves at sunset in the face of no indication of any hostile presence or move. In one case the unit concerned lay in second line behind extensive wire barriers and with a strong friendly force to its front.

This forced General Vandegrift to issue orders placing a hold on the commitment of regimental reserves without authorization from division headquarters. Given a few hours' rest, a cup of coffee, and a can of C rations, these officers' mood of apprehension would pass. In desperate battle I had seen these same officers totally unaffected by surrounding circumstances of the most daunting character.

In another incident a battalion commander, an old friend, called me directly at two o'clock in the morning and asked for tank support. He believed the Japanese were moving down the Lunga along his right flank, actually using the river itself. It was during a torrential downpour, and the Lunga was in full spate. Commitment of tanks at that hour and that place was out of the question. I called the commander of a battalion occupying the adjoining position across the river. He told me there were no Japanese, just logs and snags washing down the boiling stream. The officer who asked for tank support had been engaged for three days of continuous fighting against a major Japanese force. He and his men had triumphed, but at the cost of a devastating physical and psychological fatigue that would take more than a good night's sleep to repair. These officers were outstanding beyond compare in their courage, leadership, and battle acumen. They were the best we had, and each proved it on every encounter with the Japanese enemy. Their feats are legendary; they will be remembered as long as the Corps exists. But there is a limit to human endurance, and some had nearly reached it.

Ernest Hemingway, himself seriously wounded in World War I, displays his understanding of and concern for psychological damage in his short story "A Way You'll Never Be." This tale is the classic account of the moral and mental deterioration that is the inevitable accompaniment of unreasonably long contact on a remote front with an unrelenting antagonist. My experience with an over-the-hill Marine was an uncanny reenactment, even to the stench, which lingered in the dugout for hours. Hemingway's text provides an excellent example of the psychological relationship to the siege mentality as set forth in this chapter. Guadalcanal's environment also brought on instances of psychological deterioration as diverse as Vandegrift's gloom and orders to prepare a plan to move up the Lunga to Butch Morgan's rage at his best friend. Anyone who served on Guadalcanal would understand what I am saying.

Late in the Guadalcanal campaign, two Marines, both in normal condition, brought in a third, describing him as a man missing from a patrol that had returned a few days earlier. He was in bad shape: ragged, gaunt, filthy, soaking wet, and smelling horribly of the dank, corpse-strewn battlefield where he had somehow existed for days. The man was lucid only to an extent but conveyed to me the message that he had located a Japanese battery of two guns on the lower northern slopes of Mt. Austen to our south. The guns were deserted, and he believed ammunition was buried nearby. This information checked with a suspected location, and the rest of the account was consistent with the strange Japanese practice of leaving their guns unguarded. I then asked if the breech mechanisms of the guns had been removed. My questions as to this particular detail seemed to disconcert him. I told him to go back to his organization and later called his company commander. The man had never checked in. He was eventually listed as "missing, presumed KIA." Much later and to my great sorrow I learned that he had apparently misinterpreted my questions about the breech mechanisms as a criticism of his performance of duty and had gone back to remove them.

With all this going on, I had made little or no progress on preparing a plan for withdrawal up the Lunga River, as earlier directed by General Vandegrift during the chaotic period characterized by Edson's famous stand on the Ridge that was to bear his name.[1]

However, one drizzly morning Jerry Thomas phoned and told me, "The Old Man is talking again about going up in the hills and falling on his sword. He's coming up to see you. For Chrissake, be careful about what you say." The sky was alive with scudding dark clouds. I didn't need Jerry's gloomy message. Besides, why was the general coming to see me instead of vice versa?

In a few minutes the general appeared, looking craggier than usual and wearing his grim, no-nonsense expression. He took me aside, saying, "I want you to prepare a plan for withdrawal up the Lunga using our amphibian tractors."

Apparently he had forgotten his 13th of September directive to Jerry up at Robbers' Roost. I didn't remind him of it.

He then issued peremptory orders to burn all of our classified files and all our other records except what could be carried in one mailbag. He stayed right there while Sgt. Bob Brant started a fire and we began the burn. Then he left with Captain Compton, USN, who had come to discuss matters connected with the newly established naval station on Guadalcanal. Sgt. Dick Kuhn got a mailbag from the sergeant major. I gave my two enlisted assistants a lame excuse about raising security levels, which forbade us to continue holding such materials in our shrapnel-torn, old field safe.

This burn, however justifiable at the time, represented a tremendous loss of historical material, especially in the case of our daily operational report to ComSoPac and his messages

1. See page 108.

to us. I particularly regretted the loss of Carlson's reports on his famous Guadalcanal raid.

When the old man left me after giving his instructions, I tried in vain to figure out what change in our circumstances had brought these desperate orders about. I knew of nothing alarming on the horizon to cause it and simply assumed he was privy to some highly classified eyes-only material that he could not divulge to me or even to Jerry, his chief of staff. I still don't know.

General Vandegrift had borne a deadening burden of responsibility and concern for too long. It was disheartening to witness the decline in the optimism that had sustained him throughout these months of travail. Admiral Halsey's assumption of command had given us all our first great hope, yet his was a stormy course as well, fraught with dismaying losses as well as triumphs at sea. There were moments of doubt along the way that all of us shared.

The idea of a withdrawal up the Lunga to a final defensive position was totally impractical, and my task seemed hopeless, but I was determined to give it a try. I inquired discretely among those who would have to be critically involved.

Martin Clemens had never been all the way up the Lunga, as I recall, but he indicated that the route would be rough going even for foot soldiers unless they were in extremely fine condition and carrying only light loads. Even his native scouts considered it a very difficult route, and already our Marines were beginning to show the weakening effects of malaria, suppressed only by their daily doses of Atabrine.

I had been on a short patrol up the river with Lt. Col. Bill Whaling early in the game. Once the Lunga approached the hills, it became a boulder-strewn mountain stream. Use of wheeled transport was out of the question. The only artillery that could accompany us were the 75mm pack howitzers broken down into their separate loads and carried by hand. Lt. Col. John Bemis indicated what I already knew: Moving the guns over long distances was a job for hardy mules, not exhausted men.

As for the LVTs, Lt. Col. Walter W. Barr, their commander, agreed that the best LVT yet made did not possess the all-terrain capability that would be required for the proposed route. Many of them had been used as improvised pontoons for bridging; others had been cannibalized for parts. Each had already been stripped of its five-machine-gun armament to provide a priceless augmentation of our firepower along the perimeter. General Vandegrift definitely knew the condition of these vehicles, for in early November he informed the commanding general of I Marine Amphibious Corps (IMAC), newly established at Noumea, that "as you know, the amphibian tractors are shot."[2]

Yet another circumstance militating against a successful withdrawal up the Lunga (if one were needed) was the fact that the river veered to the west into territory accessible to the enemy at all times and at every point. In fact the Japanese already dominated the area, although they did not have a strong military presence. This was the Big Bend country where Daniel Boone had spotted the smoke of many rice fires on the evening of 24 October.

The trail up the Tenaru, which was in use even during this time by Australian gold miners, did not suffer from this disadvantage. It was an easier and shorter route and had been improved by the miners. Furthermore, its distance to the east of Lunga Point offered the depth necessary for organizing the march into the hills. The Tenaru trail was relatively out of reach of the Japanese, whereas the Lunga route would become a veritable fire sleeve, with our slender column exposed to hostile observation and fire along every yard of its forlorn journey to oblivion.

The clincher, of course, was the fact that a withdrawal inland would cut us off from contact with our navy forces, thereby denying us any possibility of reinforcement, resupply, or even evacuation by sea. Such help would be a reasonable expectation if we could preserve contact and maintain

2. A. A. Vandegrift, *Once a Marine* (New York: Ballantine Books, 1964), p. 200.

ourselves as a credible fighting force still in being—a force that bolder souls than Ghormley might consider worth salvaging.

I therefore began work on an alternate plan involving a slow retrograde movement eastward along the coast. This plan permitted withdrawal through flat, easily traversable terrain, an important consideration in view of the deteriorating physical condition of the command. The same favorable terrain factors would allow full use of our wheeled transportation in moving artillery and supplies, enable employment of tanks and half tracks, and permit employment of the remaining LVTs on the type of terrain for which they had been designed. Some resupply by air could be continued by means of airdrop or even the possible construction of temporary dirt landing strips in the numerous large, open, grassy plains to the east. Last, but by no means least, would be the continued availability of our large boat pool, operated by Lieutenant Commander Dexter, Coast Guardsman turned navy turned Marine. It had already become a key element in our logistics and would be of great value in any movement along the coastal strip.

The actual tactical scheme envisioned in the alternative plan was the successive defense—as we fell back—of each of the major river lines running northward from the axial east-west spine of the island. No great obstacles in themselves, they nevertheless would require bridging by the Japanese to bring forward their artillery and wheeled transport. The rivers' chief value would be as unmistakable phase lines so vital to the control of a retrograde movement and the delivery of its supporting fires. We would occupy two river lines at a time, beginning with the Nalimbiu and the Metapona. Nalimbiu, the westernmost, would be held as a main line of resistance (MLR), supported by artillery from areas east of the Metapona.

Approximately half the infantry strength would be held as a general reserve east of the Metapona. This force would be assigned the missions of developing a reserve line, counterattacking promptly against any enemy attempt to envelop the north flank by a shore-to-shore amphibious operation, and,

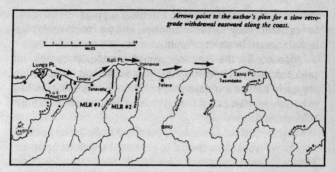

Arrows point to the author's plan for a slow retrograde withdrawal eastward along the coast.

Tentative plan of withdrawal from Lunga Point employing a series of delaying actions along each river to the east.

finally, moving against an enemy blocking force, should one be landed at a distance to the east.

When compelled to give up the MLR position on the Nalimbiu, the infantry force there would withdraw to the east supported by the Metapona position and proceed across the Balesuna (next river to the east) to take over the reserve role. In turn, the original reserve would become the MLR force along the Metapona and take over the front-line mission. This sequence would be repeated as we were driven to the east.

Optimistic? Yes. But this whole campaign had been conducted at every level largely on the basis of optimism alone. I still recalled that the JCS directive for the operation enjoined us to "be in New Britain, repeat New Britain, by 20 September."

This plan would be found fatally flawed if the Japanese could put a major force, particularly a fresh force, ashore to the east to block our line of withdrawal. We would then certainly have been caught between the proverbial rock and a hard place. But in our situation there was one luxury we could not afford—taking counsel of our fears.

In pursuing us, the Japanese would encounter major problems of their own. The physical condition of their soldiers had deteriorated markedly due to lack of an organized medical service and evacuation facilities. They had very little motor transport and almost no boats. Engineer support was virtually nonexistent. They had few supplies, and we (mistakenly) believed them to be short of ammunition.

Undoubtedly, the Japanese would rely almost entirely on captured material and supplies, just as we had done during our early half-ration days ashore. Therefore demolition had to be a major part of our plan. What could not be moved must be destroyed.

Movement would have to be confined to the hours of darkness as we would be exposed to continual attack from the air. This certainty of air attack added emphasis to the idea of demolition as a major element of this particular plan. Henderson Field would have to be destroyed to the maximum extent possible, perhaps using our own bombs or five-inch ammo for the purpose. Without engineering equipment, the enemy would be hard pressed to put it back in operational condition.

The general told no one about the instructions he gave me, and the subsequent tentative plan was never completed beyond a penciled outline in a notebook that I carried at all times—and in my mind. If that appalling moment ever arrived, it would then be necessary to call in the specialists of the 11th Marines, the 3d Defense Battalion, the 1st Engineer Battalion, the Seabees, the Motor Transport Battalion, the Boat Pool, and many other units that could contribute to, weigh the feasibility of, and build on the framework I proposed. This could not be done in advance under restrictions imposed by General Vandegrift due to the vital necessity of preventing even rumors that such a plan existed.

I believed that when push came to shove General Vandegrift would accept my plan as a more orderly and promising alternative than a hasty withdrawal to a final defensive position in the hills where no help could ever reach us. I intended to seek permission to initiate the active planning if and when we ever lost possession of the crossing at the mouth of the Matanikau, thereby permitting the enemy to place his artillery in positions commanding Lunga Point and interdicting Henderson Field. This never came about, thanks largely to Lieutenant Colonel McKelvy's 3d Battalion, 1st Marines.

Supported by the massive artillery fires of the 11th Marines, the 3d Battalion threw back a major tank-led attack across the sandbar on the night of 21 October, and the land battle for Guadalcanal was decided once and for all.

General Vandegrift, far more than the rest of us, labored under a terrific burden of responsibility heightened by doubt and misgivings. His apprehensions centered not upon the sincerity of those who now sought so desperately to intervene on our behalf but upon their ability to do so effectively before our time ran out.

General Geiger did not share these apprehensions to the same degree and seemed to appreciate my insistence that the division as a whole had never become totally engaged and in a final showdown remained capable of putting up a finish fight exceeding anything the Japanese had ever encountered. He would nod approvingly whenever I made this point. Any outright sign of approval from that old warrior was rare indeed.

As for the rest of us, we became largely a group of introverts, short tempered and unable to coordinate our activities as effectively as before. For example, a promising push across the Matanikau River had to be abandoned due to lack of truck fuel to support an advance past Kokumbona. We had been so concerned with maintaining our absolutely vital stock of avgas that we had failed to notice the increasing expenditure of lower octane fuel due to additional motor vehicles coming in with the reinforcements. This should never have happened.

Following this bungle, we began to suffer a series of small but damaging night intrusions by the Tokyo Express staging a revival of a threat we thought had been thwarted by our dive bombers. One such raid destroyed most of our field hospital, to the great distress of our wonderful division surgeon, Capt. Warwick Brown, USN. Brown, who had long ago been described to me as "a very determined man," now took a personal interest in the war, demanding explanations and action.

The Tokyo Express was the nickname that Marines and sailors gave to units of Japanese surface vessels, operating from Rabaul, New Britain, that normally arrived off Lunga Point after dark to bombard Henderson Field or bring supplies and reinforcements to Guadalcanal. These ships were usually fast and of various types and numbers depending upon their assignment.

Coast Watchers could normally see and report these enemy vessels as they sped southeast along their nearly 600-mile route. The southern half of this much-traveled beat was called the Slot, a body of water about fifty miles wide that entered south of Bougainville and extended through the Solomons chain to Guadalcanal.

Lt. Col. Al Cooley, USMC, commanding the bomber group, told me the Japanese were not coming directly down the Slot but approaching us circuitously from the north through an adjacent patrol sector that ComAirSoPac had not authorized our Cactus Air Force to enter. He volunteered to go up there with a strike force if I would give the word. True to his promise, the following night Cooley's SBD's (Douglas Dauntless) found their quarry and badly damaged a Japanese cruiser. For a few days we enjoyed comparatively peaceful nights, and Doctor Brown felt vindicated.

But that was not quite the end. A plane carrying Rear Adm. Aubrey W. Fitch, who had relieved Vice Adm. John S. McCain as ComAirSoPac, landed briefly at Henderson Field where Fitch admonished Vandegrift about our planes straying out of their sectors. Apparently our general was not greatly impressed. He never mentioned the matter either to Cooley or to me.

Everyone became nettlesome and irritable. Loss of perspective and proportion became manifest, and tempers flared up over trifles. All this was accompanied by a submergence of the English language and polite communication into a flood of foul speech born of months of deep frustration. One afternoon our D-2 (intelligence) officer, Lt. Col. Edmund J. "Buck" Buckley, and I, having engaged at length in some feckless dispute, decided to go down to Butch Morgan's galley and cool off over a cup of hot coffee. Butch and his striker, Shorty Mantay, were happy to oblige. As we sat there, we could hear Butch in his cook shack pounding away with his cleaver on God knows what for supper. Then we saw our police sergeant, Hook Moran, and his cleanup crew coming home after tidying up the usual mess caused by an air raid earlier in the day. Moran, soon to become a highly regarded sergeant major, had volunteered for the humble job because at the moment there was little need of clerical assistance on Guadalcanal. His crew consisted of a small group of very young Marines, boys in their early teens, who had somehow gotten by the recruiting sergeants in the first hectic days after Pearl Harbor. Jerry Thomas, from the depths of his recollection of another war and the dictates of a compassionate heart, had collected these "drummer boy" types who were simply too undeveloped physically for arduous and prolonged frontline duty despite their eagerness to serve.

As they straggled past, Butch leaned out and shouted at his old friend Hook, "Ya, ya, ya, here comes Snow White and his seven 'dwuffs'!"

Unshaken by his tormentor, Moran, who then sported a neatly trimmed Vandyke on his square jaw, turned his head and responded, "Hi, how ya doin', Bubbles?"

I know not the connotation of the word "Bubbles," but the effect was terrific. Cleaver in hand and in a sudden paroxysm of merciless rage, Butch came back with something that began, "Hook Moran, you piss-whiskered billy goat, one more crack like that and I'm comin' through this screen and sock this here cleaver right between your horns. You . . ."

Buck and I looked at each other and shrugged. Not to worry; it was just a couple of old friends engaging in some idle chaff on a quiet Guadalcanal afternoon. We finished our coffee and, having buried our own hatchet, went our separate ways.

CHAPTER 14

Decisive November

After the Koli Point affair and Carlson's raid, the tempo of ground fighting moderated during the crucial month of November. The war shifted abruptly to a series of battles fought at sea and in the skies by the major forces of the antagonists. On the ground the decision was to maintain a cautious and continuous threat west of the Matanikau while strengthening the perimeter against the possibility of a disastrous turn in our fortunes that would permit the enemy to land and support fresh forces in strength sufficient to overwhelm us.

The defeat of the Sendai Division and in particular the humiliation inflicted on its premier regiment, the 29th Infantry, had aroused their fury and had reinforced their determination to destroy us. We could feel the heat and hoped that the Japaneses' ungovernable passion for revenge would lead to their undoing.

Operations west of the Matanikau River were conducted largely by newly arrived forces, principally the 6th Marines and the 164th Infantry of the Americal Division. These were useful efforts of limited active defense designed to cover the development of the forward battle position along the right (east) bank of the river.

The first of these met with considerable success but was halted when General Vandegrift received information of an impending large-scale enemy reinforcement effort launched from Rabaul. It was considered necessary to pull all forces back to the east of the Matanikau River to insure the operational integrity of Henderson Field during what promised to be the decisive air and naval phase of the campaign. This was

completed on 11 November by a daylight withdrawal made
under little or no enemy pressure. It was not particularly well
executed and involved the loss of some of our heavy weapons
for no apparent reason. This was something new to us, and
Jerry Thomas instructed me not to say anything about it to
upset the general. It was a shocking experience. I believe the
weapons were eventually recovered.

The predicted attack came quickly and in great force. The
next few days were a confused melee of fighting at sea and in
the air. The weather favored the Japanese with a series of
heavy downpours that at times made Henderson Field totally
inoperable due to flooding, particularly the fighter strip. In
addition, there was a continuing enemy effort to knock the
field out of operation by bombardment in order to prevent air
attack on the large approaching transport convoy carrying the
Japanese 38th Infantry Division down from Rabaul. For a
few days the "unsinkable carrier," Henderson Field, and its
Cactus Air Force were the center of world-wide attention.
These airmen knew the hour had come, and they hit hard with
everything they had. Losses of pilots and planes were staggering. Admiral Fitch, ComAirSoPac, comprehended the
threat and gleaned replacements from all over the South Pacific. Marine squadrons arrived from Espiritu Santo, and
eight AAF P-38s flew in from Milne Bay, New Guinea. Offshore the surface navy battled desperately and successfully
day and night to prevent destruction of the field, its planes,
and installations by enemy naval gunfire bombardment.

Along the way our navy suffered losses such as no navy in
modern times has had to endure both in ships and in men, including two outstanding flag officers, Rear Adm. Norman
Scott and Daniel Callaghan. On our part there was full realization that in the final analysis we ashore in the Lunga
Perimeter were the personal beneficiaries of these events. It
was an awesome and inspiring experience. The Japanese had
exhausted their previous run of good luck. On one night they
came in with common or bombardment shells in the trays at
the guns; our navy replied with armor-piercing projectiles, to
the great discomfiture of the Japanese. On the next occasion

the enemy did not repeat their error, but the weather intervened on our behalf. The continuous tropical downpour so softened the soil beneath the Marston matting on the runways that for the most part the Japanese armor piercing projectiles failed to explode. Possibly they are still there.

At the operations center we carefully followed the TBS (talk between ships) radio transmissions during these actions. I vividly recall the night of 14 November, when Adm. Willis A. "Big Ching" Lee's Task Force 64 passed Lunga Point en route to his victory over Admiral Kondo. Unsure of us and worried about attack by our own then-inexperienced PT boats, his flagship resorted to a blaring boom-box singsong chant over his TBS as they approached Lunga Point. It went something like this: "This is Big Ching Lee, Big Ching Lee coming through fast. Don't shoot at me, little PT boats. This is Big Ching Lee, Big Ching Lee, and I'm . . ."

Not in the signal manual exactly, but it worked, and Lee went on to sink *Kirishima*, the second battleship kill of the week. Henderson Field was not bombarded that night. During that week of desperate night battles there was little we could do to help. Lieutenant Commander Dexter's boat pool swept Ironbottom Sound each dawn to pick up survivors and fight off the sharks. A few of the wounded were rescued, then treated in our field hospital before evacuation by air to Espiritu Santo. Floating bodies were recovered and buried in our division cemetery.

Our shore batteries, manned by 3d Defense Battalion, participated to the extent offered by fleeting opportunities. In one instance they inflicted three quick hits on an enemy destroyer before her skipper took Nelson's advice: "A ship's a fool to fight a fort," and hauled out of range.

Our frustration found relief—for one night at least—in an unusual way. A warrant officer, highly skilled in the technical aspects of communications, came into our shelter to make some minor repairs to our equipment. It was early evening and a Japanese flotilla on a Tokyo Express mission was approaching Lunga Point. Our visitor offered to give us a demonstration of the techniques of interfering with enemy communications by jamming. The term sounded like some heavy-handed electronic method of keeping the enemy off the air with a continuous deafening electronic blast. But it was nothing as crude as that, we were promptly informed. Such a performance would interdict our own communications as well. Carefully he tuned in on a two-ship conversation, then selected one ship as his target. Each time it attempted to reply to the other, he would interfere with a faint signal just strong enough to prevent clear reception. There would then follow a polite, routine discussion between operators conscientiously seeking to eliminate the interference. With fiendish glee our man would lean back and laugh, then come in again, laying the interference on stronger than ever. This procedure continued for some minutes, soon leading the two Japanese radiomen from proper technical corrective phraseology to raised voices. Eventually, violent recriminatory outbursts filled the air. Although we couldn't understand the words, their tone conveyed all the meaning we needed. Our mentor would then search for two new "victims" to terrorize. It was better theater than Tokyo Rose.

During this same period we had another strange experience in the field of TBS radio communications. At sunset we began intercepting fragments of a ship-to-shore communication we couldn't account for involving a landing operation. The voices were distinctly American, and they grew clearer and louder as the evening progressed. No such operation was taking place anywhere in the Solomons, and we were at a loss, for TBS is a short-range radio system. Someone suggested it was a beach jumper record being tested on us at Guadalcanal. Beach jumping was a proposed method of deception by using radio broadcasts of records of a simulated operation to make the enemy believe we were landing at a false location. This could be accomplished by a small raider-type group landing from a submarine and was seriously considered at one time.

We later discovered that we had been listening to a freak or skipping TBS conversation occurring during a rehearsal landing being conducted at Espiritu Santo, hundreds of miles away, by U.S. Army forces preparing to come to Guadalcanal.

The two night naval battles of November 13–14 and 14–15 put an end to the series of devastating bombardments of Henderson Field. On 14 and 15 November the Cactus Air Force of army, navy, and Marine Corps planes had their most memorable days, first in defeating and then in destroying the largest reinforcing operation ever launched against Guadalcanal. Eleven Japanese merchant ships, crowded with thousands of soldiers and escorted by eleven cruisers and destroyers, were subjected to an overwhelming air attack while still distant from their objective. Adm. Gunichi Mikawa recalled the ships of the naval escort and ordered them to safety. The unarmed merchant ships were kept on their course and sent on a hopeless saltwater banzai charge toward the beaches near Doma Cove.

General Vandegrift was observing activities unobtrusively from the edge of Henderson Field. I had accompanied him. The new Cactus Air Force commander, Brig. Gen. Louis Woods, USMC, came by, explained the developing situation, and asked, "Who do we go for, the cruisers or the transports?" The general's unhesitating reply may not have been in accord with the dictates of Adm. Alfred Thayer Mahan, but as usual it was sensible: "The transports."

The experience was sickening to those of our flyers who participated in the unavoidable slaughter that followed. Only five of the merchant ships made it to Guadalcanal, where they were deliberately grounded on the beach only to become the targets of our ships, planes, and shore-based artillery. It was a ghastly business with little profit to the enemy, who had landed only 2,000 men—many wounded and without weapons—200 bags of rice, and a small amount of ammunition. It was the final curtain of the Japanese effort to recapture Guadalcanal.

CHAPTER 15

Closing Out

On 16 November we received word from Adm. Kelly Turner that the 1st Division would be relieved by U.S. Army forces at an early date. Battalions were to be relieved in the order of their arrival in Guadalcanal proper. 2d Marines (less 3d Battalion) would go out after the 1st Division regiments because it was in better physical condition due to its less arduous service on Tulagi prior to 1 November, when it crossed over to Guadalcanal. However, the battle-tested 3d Battalion, 2d Marines, which had been on Guadalcanal almost from the beginning, was to be evacuated to New Zealand at the same time the 1st Division left for Australia. First Raiders and survivors of the 1st Parachute Battalion had already been taken out.

Army replacements poured in, and preparations for the takeover went smoothly. Marines, who habitually live out of their packs, wondered what the soldiers kept in those big blue barracks bags they brought along. We noted that the soldiers still had no combat uniforms and no field shoes. A few wore one-piece coveralls, which is about as poor a combat uniform as can be imagined. This gave rise to a scatological little ditty:

> U.S. Marines what a blessing.
> We can crap without undressing.

They were otherwise well armed, well equipped, and well trained. No rifle grenade had as yet been made to use with their new M-1 rifles, and they soon realized that in jungle warfare some support weapon is still needed even in units as small as the rifle squad. We expected to get M-1s in Australia, so we gave them 800 Springfields complete with *tromblons*. These are bell-shaped devices that fit over the muzzle of a service rifle to hold a grenade in place when firing and give a degree of initial guidance to the grenade's trajectory, the impetus being supplied by a blank rifle cartridge. We also included our remaining stocks of rifle grenades. Men always wanted these grenades. In the hands of an experienced man, they could be fired with remarkable accuracy up to 300 yards. Just as our last transport was leaving Lunga, an army boat went alongside and asked for 800 bayonets to go with the rifles. The bayonets were dropped into the boat, but Marines are still wondering how a soldier with a *tromblon* on the end of his rifle can use a bayonet.

Wearing a Marine Corps field uniform, Maj. Gen. Alexander M. Patch, U.S. Army, and the rest of his Americal (American-New Caledonian) Division staff arrived on Guadalcanal on 19 November but did not immediately take over. Patch gave me a sharp look when we met, no doubt recalling our prior meeting in Noumea, when he had instructed me to inform General Vandegrift not to expect any help from the Americal Division in connection with the forthcoming Guadalcanal operation.

His staff appeared competent and well organized. The army usually had admirable staffing. Unlike the army, which regarded staff duty as a prize assignment and the route to promotion, the Marine Corps regarded troop duty as far preferable, and people like my old friend Chesty Puller always referred to those of us on the staff as "paper shufflers" or "potted palms." Patch had an excellent staff and used it to advantage.

From the beginning there had existed a strange divergence between the army and Marine Corps viewpoints on overall strategy, and it now became critical. Our first army visitor, Maj. Gen. Millard F. Harmon, commander of U.S. Army Forces, South Pacific, insisted that Mt. Austen to the south of the perimeter was the key terrain feature, dominated the area, and should be held in strength. In a way he was right. Its possession would have been crucial to two field armies slugging it out in its very shadow and equipped with every engine of war from bulldozers to eight-inch artillery. But for a bobtailed, two-regiment Marine division and the enemy as well, it was "off the battlefield" and of slight practical significance to either side.

No doctrinaire soldier but an experienced banana war campaigner, General Vandegrift had reached that conclusion at exactly twenty seconds after sunrise on 7 August, when, standing on the deck of *McCawley*, he exclaimed, "Good God, Jerry, can that be Mister Widdy's grassy knoll? Change the objective to the airfield and tell Cates to reorganize there."

That had been the first order of the campaign, and under the circumstances, it was a remarkably prescient one.

Mt. Austen was a huge, nightmare hunk of fantastic terrain. All the navy's Seabees could never have built a road to its forward crest overlooking Lunga Point. Both sides sent periodic patrols across its slopes. Carlson's 2d Raiders had their last contact near the crest, but they did not linger. Mt. Austen afforded an excellent view of our activities, but the inadequacy of Japanese field radio prevented them from establishing reliable communications, as was evidenced by the total lack of coordination of their attacks on our perimeter and their inability to interdict Henderson Field with artillery.

The Japanese used the northwest slopes of the mountain as a dishonorable banishing ground for failed units, which in accordance with the Samurai code should never be permitted to rejoin the ranks of those undefiled by defeat. There were numerous such groups scattered over the area. Suffering and starving, they received occasional rice but no medical support. The smaller posts were soon overrun and plundered by our native patrols. In some cases the natives would first cut the enemy off from where their arms were stored and then "deal" with them using clubs and stones instead of weapons in order not to reveal their own presence to nearby troops. The resultant accumulation of Japanese weapons in the hands of native civilians proved worrisome to both Martin Clemens and John Mather, but it was unavoidable.

The largest and strongest of these Japanese contingents

held a strong point known as Gifu. It was established and operated by our old friend Colonel Oka, who had suffered complete loss of face. Why the Japanese called it Gifu remains unknown. One theory prevalent at the time was that the real Gifu, a somewhat remote and minor prefecture in Northern Japan, had its name used as a reflection of Japanese humor in the same sense that Americans sometimes use the word *Siberia*.

The army decided to clear these areas out before starting their final drive to the west. Successful in mopping up the smaller spots, they met determined resistance when confronting Gifu. It was eventually overrun, but at a heavy cost. Oka's fate is not known, but he was a great survivor. A Colonel Oka was present on Saipan later in the war, but no one knows whether or not it was the same officer.

These events delayed the main attack until 16 January 1943, long after we had left the island for Australia, but the question remains unanswered: Was this Mt. Austen force a sufficient threat to U.S. operations to warrant the loss of life and the long delay involved? Theoretically these Japanese did offer a threat to our major force advancing westward along the coast, but as a practical matter these isolated groups were composed of sick and starving men unable to do anything more than die in place. In one case a Japanese platoon at Gifu that heard our broadcast urging them to surrender decided they were too ill and weak even to walk to the American lines.

Under the circumstances disclosed by subsequent events, it is obvious that Mt. Austen was just part of the scenery and of no significant import to either of the antagonists. In this context General Vandegrift had again displayed a masterful capacity for correctly gauging the event itself uninfluenced by textbook theory, but to the army it remained an article of faith.

Nothing of particular importance occurred in the ground fighting during this period of overlapping command, for on 23 November, General Vandegrift decided to halt our push to the west and hold what we had. This decision was based on the necessity to shuffle army and Marine units in preparation for our departure and because intelligence sources still reported planned movements of Japanese sea and land forces.

November 28, 1942, was my fortieth birthday, and I received two presents. Both were from the decoding of Japanese messages. One was a Japanese 17th army message directing establishment of a large encampment at Numa Numa, a remote spot on the east coast of Bougainville, for the cantonment of "forces evacuated from Guadalcanal." This was definite indication that, at the 17th army level at least, the decision to accept defeat had been made. Numa Numa appeared to be an ideally remote location for the establishment of a huge Gifu for what remained of their 2d (Sendai) and 18th divisions. Withdrawal would require an imperial rescript and other time-consuming paperwork, but obviously General Hyakutake had accepted defeat and was taking time by the forelock in an attempt to salvage as much of his defeated force as possible.

The second of the two messages received on my birthday reminded us that the war at sea was far from over. It warned us that an enemy force of ten destroyers bent on a resupply mission would reach Doma Cove, northwest of Kokumbona, at 2230 on 30 November. The good news was that a U.S. Navy task force was being ordered to intercept the enemy.

Acting on this unusually precise information, I asked Brig. Gen. Pedro del Valle, 11th Marines (Artillery), to move a 155mm gun battery to a site in the Matanikau area to be in position to pick off any disabled ships that might be within their range at daylight. Don Pedro complained bitterly as usual but complied and later became so intrigued with the idea that he left the guns there permanently.

A small observation post adjacent to the division command post provided a good view of the Doma Cove area, and I watched from there. The forces made contact almost exactly on schedule. There was no illumination and exceptionally little naval gunfire. Then the action ceased. It was totally unlike the desperate night battles I had witnessed before. I was mystified and dumbfounded.

Activity of some sort continued into the night, and it was

apparent that there were ships off Lunga Point. But whose? Nobody had any information, and none of the ships replied to our signals. We began to hear fragmentary intercepts in English talking of "torpedo hits" and "hull damage."

The right flank of Col. Red Mike Edson's 5th Marines rested on the beach about 1,000 yards south of Kukum, and the observation post there sighted an unidentified ship. At 0200 Edson reported "our right flank observation post has spotted an enemy transport off Lunga disembarking troops into landing boats" and called for fire from our five-inch seacoast battery position on Lunga Point. I refused and continued my own efforts to ascertain what was going on out there. Then I learned that the "enemy transport" was our heavy cruiser *Minneapolis* (CA-36). She had taken a crippling torpedo hit, and the crew was trying to get her to the safety of Tulagi Harbour. The "landing boats" were small naval and Coast Guard craft clustered around her in an attempt to keep her on a course toward Tulagi. She either ignored our signals or was unable to make a light.

Minneapolis finally made it to Tulagi. The heavy cruisers *Northampton* (CA-26), *Pensacola* (CA-24), and *New Orleans* (CA-32) were also hit by torpedoes. *Northampton* sank. This substantial damage was a severe blow. Three of the four cruisers hit were eventually repaired, but for the time being they were out of the war. The Japanese lost one destroyer, the *Takanami*.

How could this occur? The Japanese Long Lance torpedoes were far more powerful and reliable than any of ours, and on this occasion they were fired with a high degree of skill and fantastic luck. We ashore could take consolation only in the fact that we had not, by rash action, added tragedy to the misfortunes of the night. Edson never completely forgave me for being right.

Hyakutake conducted a masterful delaying operation, and although he was attacked along the coast from two sides by U.S. Army and Marine units, he successfully evacuated his entire force of 11,000 men. For once there appears to have been remarkably close cooperation between the Japanese

army and naval forces in successive night evacuations using
destroyers as high speed transports.

The general wanted to leave a final message. I had noticed
the broadening in his point of view over the long months
of unending struggle. We were all in this together. There was
no room in his mind for petty, parochial, interservice strife.
For example, an Army Air Corps B-17 from Espiritu Santo
scored a damaging hit on an enemy destroyer. General Vandegrift was a witness. In their daily summary the Cactus Air
Force credited the hit to someone else. The general was out-
raged and had the dispatch cancelled, corrected, and retrans-
mitted. He was a fair man and insisted on equitable treatment
in every respect. These qualities made him a respected and
successful commander of a complex and ill-ordered, all-service
force of fighting men.

His farewell statement issued on 7 December was written
to reflect these views.

> In relinquishing command in the Cactus Area I hope
> that in some small measure I can convey to you my feeling
> of pride in your magnificent accomplishments and my
> thanks for the unbounded loyalty, limitless self-sacrifice
> and high courage which have made those accomplish-
> ments possible. To the soldiers and Marines who have
> faced the enemy in the fierceness of night combat; to the
> Cactus pilots, Army, Navy, and Marine whose unbeliev-
> able achievements have made the name "Guadalcanal" a
> synonym for death and disaster in the language of our
> enemy; to those who have labored and sweated within the
> lines at all manner of prodigious and vital tasks; to the men
> of the torpedo boat command slashing at the enemy in
> night sorties; to our small band of devoted allies who have
> contributed so vastly in proportion to their numbers; to the
> surface forces of the Navy associated with us in signal tri-
> umphs of their own, I say that at all times and in all places
> you have faced without flinching the worst that the enemy
> could do to us and have thrown back the best that he could
> send against us. It may well be that this modest operation

begun four months ago has, through your efforts, been successful in thwarting the larger aims of our enemy in the Pacific. The fight for the Solomons is not yet won but "tide what may" I know that you, as brave men and men of good will, will hold your heads high and prevail in the future, as you have in the past.

The actual change of operational command occurred about 1100 on 9 December 1942. Earlier in the morning Generals Vandegrift and Patch had left the perimeter to see a newly arrived National Guard regiment move into a defensive position down at the Matanikau. There was a little random rifle fire up ahead, and the advancing column instinctively "hit the grit"—and stayed there. This is just the moment when you need sergeants with number 12 combat boots to get things going again. There were none. One soldier even threatened to write his congressman.

General Patch was incensed. General Vandegrift, embarrassed, departed the scene. He took this opportunity to walk to our simple cemetery and bid farewell of the nearly 700 men and officers buried there.

Patch was still boiling two hours later when he entered the operations tent. He was looking for a dog to kick, and I was the victim. He strode over to my situation map, the beat-up homemade affair that had been pored over and studied by Admirals McCain, Turner, Halsey, and Nimitz, and shouted to my relief, "Surely we can do something better than this!" With that he put his stick under my map and flipped it off the plywood board.

My relief, who had been standing there holding something behind his back, stepped smartly forward and unrolled a beautiful map of Guadalcanal, something we had dreamed of but never expected to see. It was a copy of the map the army engineers had made for us in Australia, which had been "lost" en route to Auckland before the Guadalcanal operation began. How many of our Marines died or were wounded because we didn't have that map? We appreciated those 800 cavalry sabers the army sent us to use as machetes, but a half dozen copies of that map would have been priceless.

I picked up the pieces of my old map (I left the thumb-tacks) and departed, but not before hearing my relief launch into an impassioned harangue to his assembled henchmen, beginning with the exhortation: "If we are to avoid the mistakes of our predecessors we must . . ." Sure, we had made mistakes, but Old George had taken and held Guadalcanal and had shown a touch of class along the way, something quite unknown to our successors.

The whole stupid business put me in mind of Gen. U. S. Grant's story of the youthful Spartan warrior returning home from his first battle bearing the arm of a dead Persian on his shield. His veteran father asked, "Why did you not bring back your enemy's head instead of his arm?" The unthinking youth replied, "Because someone had cut that off before me."

The next two days were spent in an orgy of catch-up paper-work, reports, citations, recommendations, field promotions, and the like. I think everyone got some form of recognition. I recommended my two sergeants, Brant and Kuhn, for field appointments as second lieutenants. Jerry Thomas knew and admired both of these young men and gave my recommendation a fair wind. Both served throughout the war, went to college, qualified for regular commissions, and enjoyed full careers in the Corps. Kuhn retired as a lieutenant colonel. Brant became a colonel and eventually served as chief of staff of the 1st Marine Division.

Bill Buse and Ray Schwenke, my able assistants, served full careers, and Buse became a general officer. My jeep driver, Northrop, became a combat correspondent and reached high noncommissioned rank before leaving the Corps. They were a fine group and more than deserved the recognition they received for their superb performance of duty.

The night of 10 December we even had a social occasion. Brigadier General Rupertus invited us to supper at his command post on the beach at Block Four outside the old perimeter. No cocktails, of course. But in the beautiful beach environment we had, of all things, a concert by the 7th Marines band, which just a month before had been carrying wounded for twenty-four hours down the rocky slopes of Hanneken's Ridge during the two-day fight with Colonel Oka. The band had suffered several casualties but the resourceful bandmaster had fleshed it out for this occasion with volunteers. They played "shipping over music," as Marines call it, and we all enjoyed these triumphant compositions immensely.

After supper we went into the matter of a 1st Division shoulder patch, which General Vandegrift wanted because he knew we would have to wear U.S. Army or Australian uniforms, at least temporarily, as we had none of our own. I had been designated for the chore, and I brought along some excellent sketches made by Lt. Don Dickson, a former art editor of our monthly magazine, *The Leatherneck*. Unfortunately all these designs depicted classified code words pertaining "to the Guadalcanal operation, words such as "Lone Wolf," "Cactus," and "Watchtower." It was therefore thought best not to use any of these despite their artistic merit.

General Rupertus suggested a simple shoulder strip, bearing the word "Guadalcanal," a device commonly used by the British, but General Vandegrift, who for some reason disliked shoulder strips, disapproved. I'd have to come up with a bright idea before we reached Australia. Over a year later General Rupertus, who then commanded the division, authorized such a strip for the Cape Gloucester operation in New Britain. An unrelenting Vandegrift, now commandant of the Marine Corps, told him to "get rid of it."

That night a steady rain set in. We began to worry. The right combination of bad weather and flooded runways could give the Japanese another clear chance. Lt. Col. Thomas F. "Muggs" Riley, USMC, and his 1st Aviation Engineer Battalion had come in on 1 December. Jerry Thomas instructed me to keep them working under division control until adequate drainage had been provided for fighter strip one, which was most subject to flooding. They were working hard at the task.

This strip was the first of several we eventually completed. We simply called it "the fighter strip" to distinguish it from the main runway. When we completed an additional strip near the beach on the other side of Lunga, we had to number them one and two to avoid confusion leading to accidents.

Our last full day on the island was 12 December, and it was still raining. There seemed to be no limit to the paperwork— we were totally unused to it. Sometime after midnight I put on my only pair of starched and pressed khaki trousers— saved for months for the trip out. I had to go to the general's tent, where he was waiting to sign a recommendation for an award to Col. Bryant Moore, U.S. Army, who had commanded the 164th Infantry.

It was still raining. The ground was flooded. This familiar area was darker than a tomb. I tripped over the root of a banyan tree and fell headlong into a puddle. I spent most of the rest of the night scrubbing my pants in a bucket of freshly caught rain-water. They were still damp when we got to Noumea the next day. Colonel Moore received his well-deserved citation.

After daylight on the morning of 13 December I rode to the airfield with Jerry Thomas. We stopped at the fighter strip and looked around; despite the rain, for the first time it was dry and operable. Jerry remarked, "If the Japs come down today, they'll get a rough reception. Muggs Riley has done a fine job. Now he can build all the showers and shacks the fly-fly boys can use."

As our plane to Noumea lifted off Henderson Field, we looked down on the "unsinkable carrier" that had turned the tide. We had prevailed. The Japanese would never advance again. Above and beyond that, the long battle for Guadalcanal had defined the war in the Pacific and set the pattern for victory—joint action by and between all forces at all times and in all places.

CHAPTER 16

Australian Interlude

The trip from Noumea to Brisbane, Australia, by Qantas Airlines was very pleasant. General Vandegrift seemed unusually affable and "visited" up and down the aisle. Worried about the matter of the 1st Division shoulder patch, I was doodling with a lead pencil on the fly leaf of an old notebook when I was surprised to find him looking over my shoulder. He took a close look at it and, in his very small handwriting, initialed it with an "AAV." Handing it back, he said, "Now, get it done," and moved on to the front of the plane.

We were well received by the U.S. Army in Australia. The working staff was very interested in what we had to say and in turn showed us things we knew little or nothing about. These included samples of their new field uniform made of camouflage material and modern weapons including the M-1 carbine. This carbine would largely replace the Colt .45 carried by officers and senior NCOs in forward areas and give them substantial firepower in emergency situations. There would be no difficulty in rearming the division with the latest weapons from M-1 rifles to Sherman tanks.

A complete replacement of all items of uniform clothing and equipment was utterly essential. The wear-and-tear of jungle fighting had reduced the Marine herringbone twill field uniforms to unsightly rags. Shoes were destroyed by wear, water, and tropical mold. Items of web equipment had suffered equally. Only the battered metal helmets had survived the six-month ordeal. We were supplied with U.S. Army dress shoes plus khaki shirts and trousers. The Australian Army provided dark green woolen jackets, similar to our own Marine Corps winter uniforms.

General Vandegrift and senior staff officers were billeted at Lennons Hotel in downtown Brisbane, an exceptionally pleasant place. General MacArthur and his family had a large apartment on the upper floor. We often encountered their small son playing on the staircase or accompanying his Chinese amah to the park across the street. General MacArthur was in Port Moresby, New Guinea, at the time, and General Vandegrift reported to him there.

Only two of our regiments, 5th Marines (Edson), and 11th Marines (del Valle), our artillery regiment, had reached Brisbane. They were assigned to Camp Cable, a vacant Australian cantonment forty-five miles from Brisbane. It was far from being a desirable place to rehabilitate a division fresh from the devastating trauma of Guadalcanal. Facilities were scant and of the most primitive sort. The surroundings were depressing. Limited transportation would allow only brief six-hour "liberty" visits to Brisbane for not more than 500 men per day, and there were no adequate training facilities anywhere within practical reach of those who would need them.

We moved in at once, completing most of the operation at night. To everybody's sorrow we had one casualty, the well-known and well-liked Stinky Davis. Having survived bullets, bombs, bayonets, and malaria on Guadalcanal, he was struck by a truck while making camp in the dark. Badly injured, he recovered and was at the top of his form again on Tinian and Okinawa.

The camp was situated in an area infested with malaria-bearing anopheles mosquitoes, making it utterly unacceptable for troops already infected with the disease. Even the new replacements began to contract malaria during the few weeks we were there.

Our division surgeon, Captain Brown, again lived up to his well-deserved reputation for being a very determined man. He proved his case concerning the unsuitability of this region beyond contradiction and was soon joined by the local health authorities, who had not been made aware how prevalent malaria was in the newly arrived 1st Marine Division.

On 27 December I was ordered to proceed to South Australia, an area of more temperate climate, to find a malaria-free area suitable for the rehabilitation of the division. I was accompanied by Col. Harrison Heiberg, Corps of Engineers, U. S. Army, an outstanding graduate of West Point. He was most helpful, for he knew Australia and understood our numerous problems.

We visited Sydney. Like Brisbane, it was overcrowded with military personnel and unfriendly. It was the home of a vast U.S. logistics establishment of a size obviously far exceeding the present requirements of our small army in the Southwest Pacific. The headquarters was established in a great skyscraper in downtown Sydney. I noted that an entire floor was devoted to handling paperwork connected with artillery camouflage nets.

This swollen bureaucracy was commanded by a Colonel Marshall, a relative of Gen. George Catlett Marshall. He informed us—somewhat icily—that they were not willing to do anything for us. So we proceeded to Melbourne.

This beautiful city was now somewhat out of the war, for only a small U.S. military presence remained after General MacArthur moved his headquarters north to Brisbane. Melbourne was located around an extensive harbor that afforded protected areas and beaches appropriate for amphibious training. Also nearby were other areas suitable for training and maneuver. In addition, there was a brand-new hospital manned by an American unit from Cleveland, Ohio. They had everything except patients. The 1st Marine Division could provide plenty of those. Best of all, the people here would be glad to see us.

I had come off Atabrine when we left Guadalcanal, and the fever returned, as I expected it would. I spent New Year's Day in bed at the Australia Hotel. Next day we scoured the area and produced a billeting plan. The 7th Marines (Sims) would go to Balcombe, a suburban area on the bay, while Edson's 5th Marines moved into adjacent Mount Martha. Small camps, which we could quickly expand with our own resources, already existed at both places. The 1st Marines (Whaling) would be billeted in central Melbourne at the cricket grounds using the huge grandstand as a semiprotected barracks. It was a strange arrangement, but it proved highly successful. The men liked the location because it gave them a head start in crashing the gate with the local girls. The 11th Marine Artillery (del Valle) went to Ballarat, a small city twenty-five miles from Melbourne. They liked it so well that some Marines came back and settled down there after the war. To this day there is a small chapter of the 1st Marine Division Association in existence in Melbourne.

The 7th Marines were the last of our regiments to reach Australia. They came directly to Melbourne. I met them at the dock and was shocked at their condition. A single month of good living in Australia had made us forget that only a short time before we also looked like that. It was necessary to station men along and at the foot of the accommodation ladder to assist the disembarking Marines, some of whom, under the weight of their packs and equipment, were unable to decelerate as they came down the steeply slanting gangway. Plenty of milk and a few days on "styke and aigs" would cure all that. The Melbourne paper restrainedly remarked that "the newly arrived troops did not look especially fit." For the Marines, Melbourne was the single pleasant experience of a long war that for Old George did not end until 1947 in North China.

Our first step in rehabilitating the division was to get them well again. This seemed easy to accomplish in our pleasant new surroundings, but as Marines were taken off the routine dose of Atabrine, malaria recurred in an alarming number of cases and in a peculiarly virulent form. It would strike without warning. A Marine on liberty walking down a pleasant city street would suddenly fall flat, a delayed casualty of Guadalcanal. Malaria attacks were sometimes accompanied by amnesia or other complications. The large hospital in Melbourne operated by the Cleveland Medical Unit was filled to capacity, and the excellent Australian medical service found beds for hundreds more in other cities as far away as Perth. Maj. Jim Murray, our very active and conscientious D-1 (personnel officer), was at his wit's end trying to maintain an accounting of this dispersion of the division's members. Eventually all personnel returned, and this strange portion of the division's history came to a close.

How many cases of malaria did the 1st Division suffer? Captain Brown reported a 75 percent admission rate, but this takes no account of thousands who never sought treatment. I personally remember only one noncasualty in the entire division headquarters group: General Vandegrift, the old coconut warrior. The mosquitoes had given up on him years ago. In my own case I continued to suffer recurrent attacks until 1946, when an early wonder drug, Chloroquine, became available.

One of my first jobs on reaching Melbourne was to get the division shoulder patch job taken care of. It was surprisingly easy. I took the design the general liked to the Australian Knitting Mills in Melbourne, and they accepted the task cheerfully. I pledged the credit of our post exchange in lieu of payment, though I think they would have done it for nothing. Eventually they produced tens of thousands of these distinctive patches, which Marines bought up eagerly for two shillings apiece in our post exchanges. (Coffee cups and other small items marked with the 1st Division patch, plus decals, are still selling well today in the post exchange at Camp Pendleton.) The whole drill proved unnecessary in a sense, because the problem of identity never arose. Marines who had lost or destroyed or worn out everything they possessed except their '03 Springfield rifles had hung on to their globe-and-anchor collar devices and wore them proudly on their Australian jackets. This delighted General Vandegrift. After the war I asked the general to do away with all unit patches because of their divisive effect in the small peacetime Corps. He agreed and issued the necessary order. But during the war our distinctive unit patches served a useful purpose.

General Vandegrift had many notable guests at the house in the quiet Toorak area of Melbourne where he maintained his headquarters staff mess. Among these were Adm. William F. Halsey; Adm. Arthur J. Hepburn, investigating the Savo Island battle; Lt. Col. John Thomason, USMC (Ret.), author of *Fix Bayonets* and many other excellent Marine Corps books and stories; Ambassador and Mrs. Nelson Johnson, who lived with us a short time while awaiting appointment to head the Australian embassy; and Rear Adm. Samuel E. Morison, the noted naval historian.

Morison dropped by the D-3 section and asked to see one of the highly unofficial "George" medals, which had just made their mysterious appearance. He was amused but did not seem interested in looking over our records of the recent operation on Guadalcanal. I was relieved to escape the embarrassment of having to tell him that we had very little such material to offer.

Soon after we were settled in our new surroundings, General Vandegrift and Colonel Thomas were called to Washington for a lengthy stay. Brig. Gen. William H. Rupertus assumed temporary command of the division, and I was designated to act as division chief of staff. This brought me into contact with a quite different world, where it was necessary to deal with such heretofore remote matters as public relations, joint command, army and navy forces, and complex matters of both U.S. and Australian concern. It was a challenging and revealing experience for me.

Relations with the U.S. Army were never particularly difficult. The army provided full support for our activities; it was always ample, timely, and appropriate to our peculiar needs as an amphibious division. We in turn adjusted to the requirements of service with the army in every respect in an effort to contribute to rather than complicate their mission in the Southwest Pacific. There was little formal communication between the two staffs because there was little need for it; the relationship was both pleasant and effective.

Marines got along famously with Australians at almost every level. Less reserved than the always polite New Zealanders and more like Americans in their habits, faults, likes, and dislikes, the Australians were easier to empathize with. Of course, this cut both ways.

We were rationed by the Australian army and furnished with their rations, which was abundant and for the most part very acceptable. But there were exceptions, notably the old gripe about the American soldier's dislike of mutton. Like New Zealand, Australia had abundant stocks of every variety of food, but our requests for mutton substitutes fell on deaf ears. It reached the Australian press, and the Op-Ed sections were filled with fiery blasts, all to the effect that "what's good enough for our Australian boys is good enough for the Yanks. Eat it and shut up!" In New Zealand, under exactly similar circumstances, they had simply laughed at our, to them, absurd prejudices and substituted beef, pork, or fowl.

Now the result was predictable: "What's for chow, Mac? Mutton! What, that goddamn dog again? Three times this week already! C'mon, let's go over to the slop chute and get a face full of 'styke and aigs.'"

This insistence on issuing mutton to our Marines led in turn to considerable waste, which was duly noted in letters to the editor. Some of these zealots had even inspected our garbage.

Another altercation came about when the same small group of wowsers originated the accusation that we had defiled the community with venereal disease. Hardly likely, since we had just come from several months of enforced monasticism on Guadalcanal, where few if any Marines had even laid eyes on a member of the opposite sex. We were probably the most venereal disease–free group in the history of the armed forces.

The matter of intermarriage, however, was more perplexing. When the problem was first recognized by the local ministry and our own navy chaplains, steps were taken to deter impulsive unions, not all of which would survive the combined onslaughts of war, time, and distance. We resorted to administrative procedures designed to introduce an element of delay. Of doubtful legality, although benign in purpose, they gave our small number of detractors grounds for another spurious complaint. I can only state that the numerous such marriages among my own friends and acquaintances seem to have been unusually successful. In several cases the newly married couples established themselves permanently in Australia or New Zealand after the war.

While General Vandegrift was still in Washington, large numbers of Australian troops withdrawn from the desert forces of North Africa began arriving home to join the Australian contingent of MacArthur's army driving northward in New Guinea. General Rupertus diplomatically decided to contribute toward amicable relations by holding a large get-together at the cricket grounds. It was a king-sized entertainment, organized and conducted to perfection by Bandmaster Leon Brusiloff of our splendid 1st Marine Division Band, which had recently rejoined us in Australia. It was a howling success, with live entertainment and other smoker-type events. Beer was in generous quantity and was served in paper cups at Brusiloff's express direction.

Relations got off to a good start, and there were no fights during the party. Not that fights between Marines and Australian soldiers were unknown in Melbourne. As elsewhere in Australia, fights were a national tradition. Every Saturday afternoon the battle royal started down on Flinders Street near the railroad station and continued for hours, blocking traffic in both directions. The police intervened tentatively and ineffectively, but their hearts were not in it. With the return of the Aussies from North Africa, the fights took on a new dimension. Marines sometimes got involved on both sides and became quite enthusiastic.

Somebody, probably Rudyard Kipling, wrote about soldiers fighting on a Flinders Street somewhere in the United Kindgom: "Nothing dirty mind you, no knives or broken bottles like them Frogs and Wops in Shanghai, knock a man down and he'd get right up and come at you! Never saw anything like it." I can't find the reference, but the underlying tradition seems to have survived intact its transplant to Australia.

Of all our gracious visitors and guests to General Vandegrift's headquarters and mess, one was unique. Lt. Gen. Walter

Krueger, U.S. Army, MacArthur's senior general commanding the Sixth Army, was probably the most unpleasant man I
have ever known. An old "smoothbore" born in Prussia and
risen from the ranks with long service dating from before the
Spanish-American War, he seems to have been a great favorite of General MacArthur. What they could have had in
common I cannot imagine, unless it was their mutual dislike
of Gen. Dwight D. Eisenhower, who had served both of them
as a chief of staff, with scant loyalty, it would seem.

Krueger and many of his staff stayed with us for several
days while General Rupertus was acting division commander
during General Vandegrift's trip to Washington. The purpose
of Krueger's visit was not clear, as the army presence in Melbourne was very small. I imagine he was conversing with
top-level Australian military officials about forthcoming operations. He was a careful observer of a two-day amphibious
operation we put on in Port Philip Harbour in conjunction
with elements of the U.S. and Australian navies. His only
comment was, "There's a lot more to amphibious warfare
than just jumping in and out of a boat."

Krueger considered himself an expert on landing beaches.
"Give me," he would say, "a long, gently sloping beach where
men can get out of the boats in waist deep water and wade
ashore."

This is the typical Hollywood beach, the kind that Julius
Caesar picked for his landing in Great Britain and on which
he almost lost his famed Tenth Legion. Men are helplessly
exposed as they slowly struggle through the restraining water
and slippery sand. Then, when the tide goes out, the landing
of supplies and ammunition is interrupted for hours at a time.
Sometimes, however, as at Tarawa, you must take what you
can get.

At that time the naval forces assigned to commander, Southwest Pacific, were totally inadequate for a large operation.
Krueger's staff was studying the practicability of conducting
a gigantic shore-to-shore operation from Northern Australia
to New Guinea, directly across the Great Barrier Reef, using
whatever ships, boats, and landing craft they could lay their

hands on. I shuddered, but on second thought realized that some good might come of the idea. It would so shock the navy that in their desperation to prevent it they would somehow dig up the necessary shipping for a more realistic effort.

Despite his personality, General Krueger stayed the course and was the driving force behind the Allied army in its victorious drive from New Guinea to the Philippines. Perhaps his kind of leadership was the kind that was needed by that army at that hour of the war. But as one authority ruefully puts it, "He possessed a sometimes volatile temper."[1]

England still maintained its attitude of colonialism toward Australia in the matter of limitations or prohibitions placed on the manufacture of spirituous liquors. The supply of these was cut off due to the exigencies of war, and Australia was forced to create a new industry. They developed a form of fiery whiskey under the trade name "Corio." It was dreadful stuff, reminiscent of the Mason jars of "corn licker" we used to buy from the Virginia farmers in the days of Prohibition. Fortunately, their beer was both excellent and adequate.

This same surviving spirit of colonialism extended into the field of people-to-people relations in a strange way. The growing friendship and respect between Australians and Americans embarked together against a common enemy apparently became a disturbing factor at the lower levels of the British government. British Major General Dewing was sent out on a subtle mission of dissuasion. He gave a series of interesting discourses before groups of comparatively influential people on the subject of the war in North Africa—a rare treat for listeners starved for hard news of the war abroad. I heard one of these and noted that his attitude toward the American effort in North Africa was politely deprecatory. For the first time I learned that inexperienced American soldiers had suffered a severe reverse in the February 1943 battle of the Kasserine Pass. They had been broken, and their general had been replaced by Gen. George S. Patton, USA. He

1. Thomas Parrish, ed., *Encyclopedia of World War II* (New York: Simon & Schuster, 1978), p. 348.

pointed out correctly enough that "no army is worth a damn in its first fight" and closed on an upbeat note, but subtle damage had been done. Under what authority and to what purpose had he released depressing news of this nature to civilians, news to which our most senior officers were not yet privy?

Immediately thereafter I had access to a British inspired confidential news release plan about the movement of a single squadron of the famous Spitfire fighters to New Guinea from England. It provided several successive story line steps as a guide to reporters. It went something like this, only in great detail:

Step 1: Spitfires reach New Guinea . . .
Step 2: Spitfires engage Zeros . . .
Step 3: Spitfires score first success . . .
Step 4: Spitfires overwhelm Zeros . . .

The Spitfires' arrival was duly noted in the press, but I saw no further mention of them thereafter. I understand they had tried to dogfight the super-nimble Zeros (no one could do that) and had suffered resounding losses in return.

This strange proceeding had not gone unnoticed in Washington. An Army Air Force colonel from the general staff came out to take a look. He told me, "That British General Dewing is not doing us a bit of good."

General Vandegrift and Colonel Thomas returned from Washington at about this time full of plans and changes to be made. General Vandegrift would go to Noumea, New Caledonia, and relieve Maj. Gen. Clayton B. Vogel, USMC, as commander of I Marine Amphibious Corps (IMAC) for the forthcoming operation against the Shortland Islands, adjacent to southern Bougainville. Upon completion of the operation, he would return to Washington to become commandant of the Marine Corps upon the retirement of General Holcomb. Vandegrift would also reorganize the command structure of the 2d Marine Division, now at Wellington, New Zealand, before it proceeded to the Central Pacific for a combat mission (Tarawa) under control of Maj. Gen. Holland M. Smith, USMC. This reorganization was begun from Melbourne on the basis of agreements reached in Washington.

Col. Merritt A. Edson flew to Wellington to become chief of staff. Brig. Gen. Alphonse de Carre and his colonels were replaced. Col. David M. Shoup came from the States to become the D-3, and Maj. Gen. Julian C. Smith was given command of the division. These changes, long overdue, would greatly strengthen the command structure of the 2d Marine Division in advance of Tarawa.

Epilogue

Major General Vandegrift had expected to proceed directly to Washington from Australia to take over the duties of commandant of the Marine Corps upon the retirement of Lieutenant General Holcomb. However, Admiral Halsey needed his assistance to reorganize and strengthen the command of our newly formed I Marine Amphibious Corps (IMAC), composed of the 2d and 3d Marine divisions plus support units. This organization had been assigned to plan and conduct the New Georgia operation, the first major advance up the Solomons chain toward Rabaul. Corps planning clearly indicated that two divisions would be required rather than the one division force visualized by ComSoPac planners. The latter remained obdurate, and the New Georgia operation was reassigned to U.S. Army forces, who agreed to the one-division limitation.

Nevertheless, it became necessary to throw large additional forces, army and Marine, into the confused and protracted operation that followed. This may have vindicated the military judgment of the then commanding general IMAC, Maj. Gen. Clayton B. "Barney" Vogel, USMC, but it did nothing to solve the problems faced by Admiral Halsey, particularly when General Vogel, in an apparent fit of pique, took off on a protracted inspection trip of the South Pacific. This was the situation that caused ComSoPac to ask General Vandegrift to assume command of IMAC and set matters aright before proceeding to Washington to assume the commandancy of the Marine Corps.

Accompanied by a small command group consisting of

Colonel Thomas, myself, Lt. Col. Edward W. Snedeker, Maj. James C. Murray, and Maj. Ray Schwenke, the general reached Noumea on 7 July, took over command of IMAC, and cleaned house.

His house cleaning was radical and widespread; some of it had begun even before the general left Melbourne. We had advance notice that the 2d Marine Division would be sent against Tarawa. This was serious business, and Vandegrift's experiences on Guadalcanal left him with the impression that the 2d was not receiving the active, aggressive leadership the situation demanded. He sent Edson to be chief of staff and persuaded the commandant to send Maj. Gen. Julian C. Smith, USMC, out as the new commander. None of the 2d Marine Division infantry colonels who had been on Guadalcanal were retained, and new faces and aggressive officers like Dave Shoup joined the completely reorganized unit. Vandegrift did this completely on his own. On Guadalcanal where these ideas must have originated, I had never heard him utter one word in derogation of this fine unit or any of its members.

IMAC's control of the 2d Marine Division was administrative only, but we were still able to help them in one vital respect. A glance at coral-encrusted Betio Island underscored the vital necessity of amphibian tractors (LVTs) to cross the reefs. There were 114 of these vehicles held up on the docks at San Francisco by some bean counter who didn't think we needed them. When General Vandegrift left Noumea for Washington, I was designated to ride herd on the newly organized supply system to see that these tractors reached the 2d Division posthaste. I followed through, and the gators were shipped in time for Tarawa, where their presence may well have been decisive. Many people have claimed credit for this act; it was General Vandegrift in person who detected the need and took steps to meet it.

I was not privy to any of the intramural bloodshed that accompanied the reorganization, for I was appointed operations officer of the IMAC and handed the job of immediately preparing an operations plan for the seizure of the Shortland

Islands at an early date. As my assistant C-3 (operations), I was assigned the services of Maj. Wilbur J. McNenny, USMC, a recent graduate of the Army Staff College at Leavenworth, Kansas. Facing an early deadline to prepare a preliminary plan, we were immersed in work day and night from that time forward.

The ComSoPac directive gave us little reliable information. The estimate of enemy strength seemed to be so highly inflated as to make one wonder how our small force could be expected to attack at all. But we had faced this situation before and were not too greatly concerned.

The Shortland Islands lie just off the southern tip of Bougainville Island, a former German protectorate taken over by the British under the treaty of Versailles in 1919. Most, but not all, of the inhabitants favored the Allied cause. Here again Coast Watcher assistance would be vital.

The Shortlands themselves were not remarkable in any way, but they provided an extensive fleet anchorage and a strong air base on the island of Ballale, adjacent to the main island. Accessible landing beaches seemed almost nonexistent, although as yet we had almost nothing in the way of photographic intelligence and would be unable to obtain any pending confirmation of the task assignment. The new staff people at ComSoPac seemed to have learned little or nothing after eighteen months of war. Their operation plans still had about the same degree of realism as a four-year-old's letter to Santa Claus.

We adhered to General Vandegrift's maxim to avoid heavily defended beaches if by any combination of march and maneuver it was possible to place troops ashore unopposed but within striking distance of their objective. Such resort was not possible at places like Tarawa and Iwo Jima, where the nettle had to be grasped despite heavy initial losses. But in the Shortlands, by using LVTs in advance waves, we believed we could land at points that would in all probability be lightly defended. By selecting landing beaches remote from the main defensive zone, we would likewise have time to reform and move forward before serious hostile interference could materialize. It was essentially the same type of maneuver we had employed at Guadalcanal. General Vandegrift and Jerry Thomas studied the plan in detail and with great care. The general gave it tentative approval pending receipt of further and more specific intelligence as to enemy strength, hydrography, and the character of landing beaches. It was already apparent that existing studies were inadequate and that we would be largely dependent upon aerial photography and our own onshore patrols landed from submarines.

General Vandegrift and the IMAC staff displaced forward from Noumea to Guadalcanal on Friday, 13 August 1943. We landed at Henderson Field in the midst of the uproar arising out of a small Japanese sneak air raid—the first in several months and the last air attack on Guadalcanal of the war. One of the new transports, *John Penn* (APA-23), was sunk off Lunga Point before our own forces could intervene. I knew we had returned to our old haunt.

The next day General Vandegrift announced the long-rumored command changes affecting Marines in the South Pacific. He would depart the area and return to Washington to relieve General Holcomb as CMC after an inspection tour of all Marine activities in the Pacific Ocean area. He would be accompanied by Colonel Thomas. Maj. Gen. Charles D. Barrett, USMC, now commanding 3d Marine Division on Guadalcanal, would take over as commanding general, IMAC. Command of the division would pass to Brig. Gen. Hal Turnage, USMC, the present assistant division commander. Col. Alfred H. Noble, USMC, would become chief of staff, relieving Colonel Thomas. These assignments would automatically result in a one-rank promotion to each of the officers involved.

The 3d Marine Division was living in an excellent tent camp near the coast east of Koli Point. Squad tents and cots with mosquito nets provided the men with a high degree of freedom from the malaria that had scourged their predecessors. The 3d was the first of the new divisions, that is, those composed of entirely new units organized after the outbreak of the war. These men were a splendid lot, but they had problems of their own. They wanted to fight. All felt they had been held back too long working on page one of the book. They had spent long months in Samoa's debilitating climate under someone's policy of acclimating the troops to a tropical environment. "Someone" had forgotten the old saying: "Three things you don't need to practice up: going on half rations, jumping out of planes in parachutes, and living in the tropics."

At best the tropical environment is deleterious to non-natives. Those who survive habitually live quiet lives in an upgraded environment. This can never be true in the case of the soldier or Marine, whose lot must, of necessity, be a hard existence to achieve and maintain physical fitness to meet the test of battle. This well-recognized factor had somehow been forgotten or ignored.

In the case of the 3d Division, the problem was greatly intensified by the fact that some of its units had been stationed in areas where they were exposed to a disease in which parasitic filarial worms block the flow of lymph, causing parts of the body to become greatly enlarged. This dreadful mosquito-transmitted disease is known as elephantiasis or, as the Islanders of the South Seas call it, "mu mu."

How such an assignment could have occurred escapes me, but to my mind it represented the ghastliest untoward incident of the entire Pacific War. Fortunately the mistake had been detected when the affliction was in its early stages and easily curable, but the psychological impact must have been terrific. To their credit the 3d Division maintained throughout a morale and spirit second to none.

The remedy for the malady in its symptomatic stage was simple enough—prompt removal of the patient from the tropical environment to an area of the temperate zone where he can be encouraged to lead an active outdoor life to divert his mind away from the horrible psychological problems accompanying the disease. Special camps were set up to receive those afflicted. One such camp in the mountains near Klamath Falls, Oregon, my home state, was especially successful.

I understand that due to the early recognition and timely treatment of the disease, no advanced cases or deaths occurred. I strongly suspect that my old friend Dr. Warwick Brown, now at CinCPac Headquarters had a leading role in straightening this out.

In early September elements of Col. Harry B. "Harry the Horse" Liversedge's 1st Raider Regiment came through Guadalcanal en route to Espiritu Santo following their Bairoko foray. They were a disgusted group. Someone found them a bottle of Scotch, which they sorely needed. I listened carefully. They had been sent on an ill-defined mission involving extreme hardship and unnecessary exposure. Finally, they brought their enemy to brook, but holding a strong position. Timely air and logistic support did not materialize, and the Marines were unable to dislodge a stronger, better-armed and better-supplied antagonist. In short, they had been required to repeat the exact sequence of events that had so often brought disaster to the Japanese on Guadalcanal. This was Kelly Turner's last appearance in the role of soldier/sailor of the Solomons.

I never ceased to be amazed at the growth that had taken place in the Guadalcanal area. From Aola Bay to Cape Esperance, there was an almost continuous chain of highly developed installations. Improved gravel roads extended everywhere. There were seven major runways and more abuilding to handle the needs of hundreds of aircraft of all descriptions. Tulagi was a major naval base, fleet anchorage, and seaplane harbor. There were even plans to bring in beer for 100,000 thirsty troops.

Food was now plentiful on Guadalcanal, but terribly monotonous: C rations, K rations, Spam, powdered eggs, and dehydrated potatoes and carrots were about the extent of it. Fresh meat and vegetables were seldom available. Malaria sufferers like myself found it extremely difficult to keep going and required continuous doses of Maalox to function. I soon found myself living on a menu consisting largely of milk toast.

I had long sessions each day with General Barrett, who

combed through our lengthy operational study line by line and word by word. He seemed pleased with the detailed planning but had grave doubts about our ability to seize the Shortlands without incurring prohibitive losses. He did not adhere to General Vandegrift's philosophy of doing what you are ordered to do and doing it to the best of your ability with the forces placed at your disposal. Knowing this, I had planned the initial landing at a remote and unlikely spot in order to get forces ashore before coming to full grips with the enemy. General Barrett understood this but still sought an easier way.

We considered landings at other points on Bougainville itself where the enemy would have to come through the swamps and jungle to meet us, thus forcing him to repeat his old mistakes we remembered from the Tenaru, Edson's Ridge, and the hopeless attack of the Sendai Division on Puller's sector of the main perimeter. But we found no acceptable landing points. Even Empress Augusta Bay seemed too fraught with uncertainty for General Barrett to consider.

This impasse continued for days. The general would send for me in the morning at around ten o'clock, and we would continue the discussion until long after midnight, fruitlessly looking for a better solution, one guaranteed to save the lives of many of our Marines.

This delay was also a great hindrance to the other staff echelons, which also had much preparatory work to do. Intelligence (C-2), Lt. Col. William F. Coleman, was concerned with the collection of intelligence data and photographs. Logistics (C-4), Lt. Col. Freddy C. Wieseman, was faced with the necessity of constructing large embarkation facilities at Cape Esperance, which required the services of one Marine Corps engineer battalion and one naval construction battalion. My own section, operations (C-3), was anxious to initiate a series of onshore patrols, which would be landed by our highly skilled submariners. None of this could be accomplished until the what, when, and where of our objective were definitely set.

I traveled widely around the island using the fine gravel roads that had replaced the indifferent government track of our earlier days. There was a vast army representation on the island embracing every conceivable type of unit and weapon. I even stumbled across an army regiment of pack artillery with hundreds of mules to carry the disassembled 75mm pack howitzers. This really shook me. I asked the island commander, Brig. Gen. Arch Howard, USMC, about it. He said the mules refused to eat the island grass, and he had to supply baled hay from Australia. He added, only half in jest, "They've got another regiment back there. If they send it up too, I'm afraid we'll have to postpone the Bougainville show."

The tentative status of the Bougainville operation continued to serve as a ball and chain, hindering our efforts to get the bandwagon rolling in the right direction. I went down to Lunga, where my brother, Maj. Gen. Nathan Twining, U.S. Army Air Force, was acting as Commander, Air Forces Solomons (ComAirSols), a rotating joint command of army, navy, and Marine air units. His headquarters was our own old 1st Division CP, and on his staff were two old friends and aviator classmates of mine, Cmdr. Charley Coe, USN, and Lt. Col. William G. Manley, USMC. It was nice to visit the old place again, but my plea for photographs fell on deaf ears. They could photograph every bomb crater on the Ballale Island airstrip twice a day but were much too busy to get us a single shot of the critical channel entrance to the Shortland Islands seven miles away.

Relations with the navy submarine people were more productive. Like all submariners I have ever met, they knew their business. I had had prewar experience in onshore patrolling and thought I knew something about it. These people were way ahead of me, at least in their knowledge of the ins and outs of landing and retrieving small groups of men under extremely difficult and dangerous conditions.

The first patrol was sent out in early September to determine the exact character of a certain small beach and to find out if the channel leading thereto was mined or obstructed. Nothing more. You do not send out a patrol to make a search with involved, complicated instructions. Simplicity is the keynote. The secret of our first patrol was not well kept, and

some high-level kibitzers horned in. One character was looking for airfield sites; another was interested in the "attitude"
of the natives. The patrol leader was overwhelmed with the
responsibility of protecting his joy riders: those interlopers
who did not have a fundamental need for information. The
patrol leader never got an opportunity to visit the vital beach
area we were interested in. Fortunately the natives had a good
attitude as they detected and located our patrol within two
hours of its landing despite our every effort at concealment.
They also provided highly effective cover during the patrol's
time ashore. Nothing worthwhile was accomplished, but at
least all hands returned in safety.

General Barrett and his second in command, Brig. Gen. A. H.
Noble, made several trips back to Noumea to discuss matters
with Admiral Halsey, who seemed to be growing impatient at
our indecision and lack of progress. I was asked to accompany them on one of these excursions. I regretted having to
go because my only really productive work periods were during these times when I did not have to spend my working
hours closeted with General Barrett in endless discussion.

In Noumea I was called in by one of the new planners on
Halsey's staff, a superannuated professorial Naval War College type who I judged was not the man taking part in making
important decisions. He was mildly critical of all I had to say,
and I soon realized that the thrust of his disenchantment was
aimed not at our proposed operation plan but against the
ComSoPac plan itself. He obviously disapproved of the idea
of seizing the Shortlands, the objective chosen by *his* boss,
not mine, so our views failed to mesh from the outset.

Before I finally left, he gave me a stern lecture on the obvious unsuitability of the beach I had tentatively selected for
the landing. I noticed that he was holding his aerial photograph of the area upside down so that elevations appeared
as depressions. I imagine this character ended the war in
some back office reviewing recommendations for medals and
awards or some other harmless task.

Upon returning from another one of these trips, General
Barrett seemed almost jubilant about a suggestion given him

by Lt. Gen. Millard F. Harmon, U.S. Army Air Corps, chief of Army and Army Air Forces in the South Pacific area. The idea was that IMAC should occupy Choiseul Island southeast of Bougainville. Having sensed our command problem, Harmon had cagily proposed palming the Marines into a diversionary handoff toward a less important objective while the army in turn would preempt the vital mission of seizing the Shortlands. I sensed the trap and made my views explicit. I expected to be relieved on the spot but was not. I realized that my usefulness was at an end.

I was also physically exhausted. You can't live on Maalox and milk toast forever. A few nights later my tent mate Eddy Snedeker discovered me delirious and with a critical temperature. I was taken to the hospital. The doctors soon found that I did not respond to any form of malarial treatment and were at a loss as to my condition. I suspected a recurrence of the intestinal cancer that had laid me low in 1938.

The Navy Mobile Hospital, commanded by Capt. "Terrible Terry" Turville, Medical Corps, USN, an old "Marine" doctor, was a field hospital and of course totally lacking in the equipment needed for establishing such a diagnosis. It was equipped to deal with only tropical diseases, wounds, and burns. Housed in carefully designed prefabricated buildings, these mobile hospitals were a remarkably successful innovation. Although they were equipped with modern plumbing, the toilets in ours were not hooked up, so we continued to use the slit trenches out behind, no easy feat for a sick or wounded man.

But suddenly the word was flashed, "Eleanor [Roosevelt] is coming—so shape up." Suddenly burlap screens appeared around every latrine on the island. Men were cautioned about exposure. The worst places were closed or cleaned up. Terrible Terry did his part. He scorned burlap screens; we went first class. He turned the water on in every head in the hospital. We were elated. This was progress. Eleanor left the island at sunset, and Terry turned the water off again. Permanently.

My two brothers on the island visited me frequently. Ed, a retread (returned to service) from the U.S. Army Field Artillery of World War I, now a major in the intelligence branch of the U.S. Army Air Force, regaled me with reminiscences of our fishing and hunting days in the Oregon of our youth. Later, near the end of the Solomons Campaign, Ed was wounded.

Nathan, a rising star in the Air Force and now ComAirSols, drew me out and listened politely (or should I say amusedly?) to my long harangues on why we weren't winning the war fast enough. I think I did convince him of one fact of life that had become abundantly clear to me—we could never win unless all branches of our armed services were willing to cooperate in every way to fight the enemy to the best of our abilities, at all times, and in all places.

Nathan also had had personal difficulties in the South Pacific. Shortly after mid-January 1943, while on a flight from Guadalcanal to Noumea, his B-17 had to be ditched. The crew took to two life rafts and drifted for six days before being found and rescued after an intensive air and sea search. During this time their only food was a seagull Nate bagged with the last round in his .45 pistol. Of course, Ed insisted on being aboard one of the search planes. I knew nothing about this until after Nate and the crew were found.

General Barrett came by to tell me that I was being sent back to a base hospital in Noumea. He bore me no ill will and was very kind. Just before my evacuation to Noumea and eventually to the U.S. Naval Hospital, Bethesda, Maryland, the general asked me for recommendations for the permanent corps staff positions.

I recommended Lt. Col. Eddy Snedeker as my own relief, based on his demonstrated ability, energy, and military character. For C-4, a vital spot, I recommended Lt. Col. Freddy Wieseman, who as a junior member of the 1st Division staff had brought the logistics of Guadalcanal under control and whose capacity to learn seemed boundless. I also recommended that Lt. Col. Bill Coleman and Maj. James C. Murray continue in their present positions on the corps staff. I thought that General Barrett was asking for my opinions only, as a matter of undeserved kindness to me, but I was heartened to learn that all these officers were confirmed in the

slots I had recommended. They performed admirably throughout the Bougainville campaign and served with distinction
during the remainder of the war as well. Even as I wrote this
paragraph, a telephone call from Headquarters Marine Corps
informed me of the death of Freddy Wieseman, who retired
as a major general. The others, Snedeker, Coleman, and Murray, still survive.

The fortunes of IMAC continued to deteriorate. Admiral
Halsey, of course, rejected the Choiseul Island plan and proposed instead a version of the Empress Augusta Bay (Cape
Torokina) operation. Even this plan, which afforded many
advantages as compared to the Shortland Islands operation,
was unacceptable to General Barrett in his unending quest to
avoid casualties. Despite all of his brilliance, personality, and
leadership, he increasingly allowed his humanitarian in-
stincts to prevail over every dictate of a dire military necessity. In short, he had forgotten why he and his Marines were
there.

Again confronted with a command problem in IMAC, Admiral Halsey for the second time sent for his old friend Vandegrift to straighten out matters in IMAC. Vandegrift was
on his way to Washington when the call came to retrace
his steps. It was too late to save General Barrett. When informed of Halsey's intentions, he returned to his quarters in
Noumea, where a few hours later he was found lying in the
courtyard, dead of injuries suffered in a fall from a second
story window.

The Empress Augusta Bay operation went forward successfully, commanded first by Vandegrift, then by Lt. Gen.
Roy Geiger, USMC, who stayed in the Pacific theater for the
remainder of the war. As a master of both air and ground warfare, Geiger was able to impart an air-ground expertise to his
troops that served them well from Guam to Okinawa. He was
another in that long list of the Old Breed—both officers and
men—who never permitted themselves to lose sight of what
their country expected them to do.

* * *

Upon arriving in Noumea, New Caledonia, after leaving Guadalcanal on 13 December 1942, I was the guest of my brother Brig. Gen. Nathan F. Twining, U.S. Army Air Force, who was chief of staff of all U.S. Army Forces, air and ground, in the South Pacific under command of Lt. Gen. Millard T. Harmon, U.S. Army Air Force.

All the army generals lived together in a joint mess established in a house on the outskirts of Noumea. I was astonished to find a violent resentment of what had been accomplished at Guadalcanal. The generals heatedly complained that the operation represented "an unwarranted intrusion" into the role of the U.S. Army involving a wasteful duplication of military resources. They insisted that there could be no such thing as a "naval campaign" and that the proper role of the navy was limited to the support of army forces ashore.

The commander of the army's 25th Division, Maj. Gen. J. Lawton Collins, U.S. Army, who was of the company, was particularly insistent and predicted that congressional action would be taken after the war to provide a national defense organization that would prevent it from ever happening again.

I was alarmed at what I had heard and informed General Vandegrift. He listened attentively but made no comment. There was a war to be won. There was no time or strength to squander on any internecine struggle.

General Collins was good as his word. The infamous "merger bill" introduced into the U.S. Congress immediately after the war was to be known as the "Collins Plan" in his honor. It was a one-page power grab that would have had the effect of diminishing the constitutional control of Congress over the armed forces of the United States.

General Vandegrift must have remembered the report I gave in Noumea, for when the Collins Plan was introduced into Congress, I was summoned to Headquarters Marine Corps and put in charge of the effort to tell our side of the unification story.

The future of the Marine Corps was under attack by the U.S. Army general staff and a hostile White House. Unlike the army and navy, the Marine Corps has always led a "zero-sum" legislative life in that it has been required, in effect, to justify its very existence before each Congress. The year 1946 was no exception. Despite our commendable contribution to the victory of 1945, we were bitterly attacked, sometimes by the very persons who had lavished fulsome praise upon us at the time of our hard-fought victories in the Pacific. One faction claimed that there would never be another amphibious operation; another, that the Marines would be an anachronism in the proposed national defense reorganization based on the militaristic trielemental theory advanced by a German writer, Dr. Alfred A. Vagts, that the army should control everything on land, the navy on the sea, and the air force in the air. This simplistic Prussian idea had helped Germany lose two world wars.[1]

After a long struggle, the Congress in 1947 exercised its power and responsibilities with respect to the armed forces and enacted a national defense act clearly defining the role and missions of each of the services, thus putting an end to the questionable political activities and aims of the old War Department general staff. This legislation, embodying much of the original Marine Corps position, has served the nation admirably for about half a century, providing effective joint action in war and security of our democratic institutions in time of peace.

In the period immediately following World War II, few of the vital lessons learned were overlooked. The Marine Corps did not, as some recent writers have charged, continue to "fight the last war" for the simple reason that we could not afford to.

Gen. A. A. Vandegrift, commandant, U.S. Marine Corps, realized that the real problem faced by the Corps was that amphibious warfare as conducted in the world war just ended would be a suicidal exercise in the face of atomic attack. For example, at Iwo Jima, the entire naval attack force, including

---

1. Alfred A. Vagts, *Landing Operations* (Washington, DC: Military Service 1946), pp. 1–8.

the landing force ashore, could have been totally destroyed by a single accurately placed atomic bomb. This was not politics but a reality extending to the vital interests of the United States, and the Marine Corps realized it.

A senior board of general officers at Headquarters Marine Corps, headed by Lt. Gen. Lemuel C. Shepherd, USMC, was appointed to devise ways and means to meet this atomic threat. A working group was also appointed by the commandant, consisting of officers at Quantico, to initiate full-time studies and make recommendations for the consideration of the senior assembly in Washington. I was appointed to head the working group, which consisted of Col. Edward C. Dyer, USMC, a distinguished officer and experienced Marine aviator, and Col. Samuel Shaw, a highly regarded officer just now returning from the Pacific after notable combat service. He would join us in a few days.

In our first conversation, Dyer asked me if we had ever seriously considered helicopters. We had. A year before Col. (now retired Lt. Gen.) Victor H. Krulak, who was then working with me, had proposed that we look into their use as troop transports. He showed me a one-page typewritten brief of the proposed subject of inquiry. I immediately called the officer in charge of the Marine Corps rotary wing section at Marine Aviation Headquarters in Washington, D.C., and was told that the matter of helicopter transports had been carefully evaluated and that such a large craft had been found to be "an aerodynamic impossibility."

Dyer scoffed at this idea and the next day flew me up to the Piasecki helicopter factory at Morton, Pennsylvania, just outside Philadelphia. There I had a ride in their "dog ship"—a twin-rotor-transport helicopter called the "Flying Banana," which was destined to become the world's first transport helicopter. This was the implement I had dreamed of when I was pondering Carlson's classic moves during his famous raid on Guadalcanal. Carlson had gained his unlimited mobility through the employment of native scouts. We could achieve the same results faster and to greater distance with whirlybirds.

Dyer, a man deeply experienced in aircraft procurement at the Pentagon level, undertook to write the necessary program, the vital sine qua non that can make or break the best of ideas. Concurrently Sam Shaw made a thorough written analysis of the technical aspects of atomic warfare, and I contributed the basic study of our proposed tactical employment of helicopters in the face of atomic attack. By utilizing the helicopter's speed and range we found that we could reap the following benefits:

1. We could disperse amphibious shipping over a transport area of sufficient size to preclude the possibility of destroying more than one vessel per bomb.
2. Despite the greatly increased distances involved, the relatively high speed of the choppers would put Marines ashore faster than existing ten-knot landing craft.
3. The troops need not be landed as a vulnerable mass at the water's edge as from boats but could be distributed initially in correctly dispersed positions inland, on or near their beachhead objective.
4. The arduous and dangerous shore party phase would be almost eliminated by landing supplies at dumps established inland, not at the water's edge.
5. The overall speed of the operation would greatly augment the element of surprise and shock, which has tactically been one of the great attributes of the seaborne form of attack.

Our proposal, when completed, was a very thorough and penetrating study of the major problems then facing the Corps. It was approved without change and used as the basis of the Marine Corps's new look when it was presented to a discerning Congress, much to the discomfiture of our opponents in their struggle to achieve dominance on a national scale in areas where the military had heretofore been forbidden to tread.

We can attribute some of the plan's origin to the imagination and initiative inherent in Evans Carlson's speed and mobility through the employment of his native scouts during his classic raid on Guadalcanal.

As was to be expected, the winged dinosaurs who ran Marine aviation at that time, with the exception of Lt. Gen. Field Harris, USMC, took fright and opposed the scheme in every way, apparently fearful that they would lose pilot seats or, worse still, have to fly whirlybirds themselves. They did everything possible to hamstring the program, one year giving the entire annual Marine helicopter appropriation to the air force to develop their flying crane, a giant lifting machine of little interest to the Marine Corps. But the helicopter made its own way through the ruck and gained warm acceptance when it first appeared on the battlefields in Korea flying Marines of the 1st Division in and out of combat. Today, helicopters are indispensable to all of our armed forces.

Viewed in retrospect, the failure of the Japanese to establish a beachhead in the Koli Point area east of our Lunga Perimeter had marked the end of their effort to retake the island with their existing ground forces. They were demonstrably unable to dislodge us, and a massive buildup would be required before they could make another attempt. Japanese moves to augment their force and our efforts to prevent reinforcement took center stage. These issues were fought out on the seas and in the skies above. Land fighting became of secondary importance, and we in the ground forces became little more than interested but concerned spectators of a larger drama.

The navy's passage back from the catastrophe of Pearl Harbor had been a stormy one, strewn with the ghosts of great ships and heroic men—the numbers of both exceeding by many times the total count of such losses over the entire history of our naval service since the days of John Paul Jones. It all ended in a series of bloody sailors' battles fought at point-blank range in the dark waters of Ironbottom Sound. Only when the last of these had been survived or won was the overall campaign of Guadalcanal finally decided.

The total vessels lost by both navies had been about the

same, but we could replace ours, even increase their numbers; the Japanese could not. Our other losses were of a different character; leaders like Admirals Scott and Callaghan are not easy to replace. Their deaths remind us that admirals still die on the bridges of their flagships while generals die in bed.

Our successful prosecution of the Guadalcanal campaign was in no small degree affected by the contrasting views of the high commands on either side. For us it was a venture of the greatest importance from the beginning, its success a desperately needed foothold on the road back. To the Japanese it began as a minor annoyance, little more than a momentary distraction from their major objective, the seizure of Port Moresby in southern New Guinea, from which they could menace northern Australia. This attitude proved fatal. Our seizure of Guadalcanal and Tulagi on 7 August had not even been considered important enough by the Japanese to be mentioned in the day-to-day journal of events kept in Tokyo by Tojo's secretaries.[2] The fact of the landings was known but dismissed—after all, the Imperial Japanese Army already held more than 300,000 Allied POWs. The handful of Marines in the Solomons would be picked up shortly and put in the bag.

The Japaneses' early victories were so astounding that they can scarcely be faulted for believing in their own invincibility. They attributed their successes to a moral and spiritual superiority over their opponents, derived from their Bushido, and tactics of the bamboo spear. In this they were mistaken. Their easy conquests in Malaya, the Netherlands East Indies, and the Philippines were due to the Allies' failure in each case to provide a logistical supporting base sufficient to keep pace with the tremendous augmentation in numbers of their own military garrisons.

When the crisis came, Allied leaders at home as well as on the scene suddenly became aware of the enormity of the

2. Edwin P. Hoyt, *Warlord Tojo* (Lanham, MD: Scarborough House, 1993), p. 124.

problem and their total inability to solve it in the narrow margin of time remaining. Thus, our vast superiority in numerical strength became a major liability. Our meager reserves of supplies were quickly dissipated, and there was no possibility of resupply. If Guadalcanal had possessed a garrison of 50,000 Marines instead of 13,000 under similar circumstances, the result might well have been the same. Support for such a force would have been impossible. The leaders in Singapore, Batavia, and Manila separately came to the same conclusion: With no prospect whatever of ultimate success, continued resistance would achieve nothing beyond useless sacrifice of human life.

The enemy's fascination with Bushido (way of the warrior) and bamboo spear tactics was in large measure a delusion. Although these were useful in building morale, they had the effect of inviting disastrous mistakes by substituting rash and impulsive reaction for reasoned tactical judgment. Although they sometimes succeeded, particularly against surprised or worn-out defenders, it was always at great cost in Japanese lives and eventually Japanese morale. There comes a time in every combat unit's experience when it no longer brags about the extent of its losses.

Nor had the Japanese military always been successful in the past. During the late 1920s and the 1930s we had noted numerous instances of small fights in which even the nondescript soldiers of Chinese General Chiang Kai-shek stood up successfully against their Japanese oppressors. In Manchukuo to the north, little known clashes with the Russians occurred constantly. Some of these incidents were serious battles hardly noted in the U.S. press. In one such clash at Nomonhon on the Mongolian border the Japanese lost 50,000 men, including an entire infantry division. The Russian loss was less than 10,000. Such disparity caused many of us to reexamine our estimates of Japanese training and the effectiveness of the Bushido doctrine on which it was based.

The ultimate act of Bushido, the banzai charge routinely used against Marines on Guadalcanal, never succeeded and came to be regarded by Marines as a sure sign of American victory. Just as routine were the scurrilous diatribes that so often preceded the banzai charges at sunset on an eventful night. Their aim, to intimidate and cow our defenders, was so wide of the mark as to cause their effort to be regarded as an entertainment event. Our aim, to infuriate and incite the enemy, goading him into reckless assaults, often succeeded. Usually repeated in series, the banzai thrusts, each lessening in force and determination, might continue until dawn. Then both antagonists would begin to look for the ritualistic green flare that signaled the enemy's withdrawal from contact.

The Japanese were quick enough to recognize that the disaster of the Ichiki detachment at the Tenaru was due in part at least to their overhasty attempt to retake Guadalcanal by raiding tactics without firm naval control of the area. This was exactly the same mistake that we had made when Admiral Fletcher at the *Saratoga* conference had announced his intention to execute an early withdrawal, thus turning the operation into a hit-and-run amphibious raid—but without the usual formality of picking up the landing force.

No major attempt by the Japanese to retake Guadalcanal was made until 21 August, when a massive task force left Truk. The mission of the enemy was to put a landing force ashore to regain possession of the island. As at Wake and Midway, the task force, including a landing force for the purpose of reoccupying Guadalcanal, embarked on high-speed destroyer transports similar in many ways to our own APDs. The size of the landing force was totally incommensurate with the requirements of its mission. It consisted of only one Rikushenti unit[3] and one battalion of Japanese infantry—a total force of only 1,500 men. On 24 August the Battle of the Eastern Solomons was joined south of the Stewart Islands. It resulted in a heartening victory for Fletcher's smaller U.S. Navy force, which inflicted severe losses on the enemy task force, including the sinking of the carrier *Ryujo*. The Japanese's mission of reoccupying Guadalcanal was abandoned, and the task force returned to Truk.

3. The term used for Japanese landing forces similar to our Fleet Marine Forces.

Their subsequent efforts, as we have seen in detail, were at best only partially successful. The enemy expended vast resources in his mistaken effort to establish power ashore without firm control of the sea through domination of the air above it. Initially we had made the same mistake, but we had learned our lesson early on and were wise enough never to repeat that blunder. The legend of Guadalcanal is the story of the men and ships and planes who turned an impending defeat into a resounding and decisive victory for the United States.

Old George was in the war to the very end, isolating Rabaul permanently by seizing Cape Gloucester in New Britain in 1943, protecting MacArthur's advance northward by a successful but costly attack on Peleliu in 1944, and finishing off the war at Okinawa. These were all hard fights, and the 1st Division's losses for the entire war totaled more than 20,000 killed and wounded.

After the peace was signed in 1945, the 1st Marine Division was sent to northern China, where it expelled the former Japanese conquerors and faced off against the Chinese Communists for more than two long, hard years. One of its scrapes with the Chinese was at Hsin Ho on the Manchurian railroad, a few miles west of Tongku at the mouth of the Pei-ho River and on the exact spot where, as a second lieutenant, I had hassled with Chinese Communists in 1927 in the days of Brig. Gen. Smedley Butler and the 3d Marine Brigade, forerunner of the 2d Marine Division.

Old George finally got home in 1947 but was off to the wars again in 1950 for years of service in Korea, adding to its colors new battle streamers that bore such names as Inchon, Chosin, and Hagaru-Ri. A comment by noted military writer S. L. A. Marshall on the Chosin battle is noteworthy: "No other operation in the American book of war quite compares with this show by the 1st Marine Division in the perfection of tactical concepts precisely executed, in accuracy of estimate of situation by leadership at all levels, and in promptness of utilization of all supporting forces."[4]

4. S. L. A. Marshall, "Last Barrier," *Marine Corps Gazette* (Jan. 1953): 16.

Old George was also among the first to land in Vietnam and stayed until the bitter end of that misbegotten war ten years later. The division fought valiantly throughout, particularly in the sanguinary "soldiers' battles" fought to stabilize and restore the situation following the Tet Offensive. The 1st Division suffered none of the unrest that demoralized some other units during the closing phases of that war.

The old magic was still there when in Operation Desert Storm, Old George broke through the Iraqis' barricades in record time, then moved into Kuwait City after sweeping aside the stunned defenders of that beleaguered nation's captured capital. Its recent participation in Somalia was a highly creditable display of professionalism in the restrained use of force in an obscure and volatile situation. Its response at every level from the overall command to the gunner on the street bespoke a discipline borne of long years of unfailing service. The Marine Corps and its 1st Division have never given the nation an unhappy moment, and they never will.

Index

251

*What if Germany invaded
America in . . .*

1901

A thrilling novel of a war that never was

by Robert Conroy

The year is 1901. Germany's navy is the second largest in the world; their army, the most
powerful. But with the exception of a small
piece of Africa and a few minor islands in the
Pacific, Germany is without an empire. Kaiser
Wilhelm II demands that the United States surrender its newly acquired territories. President
McKinley indignantly refuses, so with the
honor and economic future of the Reich at
stake, the Kaiser launches an invasion of the
United States, striking first on Long Island.

Now the Americans, with their army largely
disbanded, must defend the homeland. When
McKinley suffers a fatal heart attack, the new
commander in chief, Theodore Roosevelt, ral-
lies to the cause, along with Confederate general James Longstreet. From the burning of
Manhattan to the climactic Battle of Danbury,
American forces face Europe's most potent
war machine in a blazing contest of will
against strength.

Published by Presidio Press
Available wherever books are sold

"A definitive biography . . .
The story of this brave and paradoxi-
cal Marine is the stuff of legends."
—W. E. B. Griffin
Author of *The Corps*

BLACK SHEEP ONE
The Life of Gregory "Pappy" Boyington
by Bruce Gamble

Black Sheep One is the first biography of legendary
warrior and World War II hero Gregory
Boyington. In 1936, Boyington became an aviation cadet and earned the "wings of gold" of a
naval aviator. After only a short period on active
duty, however, he was "encouraged" to resign
from the Marine Corps due to his unconventional
behavior. Remarkably, this inauspicious beginning was just the prologue to a heroic career as
an American fighter pilot and innovative combat
leader. With the onset of World War II, when
skilled pilots were in demand, he became the
commander of an ad hoc squadron of flying leathernecks. Led by Medal of Honor winner
Boyington, the legendary Black Sheep set a blis-
tering pace of aerial victories against the enemy.

Published by Presidio Press
Available wherever books are sold

"Onward we stagger, and if the tanks come, may God help the tanks."
—WILLIAM O. DARBY

DARBY'S RANGERS
We Led the Way
by William O. Darby

From the moment they hit the beaches in North Africa to their last desperate struggle at Anzio, Darby's Rangers asked for only one thing in World War II—the chance to fight. Experts at amphibious landings, night attacks, and close combat, the Rangers were the spearhead for advancing U.S. forces. And at their helm was William O. Darby, a forceful, charismatic man who inspired, and was inspired by, his troops. Against overwhelming odds in Tunisia, through the concentrated hell at Gela, on to the final kill at Messina and the Italian mainland, Darby and his Rangers led the way. Darby's Rangers is an authentic war story, as vivid as the action itself.

Published by Presidio Press
Available wherever books are sold

"Behind the legend of the 'bad boy' squadron is the true story of the people, places, and events that made the outfit what it was."
—*World War II Magazine*

THE BLACK SHEEP

The Definitive Account of Marine Fighting Squadron 214 in World War II

by Bruce Gamble

With their renowned squadron leader Greg "Pappy" Boyington, Marine Fighting Squadron (VMF) 214 was one of the best-known and most colorful combat units of World War II. The popular television series *Baa Baa Black Sheep* added to their legend—while obscuring the truly remarkable combat record of the Black Sheep and Boyington. A retired naval flight officer and former historian for the Naval Aviation Museum Foundation, Bruce Gamble provides a highly readable account that serves to both correct and extend the record of this premier fighting force.

Published by Presidio Press
Available wherever books are sold

"Gripping . . . These men were
common warriors who fought with
uncommon courage and thus shaped
the destiny of our great nation."
—Former Senator Bob Dole

THE DEADLY
BROTHERHOOD

The American Combat Soldier
in World War II

by John C. McManus

"Do you want to know what the World War II foot
soldier felt and how he fought? What he ate and
how he liked it? What his life was like during periods he was not in combat? *The Deadly Brotherhood*
goes a long way towards answering such questions. . . . Each chapter contains a wealth of supporting comments. This approach produces an
extreme degree of authenticity. . . . This fine book
provides a comprehensive understanding of a
World War II infantryman's troubles and travails."
—*Military Review*

Published by Presidio Press
Available wherever books are sold

*Seventy-seven deadly days
in combat*

WEST DICKENS AVENUE

A Marine at Khe Sanh

by John Corbett

In January 1968, John Corbett and his fellow leathernecks of the 26th Marine Regiment fortified a remote outpost at a place in South Vietnam called Khe Sanh. Within days of their arrival, twenty thousand North Vietnamese soldiers surrounded the base. What followed over the next seventy-seven days became one of the deadliest fights of the Vietnam War— and one of the greatest battles in military history.

"In this short, readable account, Corbett describes his days at Khe Sanh in almost dispassionate prose and in great detail. . . . effectively convey[ing] the siege from a Marine grunt's point of view."
—*Publishers Weekly*

Published by Presidio Press
Available wherever books are sold